W9-AMM-550

Visit classzone.com and get connected

Online resources for students and parents

ClassZone resources provide instruction, practice, and learning support.

eEdition Plus ONLINE

This interactive version of the text encourages students to explore science.

Content Review Online

Interactive review reinforces the big idea and key concepts of each chapter.

SciLinks

NSTA-selected links provide relevant Web resources correlated to the text.

Chapter-Based Support

Math tutorials, news, resources, test practice, and a misconceptions database help students succeed.

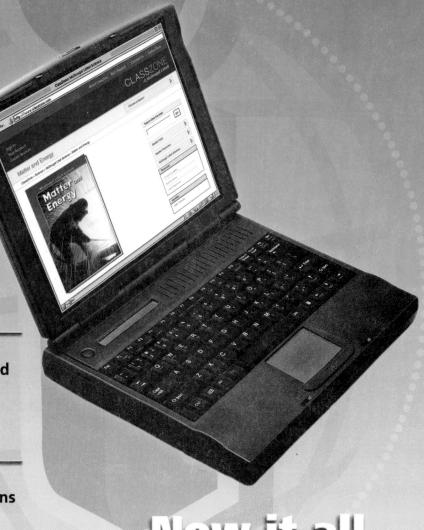

Now it all clicks!™

CLASSZONE.COM

McDougal Littell

McDougal Littell Science

Matter and Energy

radiation

mass

HEAT

physical
change

PHYSICAL SCIENCE

A ▶ Matter and Energy
B ▶ Chemical Interactions
C ▶ Motion and Forces
D ▶ Waves, Sound, and Light
E ▶ Electricity and Magnetism

LIFE SCIENCE

A ▶ Cells and Heredity
B ▶ Life Over Time
C ▶ Diversity of Living Things
D ▶ Ecology
E ▶ Human Biology

EARTH SCIENCE

A ▶ Earth's Surface
B ▶ The Changing Earth
C ▶ Earth's Waters
D ▶ Earth's Atmosphere
E ▶ Space Science

Acknowledgments: Excerpts and adaptations from *National Science Education Standards* by the National Academy of Sciences. Copyright © 1996 by the National Academy of Sciences. Reprinted with permission from the National Academies Press, Washington, D.C.

Excerpts and adaptations from *Benchmarks for Science Literacy: Project 2061.* Copyright © 1993 by the American Association for the Advancement of Science. Reprinted with permission.

Copyright © 2007 by McDougal Littell, a division of Houghton Mifflin Company.

No part of this work may be reproduced or transmitted in any form or by any means, electronic or mechanical, including photocopy and recording, or by any information storage or retrieval system without the prior written permission of McDougal Littell unless such copying is expressly permitted by federal copyright law. Address inquiries to Supervisor, Rights and Permissions, McDougal Littell, P.O. Box 1667, Evanston, IL 60204.

ISBN-13: 978-0-618-84249-0   6 7 8 9 0914 14 13 12

ISBN-10: 0-618-84249-7   4500365213

Internet Web Site: http://www.mcdougallittell.com

Science Consultants

Chief Science Consultant

James Trefil, Ph.D. is the Clarence J. Robinson Professor of Physics at George Mason University. He is the author or co-author of more than 25 books, including *Science Matters* and *The Nature of Science.* Dr. Trefil is a member of the American Association for the Advancement of Science's Committee on the Public Understanding of Science and Technology. He is also a fellow of the World Economic Forum and a frequent contributor to *Smithsonian* magazine.

Rita Ann Calvo, Ph.D. is Senior Lecturer in Molecular Biology and Genetics at Cornell University, where for 12 years she also directed the Cornell Institute for Biology Teachers. Dr. Calvo is the 1999 recipient of the College and University Teaching Award from the National Association of Biology Teachers.

Kenneth Cutler, M.S. is the Education Coordinator for the Julius L. Chambers Biomedical Biotechnology Research Institute at North Carolina Central University. A former middle school and high school science teacher, he received a 1999 Presidential Award for Excellence in Science Teaching.

Instructional Design Consultants

Douglas Carnine, Ph.D. is Professor of Education and Director of the National Center for Improving the Tools of Educators at the University of Oregon. He is the author of seven books and over 100 other scholarly publications, primarily in the areas of instructional design and effective instructional strategies and tools for diverse learners. Dr. Carnine also serves as a member of the National Institute for Literacy Advisory Board.

Linda Carnine, Ph.D. consults with school districts on curriculum development and effective instruction for students struggling academically. A former teacher and school administrator, Dr. Carnine also co-authored a popular remedial reading program.

Donald Steely, Ph.D. serves as principal investigator at the Oregon Center for Applied Science (ORCAS) on federal grants for science and language arts programs. His background also includes teaching and authoring of print and multimedia programs in science, mathematics, history, and spelling.

Sam Miller, Ph.D. is a middle school science teacher and the Teacher Development Liaison for the Eugene, Oregon, Public Schools. He is the author of curricula for teaching science, mathematics, computer skills, and language arts.

Vicky Vachon, Ph.D. consults with school districts throughout the United States and Canada on improving overall academic achievement with a focus on literacy. She is also co-author of a widely used program for remedial readers.

Content Reviewers

John Beaver, Ph.D.
Ecology
Professor, Director of Science Education Center
College of Education and Human Services
Western Illinois University
Macomb, IL

Donald J. DeCoste, Ph.D.
Matter and Energy, Chemical Interactions
Chemistry Instructor
University of Illinois
Urbana-Champaign, IL

Dorothy Ann Fallows, Ph.D., MSc
Diversity of Living Things, Microbiology
Partners in Health
Boston, MA

Michael Foote, Ph.D.
The Changing Earth, Life Over Time
Associate Professor
Department of the Geophysical Sciences
The University of Chicago
Chicago, IL

Lucy Fortson, Ph.D.
Space Science
Director of Astronomy
Adler Planetarium and Astronomy Museum
Chicago, IL

Elizabeth Godrick, Ph.D.
Human Biology
Professor, CAS Biology
Boston University
Boston, MA

Isabelle Sacramento Grilo, M.S.
The Changing Earth
Lecturer, Department of the Geological Sciences
San Diego State University
San Diego, CA

David Harbster, MSc
Diversity of Living Things
Professor of Biology
Paradise Valley Community College
Phoenix, AZ

Richard D. Norris, Ph.D.
Earth's Waters
Professor of Paleobiology
Scripps Institution of Oceanography
University of California, San Diego
La Jolla, CA

Donald B. Peck, M.S.
*Motion and Forces; Waves, Sound, and Light;
  Electricity and Magnetism*
Director of the Center for Science Education (retired)
Fairleigh Dickinson University
Madison, NJ

Javier Penalosa, Ph.D.
Diversity of Living Things, Plants
Associate Professor, Biology Department
Buffalo State College
Buffalo, NY

Raymond T. Pierrehumbert, Ph.D.
Earth's Atmosphere
Professor in Geophysical Sciences (Atmospheric Science)
The University of Chicago
Chicago, IL

Brian J. Skinner, Ph.D.
Earth's Surface
Eugene Higgins Professor of Geology and Geophysics
Yale University
New Haven, CT

Nancy E. Spaulding, M.S.
Earth's Surface, The Changing Earth, Earth's Waters
Earth Science Teacher (retired)
Elmira Free Academy
Elmira, NY

Steven S. Zumdahl, Ph.D.
Matter and Energy, Chemical Interactions
Professor Emeritus of Chemistry
University of Illinois
Urbana-Champaign, IL

Susan L. Zumdahl, M.S.
Matter and Energy, Chemical Interactions
Chemistry Education Specialist
University of Illinois
Urbana-Champaign, IL

Safety Consultant

Juliana Texley, Ph.D.
Former K–12 Science Teacher and School Superintendent
Boca Raton, FL

English Language Advisor

Judy Lewis, M.A.
Director, State and Federal Programs for reading proficiency
and high risk populations
Rancho Cordova, CA

Teacher Panel Members

Carol Arbour
Tallmadge Middle School,
Tallmadge, OH

Patty Belcher
Goodrich Middle School,
Akron, OH

Gwen Broestl
Luis Munoz Marin Middle School,
Cleveland, OH

Al Brofman
Tehipite Middle School,
Fresno, CA

John Cockrell
Clinton Middle School,
Columbus, OH

Jenifer Cox
Sylvan Middle School,
Citrus Heights, CA

Linda Culpepper
Martin Middle School,
Charlotte, NC

Kathleen Ann DeMatteo
Margate Middle School,
Margate, FL

Melvin Figueroa
New River Middle School,
Ft. Lauderdale, FL

Doretha Grier
Kannapolis Middle School,
Kannapolis, NC

Robert Hood
Alexander Hamilton Middle School,
Cleveland, OH

Scott Hudson
Covedale Elementary School,
Cincinnati, OH

Loretta Langdon
Princeton Middle School,
Princeton, NC

Carlyn Little
Glades Middle School,
Miami, FL

Ann Marie Lynn
Amelia Earhart Middle School,
Riverside, CA

James Minogue
Lowe's Grove Middle School,
Durham, NC

Joann Myers
Buchanan Middle School,
Tampa, FL

Barbara Newell
Charles Evans Hughes Middle School,
Long Beach, CA

Anita Parker
Kannapolis Middle School,
Kannapolis, NC

Greg Pirolo
Golden Valley Middle School,
San Bernardino, CA

Laura Pottmyer
Apex Middle School,
Apex, NC

Lynn Prichard
Booker T. Washington Middle Magnet
School, Tampa, FL

Jacque Quick
Walter Williams High School,
Burlington, NC

Robert Glenn Reynolds
Hillman Middle School,
Youngstown, OH

Stacy Rinehart
Lufkin Road Middle School,
Apex, NC

Theresa Short
Abbott Middle School,
Fayetteville, NC

Rita Slivka
Alexander Hamilton Middle School,
Cleveland, OH

Marie Sofsak
B F Stanton Middle School,
Alliance, OH

Nancy Stubbs
Sweetwater Union Unified School District,
Chula Vista, CA

Sharon Stull
Quail Hollow Middle School,
Charlotte, NC

Donna Taylor
Okeeheelee Middle School,
West Palm Beach, FL

Sandi Thompson
Harding Middle School,
Lakewood, OH

Lori Walker
Audubon Middle School & Magnet Center,
Los Angeles, CA

Teacher Lab Evaluators

Andrew Boy
W.E.B. DuBois Academy,
Cincinnati, OH

Jill Brimm-Byrne
Albany Park Academy,
Chicago, IL

Gwen Broestl
Luis Munoz Marin Middle School,
Cleveland, OH

Al Brofman
Tehipite Middle School,
Fresno, CA

Michael A. Burstein
The Rashi School,
Newton, MA

Trudi Coutts
Madison Middle School,
Naperville, IL

Jenifer Cox
Sylvan Middle School,
Citrus Heights, CA

Larry Cwik
Madison Middle School,
Naperville, IL

Jennifer Donatelli
Kennedy Junior High School,
Lisle, IL

Melissa Dupree
Lakeside Middle School,
Evans, GA

Carl Fechko
Luis Munoz Marin Middle School,
Cleveland, OH

Paige Fullhart
Highland Middle School,
Libertyville, IL

Sue Hood
Glen Crest Middle School,
Glen Ellyn, IL

William Luzader
Plymouth Community Intermediate School,
Plymouth, MA

Ann Min
Beardsley Middle School,
Crystal Lake, IL

Aileen Mueller
Kennedy Junior High School,
Lisle, IL

Nancy Nega
Churchville Middle School,
Elmhurst, IL

Oscar Newman
Sumner Math and Science Academy,
Chicago, IL

Lynn Prichard
Booker T. Washington Middle Magnet
School, Tampa, FL

Jacque Quick
Walter Williams High School,
Burlington, NC

Stacy Rinehart
Lufkin Road Middle School,
Apex, NC

Seth Robey
Gwendolyn Brooks Middle School,
Oak Park, IL

Kevin Steele
Grissom Middle School,
Tinley Park, IL

Matter and Energy

Energy

eEdition

Unit Features

SCIENTIFIC AMERICAN

1 Introduction to Matter   6

the BIG idea

Everything that has mass and takes up space is matter.

2 Properties of Matter   38

the BIG idea

Matter has properties that can be changed by physical and chemical processes.

What properties could help you identify this sculpture as sugar?
page 38

What different forms of energy are shown in this photograph? page 68

Features

Visual Highlights

Internet Resources @ ClassZone.com

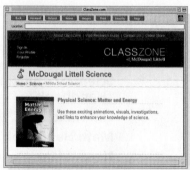

INVESTIGATIONS AND ACTIVITIES

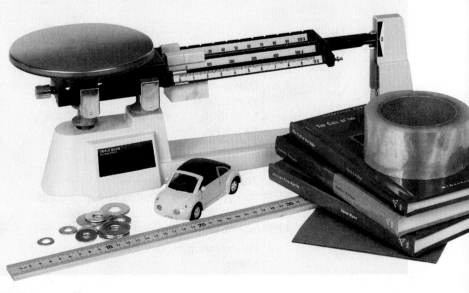

Each chapter in **Matter and Energy** covers some of the learning goals that are described in the *National Science Education Standards* (NSES) and the Project 2061 *Benchmarks for Science Literacy*. Selected content and skill standards are shown below in shortened form. The following National Science Education Standards are covered on pages xii–xxvii, in Frontiers in Science, and in Timelines in Science, as well as in chapter features and laboratory investigations: Understandings About Scientific Inquiry (A.9), Understandings About Science and Technology (E.6), Science and Technology in Society (F.5), Science as a Human Endeavor (G.1), Nature of Science (G.2), and History of Science (G.3).

Content Standards

1 Introduction to Matter

National Science Education Standards

B.1.c | There are more than 100 known elements that combine to produce compounds.

Project 2061 Benchmarks

4.D.1 | All matter is made up of atoms.

4.D.3 | Atoms and molecules are always in motion.
- In solids, they vibrate.
- In liquids, they slide past one another.
- In gases, they move freely.

2 Properties of Matter

National Science Education Standards

B.1.a |
- A substance has characteristic properties.
- A mixture often can be separated into the original substances using these properties.

Project 2061 Benchmarks

4.D.2 | Equal volumes of different substances usually have different weights.

8.B.1 | The choice of materials for a job depends on their properties.

3 Energy

National Science Education Standards

B.3.a | Energy is a property of substances that is often associated with
- heat
- light
- electricity
- mechanical motion
- sound
- atomic nuclei
- chemical compounds

Energy is transferred in many ways.

Project 2061 Benchmarks

4.E.1 | Energy cannot be created or destroyed, but it can be changed from one form to another.

4.E.2 | Most of what goes on in the universe involves energy transformations.

4.E.4 | Energy has many different forms, including
- heat
- chemical
- mechanical
- gravitational

8.C.1 | • As energy changes from one form to another, some energy is always converted to heat.
• Some systems transform energy with less heat loss than others.

4 Temperature and Heat

National Science Education Standards

B.3.b | Heat flows from warmer objects to cooler ones, until both reach the same temperature.

Project 2061 Benchmarks

4.E.2 | Energy in the form of heat is almost always one of the products of an energy transformation.

4.E.3 | Heat can be transferred through materials by the collisions of atoms or across space by radiation.

4.E.4 | • Energy appears in different forms.
• Heat energy is the disorderly motion of molecules.

Process and Skill Standards

National Science Education Standards

A.1 | Identify questions that can be answered through investigation.

A.2 | Design and conduct a scientific investigation.

A.3 | Use appropriate tools and techniques to gather and interpret data.

A.4 | Use evidence to describe, predict, explain, and model.

A.5 | Use critical thinking to find relationships between results and interpretations.

A.6 | Consider alternative explanations and predictions.

A.7 | Communicate procedures, results, and conclusions.

A.8 | Use mathematics in scientific investigations.

E.1 | Identify a problem to be solved.

E.2 | Design a solution or product.

E.3 | Implement the proposed solution.

E.4 | Evaluate the solution or design.

Project 2061 Benchmarks

1.C.1 | Contributions to science and technology have been made by different people, in different cultures, at different times.

2.B.1 | Mathematics contributes to science and technology.

3.C.4 | Technology has influenced the course of history.

9.A.3 | How decimals should be written depends on how precise the measurements are.

9.A.5 | The expression *a/b* can mean different things: *a* divided by *b* or *a* compared to *b*.

11.C.4 | Use equations to summarize observed changes.

12.B.1 | Find what percentage one number is of another.

12.B.7 | Determine the appropriate unit for an answer. Convert units.

12.B.8 | Round a calculation to the correct number of significant figures.

12.C.1 | Compare amounts proportionally.

12.C.3 | Using appropriate units, use and read instruments that measure length, volume, weight, time, rate, and temperature.

12.D.1 | Use tables and graphs to organize information and identify relationships.

12.D.2 | Read, interpret, and describe tables and graphs.

12.D.4 | Understand information that includes different types of charts and graphs, including circle charts, bar graphs, line graphs, data tables, diagrams, and symbols.

Introducing Physical Science

Scientists are curious. Since ancient times, they have been asking and answering questions about the world around them. Scientists are also very suspicious of the answers they get. They carefully collect evidence and test their answers many times before accepting an idea as correct.

In this book you will see how scientific knowledge keeps growing and changing as scientists ask new questions and rethink what was known before. The following sections will help get you started.

UNIFYING PRINCIPLES **of Physical Science**

What Is Physical Science?

In the simplest terms, physical science is the study of what things are made of and how they change. It combines the studies of both physics and chemistry. Physics is the science of matter, energy, and forces. It includes the study of topics such as motion, light, and electricity and magnetism. Chemistry is the study of the structure and properties of matter, and it especially focuses on how substances change into different substances.

The text and pictures in this book will help you learn key concepts and important facts about physical science. A variety of activities will help you investigate these concepts. As you learn, it helps to have a big picture of physical science as a framework for this new information. The four unifying principles listed below will give you this big picture. Read the next few pages to get an overview of each of these principles and a sense of why they are so important.

- **Matter is made of particles too small to see.**

- **Matter changes form and moves from place to place.**

- **Energy changes from one form to another, but it cannot be created or destroyed.**

- **Physical forces affect the movement of all matter on Earth and throughout the universe.**

the BIG idea

Each chapter begins with a big idea. Keep in mind that each big idea relates to one or more of the unifying principles.

Unifying Principles **xiii**

Matter is made of particles too small to see.

This simple statement is the basis for explaining an amazing variety of things about the world. For example, it explains why substances can exist as solids, liquids, and gases, and why wood burns but iron does not. Like the tiles that make up this mosaic picture, the particles that make up all substances combine to make patterns and structures that can be seen. Unlike these tiles, the individual particles themselves are far too small to see.

What It Means

To understand this principle better, let's take a closer look at the two key words: *matter* and *particles*.

Matter

Objects you can see and touch are all around you. The materials that these objects are made of are called **matter.** All living things—even you—are also matter. Even though you can't see it, the air around you is matter too. Scientists often say that matter is anything that has mass and takes up space. **Mass** is a measure of the amount of matter in an object. We use the word **volume** to refer to the amount of space an object or a substance takes up.

Particles

The tiny particles that make up all matter are called **atoms.** Just how tiny are atoms? They are far too small to see, even through a powerful microscope. In fact, an atom is more than a million times smaller than the period at the end of this sentence.

There are more than 100 basic kinds of matter called **elements.** For example, iron, gold, and oxygen are three common elements. Each element has its own unique kind of atom. The atoms of any element are all alike but different from the atoms of any other element.

Many familiar materials are made of particles called molecules. In a **molecule,** two or more atoms stick together to form a larger particle. For example, a water molecule is made of two atoms of hydrogen and one atom of oxygen.

Why It's Important

Understanding atoms and molecules makes it possible to explain and predict the behavior of matter. Among other things, this knowledge allows scientists to

- explain why different materials have different characteristics
- predict how a material will change when heated or cooled
- figure out how to combine atoms and molecules to make new and useful materials

UNIFYING PRINCIPLE

Matter changes form and moves from place to place.

You see matter change form every day. You see the ice in your glass of juice disappear without a trace. You see a black metal gate slowly develop a flaky, orange coating. Matter is constantly changing and moving.

What It Means

Remember that matter is made of tiny particles called atoms. Atoms are constantly moving and combining with one another. All changes in matter are the result of atoms moving and combining in different ways.

Matter Changes and Moves

You can look at water to see how matter changes and moves. A block of ice is hard like a rock. Leave the ice out in sunlight, however, and it changes into a puddle of water. That puddle of water can eventually change into water vapor and disappear into the air. The water vapor in the air can become raindrops, which may fall on rocks, causing them to weather and wear away. The water that flows in rivers and streams picks up tiny bits of rock and carries them from one shore to another. Understanding how the world works requires an understanding of how matter changes and moves.

Matter Is Conserved

No matter was lost in any of the changes described above. The ice turned to water because its molecules began to move more quickly as they got warmer. The bits of rock carried away by the flowing river were not gone forever. They simply ended up farther down the river. The puddles of rainwater didn't really disappear; their molecules slowly mixed with molecules in the air.

Under ordinary conditions, when matter changes form, no matter is created or destroyed. The water created by melting ice has the same mass as the ice did. If you could measure the water vapor that mixes with the air, you would find it had the same mass as the water in the puddle did.

Why It's Important

Understanding how mass is conserved when matter changes form has helped scientists to

- describe changes they see in the world
- predict what will happen when two substances are mixed
- explain where matter goes when it seems to disappear

Energy changes from one form to another, but it cannot be created or destroyed.

When you use energy to warm your food or to turn on a flashlight, you may think that you "use up" the energy. Even though the camp-stove fuel is gone and the flashlight battery no longer functions, the energy they provided has not disappeared. It has been changed into a form you can no longer use. Understanding how energy changes forms is the basis for understanding how heat, light, and motion are produced.

What It Means

Changes that you see around you depend on energy. **Energy,** in fact, means the ability to cause change. The electrical energy from an outlet changes into light and heat in a light bulb. Plants change the light energy from the Sun into chemical energy, which animals use to power their muscles.

Energy Changes Forms

Using energy means changing energy. You probably have seen electric energy changing into light, heat, sound, and mechanical energy in household appliances. Fuels like wood, coal, and oil contain chemical energy that produces heat when burned. Electric power plants make electrical energy from a variety of energy sources, including falling water, nuclear energy, and fossil fuels.

Energy Is Conserved

Energy can be converted into forms that can be used for specific purposes. During the conversion, some of the original energy is converted into unwanted forms. For instance, when a power plant converts the energy of falling water into electrical energy, some of the energy is lost to friction and sound.

Similarly, when electrical energy is used to run an appliance, some of the energy is converted into forms that are not useful. Only a small percentage of the energy used in a light bulb, for instance, produces light; most of the energy becomes heat. Nonetheless, the total amount of energy remains the same through all these conversions.

The fact that energy does not disappear is a law of physical science. The **law of conservation of energy** states that energy cannot be created or destroyed. It can only change form.

Why It's Important

Understanding that energy changes form but does not disappear has helped scientists to

• predict how energy will change form
• manage energy conversions in useful ways
• build and improve machines

Physical forces affect the movement of all matter on Earth and throughout the universe.

What makes the world go around? The answer is simple: forces. Forces allow you to walk across the room, and forces keep the stars together in galaxies. Consider the forces acting on the rafts below. The rushing water is pushing the rafts forward. The force from the people paddling helps to steer the rafts.

What It Means

A **force** is a push or a pull. Every time you push or pull an object, you're applying a force to that object, whether or not the object moves. There are several forces—several pushes and pulls—acting on you right now. All these forces are necessary for you to do the things you do, even sitting and reading.

- You are already familiar with the force of gravity. **Gravity** is the force of attraction between two objects. Right now gravity is at work pulling you to Earth and Earth to you. The Moon stays in orbit around Earth because gravity holds it close.

- A contact force occurs when one object pushes or pulls another object by touching it. If you kick a soccer ball, for instance, you apply a contact force to the ball. You apply a contact force to a shopping cart that you push down a grocery aisle or a sled that you pull up a hill.

- **Friction** is the force that resists motion between two surfaces pressed together. If you've ever tried to walk on an icy sidewalk, you know how important friction can be. If you lightly rub your finger across a smooth page in a book and then across a piece of sandpaper, you can feel how the different surfaces produce different frictional forces. Which is easier to do?

- There are other forces at work in the world too. For example, a compass needle responds to the magnetic force exerted by Earth's magnetic field, and objects made of certain metals are attracted by magnets. In addition to magnetic forces, there are electrical forces operating between particles and between objects. For example, you can demonstrate electrical forces by rubbing an inflated balloon on your hair. The balloon will then stick to your head or to a wall without additional means of support.

Why It's Important

Although some of these forces are more obvious than others, physical forces at work in the world are necessary for you to do the things you do. Understanding forces allows scientists to

- predict how objects will move
- design machines that perform complex tasks
- predict where planets and stars will be in the sky from one night to the next

The Nature of Science

You may think of science as a body of knowledge or a collection of facts. More important, however, science is an active process that involves certain ways of looking at the world.

Scientific Habits of Mind

Scientists are curious. They are always asking questions. Scientists have asked questions such as, "What is the smallest form of matter?" and "How do the smallest particles behave?" These and other important questions are being investigated by scientists around the world.

Scientists are observant. They are always looking closely at the world around them. Scientists once thought the smallest parts of atoms were protons, neutrons, and electrons. Later, protons and neutrons were found to be made of even smaller particles called quarks.

Scientists are creative. They draw on what they know to form possible explanations for a pattern, an event, or an interesting phenomenon that they have observed. Then scientists create a plan for testing their ideas.

Scientists are skeptical. Scientists don't accept an explanation or answer unless it is based on evidence and logical reasoning. They continually question their own conclusions and the conclusions suggested by other scientists. Scientists trust only evidence that is confirmed by other people or methods.

Scientists cannot always make observations with their own eyes. They have developed technology, such as this particle detector, to help them gather information about the smallest particles of matter.

Scientists ask questions about the physical world and seek answers through carefully controlled procedures. Here a researcher works with supercooled magnets.

Science Processes at Work

You can think of science as a continuous cycle of asking and seeking answers to questions about the world. Although there are many processes that scientists use, scientists typically do each of the following:

• Observe and ask a question
• Determine what is known
• Investigate
• Interpret results
• Share results

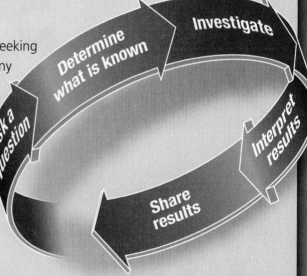

Observe and Ask a Question

It may surprise you that asking questions is an important skill. A scientific process may start when a scientist asks a question. Perhaps scientists observe an event or a process that they don't understand, or perhaps answering one question leads to another.

Determine What Is Known

When beginning an inquiry, scientists find out what is already known about a question. They study results from other scientific investigations, read journals, and talk with other scientists. A scientist working on subatomic particles is most likely a member of a large team using sophisticated equipment. Before beginning original research, the team analyzes results from previous studies.

Investigate

Investigating is the process of collecting evidence. Two important ways of investigating are observing and experimenting.

Observing is the act of noting and recording an event, a characteristic, or anything else detected with an instrument or with the senses. A researcher may study the properties of a substance by handling it, finding its mass, warming or cooling it, stretching it, and so on. For information about the behavior of subatomic particles, however, a researcher may rely on technology such as scanning tunneling microscopes, which produce images of structures that cannot be seen with the eye.

An **experiment** is an organized procedure to study something under controlled conditions. In order to study the effect of wing shape on the motion of a glider, for instance, a researcher would need to conduct controlled studies in which gliders made of the same materials and with the same masses differed only in the shape of their wings.

Scanning tunneling microscopes create images that allow scientists to observe molecular structure.

Physical chemists have found a way to observe chemical reactions at the atomic level. Using lasers, they can watch bonds breaking and new bonds forming.

Forming hypotheses and making predictions are two of the skills involved in scientific investigations. A **hypothesis** is a tentative explanation for an observation, a phenomenon, or a scientific problem that can be tested by further investigation. For example, in the mid-1800s astronomers noticed that the planet Uranus departed slightly from its expected orbit. One astronomer hypothesized that the irregularities in the planet's orbit were due to the gravitational effect of another planet—one that had not yet been detected. A **prediction** is an expectation of what will be observed or what will happen. A prediction can be used to test a hypothesis. The astronomers predicted that they would discover a new planet in the position calculated, and their prediction was confirmed with the discovery of the planet Neptune.

Interpret Results

As scientists investigate, they analyze their evidence, or data, and begin to draw conclusions. **Analyzing data** involves looking at the evidence gathered through observations or experiments and trying to identify any patterns that might exist in the data. Scientists often need to make additional observations or perform more experiments before they are sure of their conclusions. Many times scientists make new predictions or revise their hypotheses.

Often scientists use computers to help them analyze data. Computers reveal patterns that might otherwise be missed.

Scientists use computers to create models of objects or processes they are studying. This model shows carbon atoms forming a sphere.

Share Results

An important part of scientific investigation is sharing results of experiments. Scientists read and publish in journals and attend conferences to communicate with other scientists around the world. Sharing data and procedures gives them a way to test one another's results. They also share results with the public through newspapers, television, and other media.

The Nature of Technology

When you think of technology, you may think of cars, computers, and cell phones, as well as refrigerators, radios, and bicycles. Technology is not only the machines and devices that make modern lives easier, however. It is also a process in which new methods and devices are created. Technology makes use of scientific knowledge to design solutions to real-world problems.

Science and Technology

Science and technology go hand in hand. Each depends upon the other. Even designing a device as simple as a toaster requires knowledge of how heat flows and which materials are the best conductors of heat. Just as technology based on scientific knowledge makes our lives easier, some technology is used to advance scientific inquiry itself. For example, researchers use a number of specialized instruments to help them collect data. Microscopes, telescopes, spectrographs, and computers are just a few of the tools that help scientists learn more about the world. The more information these tools provide, the more devices can be developed to aid scientific research and to improve modern lives.

The Process of Technological Design

The process of technology involves many choices. For example, how does an automobile engineer design a better car? Is a better car faster? safer? cheaper? Before designing any new machine, the engineer must decide exactly what he or she wants the machine to do as well as what may be given up for the machine to do it. A faster car may get people to their destinations more quickly, but it may cost more and be less safe. As you study the technological process, think about all the choices that were made to build the technologies you use.

Identify a Need

Successful technology fills a need; it helps us perform a task we need or want to do. For example, as more cars appear on the road, noise and air pollution become serious threats to the environment and to people's health. Gas consumption also depletes precious petroleum resources. There is a need to find a fuel source for a car that will not pollute the air and that will never run out.

Design and Develop

Hydrogen fuel cells are a potential solution to this need. These cells combine hydrogen and oxygen into water, producing electricity in the process. Engineers have found a way to make fuel cells small enough to fit into a car, yet able to produce enough electricity to power an electric motor. Before arriving at this final design, engineers tried many others.

Test and Improve

Just because a technology works doesn't mean it cannot be improved. A fuel-cell-powered car has been driven from San Francisco to Washington, D.C., but it probably will be a while before it's in dealer showrooms. Engineers won't know how these cars will perform until they're driven in real-world conditions. Engineers also won't know if the average driver will be able to handle the necessary maintenance on the car until the car is made available to ordinary drivers. Improvements in the future may well bring cars powered by fuel cells into garages everywhere.

Reading Text and Visuals

This book is organized to help you learn. Use these boxed pointers as a path to help you learn and remember the **Big Ideas** and **Key Concepts**.

Take notes.

Use the strategies on the **Getting Ready to Learn** page.

Read the Big Idea.

As you read **Key Concepts** for the chapter, relate them to **the Big Idea**.

CHAPTER 2
Proper Matter

the BIG idea

Matter has properties that can be changed by physical and chemical processes.

Key Concepts

SECTION 2.1
Matter has observable properties.
Learn how to recognize physical and chemical properties.

SECTION 2.2
Changes of state are physical changes.
Learn how energy is related to changes of state.

SECTION 2.3
Properties are used to identify substances.
Learn how the properties of substances can be used to identify them and to separate mixtures.

Internet Preview

CLASSZONE.COM
Chapter 2 online resources: Content Review, Simulation, three Resource Centers, Math Tutorial, Test Practice

A 38 Unit: Matter and Energy

CHAPTER 2
Getting Ready to Learn

CONCEPT REVIEW

- Everything is made of matter.
- Matter has mass and volume.
- Atoms combine to form molecules.

VOCABULARY REVIEW

mass p. 10
volume p. 11
molecule p. 18
states of matter p. 27

CONTENT REVIEW
CLASSZONE.COM
Review concepts and vocabulary.

TAKING NOTES

MAIN IDEA WEB

Write each new blue heading in a box. Then write notes in boxes around the center box that give important terms and details about that heading.

VOCABULARY STRATEGY

Think about a vocabulary term as a **magnet word** diagram. Write related terms and ideas in boxes around it.

SCIENCE NOTEBOOK

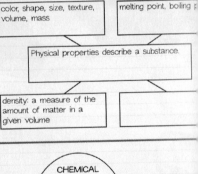

color, shape, size, texture, volume, mass

melting point, boiling p

Physical properties describe a substance.

density: a measure of the amount of matter in a given volume

burning

rusting

tarnishing

CHEMICAL CHANGE

change in tempera

change in color

formation of bubble

See the Note-Taking Handbook on pages R45–R51.

A 40 Unit: Matter and Energy

xxviii

Read each heading.

See how it fits into the outline of the chapter.

KEY CONCEPT

2.1 Matter has observable properties.

◀ **BEFORE, you learned**

- Matter has mass and volume
- Matter is made of atoms
- Matter exists in different states

▶ **NOW, you will learn**

- About physical and chemical properties
- About physical changes
- About chemical changes

Remember what you know.

Think about concepts you learned earlier and preview what you'll learn now.

VOCABULARY

physical property p. 41
density p. 43
physical change p. 44
chemical property p. 46
chemical change p. 46

EXPLORE Physical Properties

How can a substance be changed?

PROCEDURE

① Observe the clay. Note its physical characteristics, such as color, shape, texture, and size.

② Change the shape of the clay. Note which characteristics changed and which ones stayed the same.

MATERIAL
rectangular piece of clay

WHAT DO YOU THINK?

- How did reshaping the clay change its physical characteristics?
- How were the mass and the volume of the clay affected?

Try the activities.

They will introduce you to science concepts.

Physical properties describe a substance.

What words would you use to describe a table? a chair? the sandwich you ate for lunch? You would probably say something about the shape, color, and size of each item. Next you might consider whether it is hard or soft, smooth or rough to the touch. Normally, when describing an object, you identify the characteristics of the object that you can observe without changing the identity of the object.

The characteristics of a substance that can be observed without changing the identity of the substance are called **physical properties.** In science, observation can include measuring and handling a substance. All of your senses can be used to detect physical properties. Color, shape, size, texture, volume, and mass are a few of the physical properties you probably have encountered.

VOCABULARY
Make a magnet word diagram in your notebook for *physical property.*

Learn the vocabulary.

Take notes on each term.

CHECK YOUR READING Describe some of the physical properties of your desk.

Answer the questions.

Check Your Reading questions will help you remember what you read.

Chapter 2: **Properties of Matter** 41 **A**

Chapter 2: **Properties of Matter** 39 **A**

Reading Text and Visuals

Read one paragraph at a time.

Look for a topic sentence that explains the main idea of the paragraph. Figure out how the details relate to that idea. One paragraph might have several important ideas; you may have to reread to understand.

Answer the questions.

Check Your Reading questions will help you remember what you read.

Study the visuals.

- Read the title.

- Read all labels and captions.

- Figure out what the picture is showing. Notice colors, arrows, and lines.

- Answer the question. **Reading Visuals** questions will help you understand the picture.

Physical Properties

How do you know which characteristics are physical properties? Just ask yourself whether observing the property involves changing the substance to a different substance. For example, you can stretch a rubber band. Does stretching the rubber band change what it is made of? No. The rubber band is still a rubber band before and after it is stretched. It may look a little different, but it is still a rubber band.

Mass and volume are two physical properties. Measuring these properties does not change the identity of a substance. For example, a lump of clay might have a mass of 200 grams (g) and a volume of 100 cubic centimeters (cm^3). If you were to break the clay in half, you would have two 100 g pieces of clay, each with a volume of 50 cm^3. You can bend and shape the clay too. Even if you were to mold a realistic model of a car out of the clay, it still would be a piece of clay. Although you have changed some of the properties of the object, such as its shape and volume, you have not changed the fact that the substance you are observing is clay.

▽ **REMINDER**

Because all formulas for volume involve the multiplication of three measurements, volume has a unit that is cubed (such as cm^3).

CHECK YOUR READING Which physical properties listed above are found by taking measurements? Which are not?

Physical Properties

Physical properties of clay—such as volume, mass, color, texture, and shape—can be observed without changing the fact that the substance is clay.

Block of Clay

Shaped Clay

READING VISUALS COMPARE AND CONTRAST Which physical properties do the two pieces of clay have in common? Which are different?

42 Unit: **Matter and Energy**

Doing Labs

To understand science, you have to see it in action. Doing labs helps you understand how things really work.

① Read the entire lab first.

② Form a hypothesis.

③ Follow the procedure.

④ Record the data.

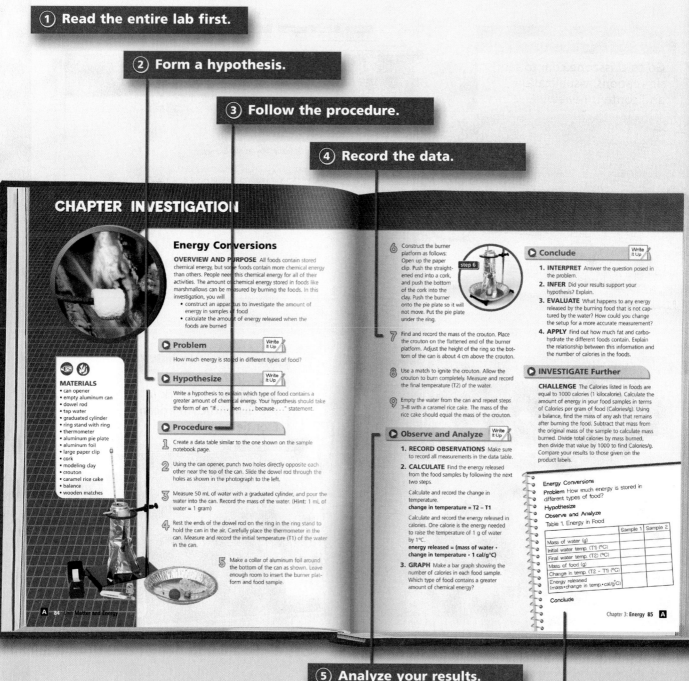

CHAPTER INVESTIGATION

Energy Conversions

OVERVIEW AND PURPOSE All foods contain stored chemical energy, but some foods contain more chemical energy than others. People need this chemical energy for all of their activities. The amount of chemical energy stored in foods like marshmallows can be measured by burning the foods. In this investigation, you will
• construct an apparatus to investigate the amount of energy in samples of food
• calculate the amount of energy released when the foods are burned

▶ Problem   *Write it Up*

How much energy is stored in different types of food?

▶ Hypothesize   *Write it Up*

Write a hypothesis to explain which type of food contains a greater amount of chemical energy. Your hypothesis should take the form of an "If . . . , then . . . , because . . ." statement.

▶ Procedure

1. Create a data table similar to the one shown on the sample notebook page.

2. Using the can opener, punch two holes directly opposite each other near the top of the can. Slide the dowel rod through the holes as shown in the photograph to the left.

3. Measure 50 mL of water with a graduated cylinder, and pour the water into the can. Record the mass of the water. (Hint: 1 mL of water = 1 gram)

4. Rest the ends of the dowel rod on the ring in the ring stand to hold the can in the air. Carefully place the thermometer in the can. Measure and record the initial temperature (T1) of the water in the can.

5. Make a collar of aluminum foil around the bottom of the can as shown. Leave enough room to insert the burner platform and food sample.

MATERIALS
• can opener
• empty aluminum can
• dowel rod
• tap water
• graduated cylinder
• ring stand with ring
• thermometer
• aluminum pie plate
• aluminum foil
• large paper clip
• cork
• modeling clay
• crouton
• caramel rice cake
• balance
• wooden matches

6. Construct the burner platform as follows: Open up the paper clip. Push the straight-ened end into a cork, and push the bottom of the cork into the clay. Push the burner onto the pie plate so it will not move. Put the pie plate under the ring.

step 6

7. Find and record the mass of the crouton. Place the crouton on the flattened end of the burner platform. Adjust the height of the ring so the bot-tom of the can is about 4 cm above the crouton.

8. Use a match to ignite the crouton. Allow the crouton to burn completely. Measure and record the final temperature (T2) of the water.

9. Empty the water from the can and repeat steps 3–8 with a caramel rice cake. The mass of the rice cake should equal the mass of the crouton.

▶ Observe and Analyze   *Write it Up*

1. **RECORD OBSERVATIONS** Make sure to record all measurements in the data table.

2. **CALCULATE** Find the energy released from the food samples by following the next two steps.

   Calculate and record the change in temperature.
   change in temperature = T2 – T1

   Calculate and record the energy released in calories. One calorie is the energy needed to raise the temperature of 1 g of water by 1°C.
   energy released = (mass of water · change in temperature · 1 cal/g°C)

3. **GRAPH** Make a bar graph showing the number of calories in each food sample. Which type of food contains a greater amount of chemical energy?

▶ Conclude   *Write it Up*

1. **INTERPRET** Answer the question posed in the problem.

2. **INFER** Did your results support your hypothesis? Explain.

3. **EVALUATE** What happens to any energy released by the burning food that is not cap-tured by the water? How could you change the setup for a more accurate measurement?

4. **APPLY** Find out how much fat and carbo-hydrate the different foods contain. Explain the relationship between this information and the number of calories in the foods.

▶ INVESTIGATE Further

CHALLENGE The Calories listed in foods are equal to 1000 calories (1 kilocalorie). Calculate the amount of energy in your food samples in terms of Calories per gram of food (Calories/g). Using a balance, find the mass of any ash that remains after burning the food. Subtract that mass from the original mass of the sample to calculate mass burned. Divide total calories by mass burned, then divide that value by 1000 to find Calories/g. Compare your results to those given on the product labels.

Energy Conversions
Problem How much energy is stored in different types of food?
Hypothesize
Observe and Analyze
Table 1. Energy in Food

	Sample 1	Sample 2
Mass of water (g)		
Initial water temp. (T1) (°C)		
Final water temp. (T2) (°C)		
Mass of food (g)		
Change in temp. (T2 – T1) (°C)		
Energy released (mass·change in temp.·cal/g°C)		

Conclude

⑤ Analyze your results.

⑥ Write your lab report.

Using Technology

The Internet is a great source of information about up-to-date science. The ClassZone Web site and SciLinks have exciting sites for you to explore. Video clips and simulations can make science come alive.

Look for red banners.

Go to **classzone.com** to see simulations, visualizations, and content review.

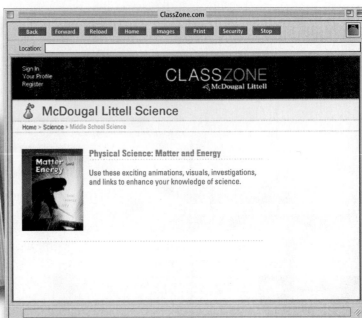

ClassZone.com

Back | Forward | Reload | Home | Images | Print | Security | Stop

Location:

Sign In
Your Profile
Register

CLASSZONE
McDougal Littell

McDougal Littell Science

Home > Science > Middle School Science

Physical Science: Matter and Energy

Use these exciting animations, visuals, investigations, and links to enhance your knowledge of science.

Watch the videos.

See science at work in the **Scientific American Frontiers** video.

Look up SciLinks.

Go to **scilinks.org** to explore the topic.

NSTA
scilinks.org
SCiLINKS

Forces **Code: MDL005**

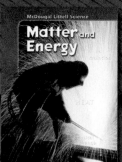

Matter and Energy
Contents Overview

Unit Features

1 Introduction to Matter   6

the BIG idea

Everything that has mass and takes up space is matter.

2 Properties of Matter   38

the BIG idea

Matter has properties that can be changed by physical and chemical processes.

3 Energy   68

the BIG idea

Energy has different forms, but it is always conserved.

4 Temperature and Heat   100

the BIG idea

Heat is a flow of energy due to temperature differences.

FUELS of the FUTURE

Where does this spacecraft get its fuel?

SCIENTIFIC
AMERICAN
FRONTIERS

View the "Sunrayce" segment of your *Scientific American Frontiers* video to learn about a cross-country race in which cars use solar power instead of gasoline.

Deep Space 1 was an experimental design. Its successful mission prepared the way to the development of more ion-propelled spacecraft.

The stream of ions glows blue as it is shot out of an ion-propulsion engine.

Ion Engines for Long Voyages

Rocket engines must provide huge amounts of energy to move spacecraft away from Earth and keep them in orbit. The fuel required can weigh more than the spacecraft themselves. That is why scientists and engineers are always looking for more efficient ways to give spacecraft and other vehicles the energy to move.

One method of powering spacecraft uses electrically charged particles called ions. The atoms of a gas—usually xenon—are first made into ions. An electric field is then used to pull these ions out of the engine at a very high speed—faster than 100,000 kilometers per hour (62,000 mi/h). This stream of rapidly moving ions works like the gases coming out of a jet engine on a plane—propelling the spacecraft in the direction opposite to the ion stream.

An advantage of ion propulsion is that its fuel is much lighter than the chemical fuel used in rockets. Ion propulsion does not provide enough thrust to be used for a rocket launch, but it can be used to move a spacecraft through long distances in outer space. This method of propulsion provides a small force to the spacecraft; however, over time the spacecraft can reach great speeds.

The space probe *Deep Space 1* was the first to use an ion engine to travel between planets. The engine generated enough speed for the probe to follow and photograph comet Borrelly in 2001.

Solar sails will reflect sunlight to move a spacecraft through space.

Running on Sunlight

Solar energy is used for travel in outer space, where there is plenty of sunlight and very little friction to slow down a spacecraft. However, once a spacecraft travels far away from the Sun—as far as the outer planets Jupiter and Saturn—the amount of energy reaching it is far less than the energy it was getting near Earth. The sunlight can be helpful only if solar cells on the vehicle can collect enough of it. One solution is to reflect sunlight. Scientists are developing solar sails, which will act like enormous mirrors. The pressure of reflected sunlight on the sails can be used to move a large ship through space—even far from the Sun.

Beaming Energy from Earth

Another way to power a spacecraft is to send energy to it all the way from Earth. This idea is called beamed energy propulsion. A beam delivers energy to solar sails on the spacecraft. The energy can be in the form of microwaves—the same energy that heats food in a microwave oven or delivers calls on a cell phone. Or it can be in the form of laser light, a very concentrated beam of visible light. This method has already been used successfully to power very small vehicles, 10 centimeters (4 in.) long. Experiments are under way with larger spacecraft.

Combined Technologies

Some recent space flights have combined common and experimental technologies. For example, the *Cassini* space probe has two regular rocket engines for propulsion. Other energy comes from three generators powered by radioactive decay. This combination of engines allowed *Cassini* to be the largest and most complicated spacecraft ever launched. Its goal is to explore Saturn.

SCIENTIFIC AMERICAN FRONTIERS

View the "Sunrayce" segment of your *Scientific American Frontiers* video to see what is involved in solar-car racing.

IN THIS SCENE FROM THE VIDEO ▶ Students from California State University, Los Angeles, work on their solar car.

CATCHING THE SUN'S RAYS Since 1990 teams of college students have built and raced solar-powered cars. The races are held every two years to promote awareness of solar energy and to inspire young people to work in science and engineering.

Solar cells on the cars' bodies convert sunlight into electricity. The goal is to make lightweight cars that convert sunlight efficiently. Today's solar cars can reach speeds of up to 75 miles per hour, but the average racing speed is 25 miles per hour. On cloudy or rainy days, the teams conserve power by traveling more slowly—or risk running down their batteries.

In 2003 the American Solar Challenge took place on historic Route 66 from Chicago to Claremont, California. At 3700 kilometers (2300 mi), the ten-day event was the longest solar-car race in the world.

Alternative Fuels on Earth

Scientists and inventors have long been looking for practical alternative fuels to power vehicles on Earth as well as in outer space. Most vehicle engines on Earth use gasoline or other fossil fuels. These fuels are based on resources, such as petroleum, that are found in underground deposits. Those deposits will not be replaced for millions of years. Solar energy, by contrast, is endlessly renewable, so it seems to be a good alternative to nonrenewable fossil fuels.

Solar-powered cars rely on solar cells, which convert the energy of sunlight directly into electrical energy that can be stored in batteries. One outstanding solar car was built by Dutch students and entered in the 2001 World Solar Challenge.

The students' car, called the *Nuna,* used several technologies that had been developed for space travel. Its body was reinforced with Kevlar, a space-age material that is also used in satellites, space suits, and bulletproof vests. During the race, the *Nuna* covered 3010 kilometers of desert in Australia, breaking solar-car speed records, and won the race.

Does the development of solar cars like the *Nuna* mean that most people will be driving solar cars soon? Unfortunately, such cars run only when the Sun is shining unless they rely on batteries—and it takes hundreds of pounds of batteries to store the amount of energy in a gallon of gasoline. As with spacecraft, the goal is to design a vehicle in which the fuel doesn't outweigh the vehicle itself.

UNANSWERED Questions

Even as scientists and inventors solve problems in solar technology, new questions arise.

- Can solar technology be made affordable?
- Is solar technology practical for large-scale public transportation?
- Are there any hidden costs to the use of alternative fuels?

UNIT PROJECTS

As you study this unit, work alone or with a group on one of these projects.

Build a Solar Oven

Design and build a solar oven that can boil a quarter cup of water.

- Plan and sketch a design for a solar oven that can reach 100°C.
- Collect materials and assemble your oven. Then conduct trials and improve your design.

Multimedia Presentation

Create an informative program on solar race cars and the way they work.

- Collect information about solar race cars. Research how they are powered.
- Examine why solar cars have specific shapes. Learn how the solar panels and batteries work together.
- Give a multimedia presentation describing what you learned.

Design an Experiment

Design an experiment that compares how well two of the following alternative energy sources move an object: solar energy, wind power, biomass (fuel from plant material), waste-material fuel, hydrogen fuel cells, heat exchangers.

- Research the energy sources, and pick two types to compare.
- List materials for your experiment. Create a data table and write up your procedure.
- Describe your experiment for the class.

CAREER CENTER
CLASSZONE.COM

Learn more about careers in electrical engineering.

CHAPTER

Introduction to Matter

the **BIG** idea

Everything that has mass and takes up space is matter.

Key Concepts

SECTION
1.1 Matter has mass and volume.
Learn what mass and volume are and how to measure them.

SECTION
1.2 Matter is made of atoms.
Learn about the movement of atoms and molecules.

SECTION
1.3 Matter combines to form different substances.
Learn how atoms form compounds and mixtures.

SECTION
1.4 Matter exists in different physical states.
Learn how different states of matter behave.

Internet Preview

CLASSZONE.COM

Chapter 1 online resources:
Content Review, two
Simulations, four Resource
Centers, Math Tutorial,
Test Practice

What matter can you identify in this photograph?

EXPLORE (the BIG idea)

What Has Changed?

Blow up a balloon. Observe it. Let the air out of the balloon slowly. Observe it again.

Observe and Think Did the amount of material that makes up the balloon change? Did the amount of air inside the balloon change? How did the amount of air inside the balloon affect the size of the balloon?

Where Does the Sugar Go?

Stir some sugar into a glass of water. Observe what happens.

Observe and Think What happened to the sugar as you stirred? Do you think you would be able to separate the sugar from the water? If so, how?

Internet Activity: Scale

Go to **ClassZone.com** to explore the smallest units of matter. Start with a faraway view of an object. Then try closer and closer views until you see that object at the atomic level.

Observe and Think Are all objects seen at faraway views made up of the same parts at an atomic level? Explain your answer.

NSTA scilinks.org **SCiLINKS**

Solids, Liquids, and Gases **Code: MDL061**

Getting Ready to Learn

◀ CONCEPT REVIEW

- Matter is made of particles too small to see.
- Energy and matter change from one form to another.
- Energy cannot be created or destroyed.

◀ VOCABULARY REVIEW

See Glossary for definitions.

particle

substance

ⓘ CONTENT REVIEW
CLASSZONE.COM
Review concepts and vocabulary.

▶ TAKING NOTES

MAIN IDEA AND DETAIL NOTES

Make a two-column chart. Write the main ideas, such as those in the blue headings, in the column on the left. Write details about each of those main ideas in the column on the right.

VOCABULARY STRATEGY

Write each new vocabulary term in the center of a **four square** diagram. Write notes in the squares around each term. Include a definition, some characteristics, and some examples of the term. If possible, write some things that are not examples of the term.

See the Note-Taking Handbook on pages R45–R51.

SCIENCE NOTEBOOK

MAIN IDEAS	DETAIL NOTES
1. All objects are made of matter.	1. All objects and living organisms are matter.
	1. Light and sound are not matter.
2. Mass is a measure of the amount of matter.	2. A balance can be used to compare masses.
	2. Standard unit of mass is kilogram (kg).

Definition	Characteristics
the downward pull on an object due to gravity	• standard unit is newton (N) • is measured by using a scale

WEIGHT

Examples	Nonexamples
On Earth, a 1 kg object has a weight of 9.8 N.	not the same as mass, which is a measure of how much matter an object contains

Matter has mass and volume.

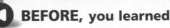 **BEFORE, you learned**

- Scientists study the world by asking questions and collecting data
- Scientists use tools such as microscopes, thermometers, and computers

 NOW, you will learn

- What matter is
- How to measure the mass of matter
- How to measure the volume of matter

VOCABULARY

matter p. 9
mass p. 10
weight p. 11
volume p. 11

EXPLORE Similar Objects

How can two similar objects differ?

PROCEDURE

① Look at the two balls but do not pick them up. Compare their sizes and shapes. Record your observations.

② Pick up each ball. Compare the way the balls feel in your hands. Record your observations.

WHAT DO YOU THINK?

How would your observations be different if the larger ball were made of foam?

MATERIALS
2 balls of different sizes

All objects are made of matter.

Suppose your class takes a field trip to a museum. During the course of the day you see mammoth bones, sparkling crystals, hot-air balloons, and an astronaut's space suit. All of these things are matter.

Matter is what makes up all of the objects and living organisms in the universe. As you will see, **matter** is anything that has mass and takes up space. Your body is matter. The air that you breathe and the water that you drink are also matter. Matter makes up the materials around you. Matter is made of particles called atoms, which are too small to see. You will learn more about atoms in the next section.

Not everything is matter. Light and sound, for example, are not matter. Light does not take up space or have mass in the same way that a table does. Although air is made of atoms, a sound traveling through air is not.

VOCABULARY
Make four square diagrams for *matter* and for *mass* in your notebook to help you understand their relationship.

 CHECK YOUR READING What is matter? How can you tell if something is matter?

Mass is a measure of the amount of matter.

MAIN IDEA AND DETAILS
As you read, write the blue headings on the left side of a two-column chart. Add details in the other column.

Different objects contain different amounts of matter. **Mass** is a measure of how much matter an object contains. A metal teaspoon, for example, contains more matter than a plastic teaspoon. Therefore, a metal teaspoon has a greater mass than a plastic teaspoon. An elephant has more mass than a mouse.

 CHECK YOUR READING How are matter and mass related?

Measuring Mass

When you measure mass, you compare the mass of the object with a standard amount, or unit, of mass. The standard unit of mass is the kilogram (kg). A large grapefruit has a mass of about one-half kilogram. Smaller masses are often measured in grams (g). There are 1000 grams in a kilogram. A penny has a mass of between two and three grams.

How can you compare the masses of two objects? One way is to use a pan balance, as shown below. If two objects balance each other on a pan balance, then they contain the same amount of matter. If a basketball balances a metal block, for example, then the basketball and the block have the same mass. Beam balances work in a similar way, but instead of comparing the masses of two objects, you compare the mass of an object with a standard mass on the beam.

A bowling ball and a basketball are about the same size, but a bowling ball has more mass.

Measuring Weight

When you hold an object such as a backpack full of books, you feel it pulling down on your hands. This is because Earth's gravity pulls the backpack toward the ground. Gravity is the force that pulls two masses toward each other. In this example, the two masses are Earth and the backpack. **Weight** is the downward pull on an object due to gravity. If the pull of the backpack is strong, you would say that the backpack weighs a lot.

Weight is measured by using a scale, such as a spring scale like the one shown on the right, that tells how hard an object is pushing or pulling on it. The standard scientific unit for weight is the newton (N). A common unit for weight is the pound (lb).

Mass and weight are closely related, but they are not the same. Mass describes the amount of matter an object has, and weight describes how strongly gravity is pulling on that matter. On Earth, a one-kilogram object has a weight of 9.8 newtons (2.2 lb). When a person says that one kilogram is equal to 2.2 pounds, he or she is really saying that one kilogram has a weight of 2.2 pounds on Earth. On the Moon, however, gravity is one-sixth as strong as it is on Earth. On the Moon, the one-kilogram object would have a weight of 1.6 newtons (0.36 lb). The amount of matter in the object, or its mass, is the same on Earth as it is on the Moon, but the pull of gravity is different.

Gravity is pulling down on both the girl and the backpack. The greater the mass of the backpack is, the stronger the pull of gravity is on it.

SIMULATION
CLASSZONE.COM

Compare weights on different planets.

CHECK YOUR READING   What is the difference between mass and weight?

Volume is a measure of the space matter occupies.

Matter takes up space. A bricklayer stacks bricks on top of each other to build a wall. No two bricks can occupy the same place because the matter in each brick takes up space.

The amount of space that matter in an object occupies is called the object's **volume.** The bowling ball and the basketball shown on page 10 take up approximately the same amount of space. Therefore, the two balls have about the same volume. Although the basketball is hollow, it is not empty. Air fills up the space inside the basketball. Air and other gases take up space and have volume.

Determining Volume by Formula

RESOURCE CENTER
CLASSZONE.COM

Find out more about
volume.

There are different ways to find the volume of an object. For objects that have well-defined shapes, such as a brick or a ball, you can take a few measurements of the object and calculate the volume by substituting these values into a formula.

A rectangular box, for example, has a length, a width, and a height that can be measured. To find the volume of the box, multiply the three values.

Volume = length · width · height
$$V = lwh$$

If you measure the length, the width, and the height of the box in centimeters (cm), the volume has a unit of centimeters times centimeters times centimeters, or centimeters cubed (cm^3). If the measurements are meters, the unit of volume is meters cubed (m^3). All measurements must be in the same unit to calculate volume.

Other regular solids, such as spheres and cylinders, also have formulas for calculating volumes. All formulas for volume require multiplying three dimensions. Units for volume are often expressed in terms of a length unit cubed, that is, a length to the third power.

Calculating Volume

Sample Problem

What is the volume of a pizza box that is 8 cm high, 38 cm wide, and 38 cm long?

What do you know?	length = 38 cm, width = 38 cm, height = 8 cm
What do you want to find out?	Volume
Write the formula:	$V = lwh$
Substitute into the formula:	$V = 38$ cm · 38 cm · 8 cm
Calculate and simplify:	11,552 cm · cm · cm = 11,552 cm^3
Check that your units agree:	Unit is cm^3. Unit of volume is cm^3. Units agree.
Answer:	11,552 cm^3

Practice the Math

1. A bar of gold is 10 cm long, 5 cm wide, and 7 cm high. What is its volume?

2. What is the volume of a large block of wood that is 1 m long, 0.5 m high, and 50 cm wide?

Measuring Volume by Displacement

Although a box has a regular shape, a rock does not. There is no simple formula for calculating the volume of something with an irregular shape. Instead, you can make use of the fact that two objects cannot be in the same place at the same time. This method of measuring is called displacement.

1 Add water to a graduated cylinder. Note the volume of the water by reading the water level on the cylinder.

2 Submerge the irregular object in the water. Because the object and the water cannot share the same space, the water is displaced, or moved upward. Note the new volume of the water with the object in it.

3 Subtract the volume of the water before you added the object from the volume of the water and the object together. The result is the volume of the object. The object displaces a volume of water equal to the volume of the object.

You measure the volume of a liquid by measuring how much space it takes up in a container. The volume of a liquid usually is measured in liters (L) or milliliters (mL). One liter is equal to 1000 milliliters. Milliliters and cubic centimeters are equivalent. This can be written as $1 \text{ mL} = 1 \text{ cm}^3$. If you had a box with a volume of one cubic centimeter and you filled it with water, you would have one milliliter of water.

In the first photograph, the graduated cylinder contains 50 mL of water. Placing a rock in the cylinder causes the water level to rise from 50 mL to 55 mL. The difference is 5 mL; therefore, the volume of the rock is 5 cm^3.

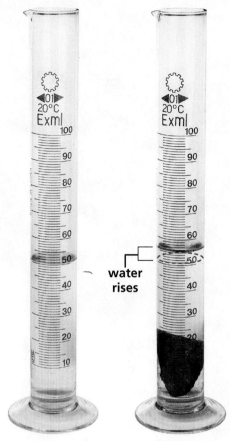

water rises

Measure the volume of water without the rock.

Measure the volume of water with the rock in it.

1.1 Review

KEY CONCEPTS

1. Give three examples of matter.
2. What do weight and mass measure?
3. How can you measure the volume of an object that has an irregular shape?

CRITICAL THINKING

4. **Calculate** What is the volume of a box that is 12 cm long, 6 cm wide, and 4 cm high?
5. **Synthesize** What is the relationship between the units of measurement for the volume of a liquid and of a solid object?

◇ CHALLENGE

6. **Infer** Why might a small increase in the dimensions of an object cause a large change in its volume?

CHAPTER INVESTIGATION

Mass and Volume

OVERVIEW AND PURPOSE In order for scientists around the world to communicate with one another about calculations in their research, they use a common system of measurement called the metric system. Scientists use the same tools and methods for the measurement of length, mass, and volume. In this investigation you will

- use a ruler, a graduated cylinder, and a balance to measure the mass and the volume of different objects
- determine which method is best for measuring the volume of the objects

▶ Procedure

1 Make a data table like the one shown on the sample notebook page.

2 Measure the mass of each object: rock, pennies, sponge, and tissue box. Record each mass.

step 2

3 For each object, conduct three trials for mass. Average the trials to find a final mass measurement.

4 Decide how you will find the volume of each object.

For rectangular objects, you will use the following formula:

$$\text{Volume} = \text{length} \cdot \text{width} \cdot \text{height}$$

For irregular objects, you will use the displacement method and the following formula:

$$\text{Volume of object} = \text{volume of water with object} - \text{volume of water without object}$$

MATERIALS
- small rock
- 5 pennies
- rectangular sponge
- tissue box
- beam balance
- large graduated cylinder
- water
- ruler

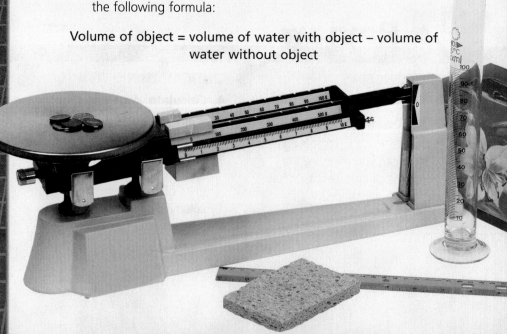

5. For each object, you will conduct three trials for measuring volume. Average the trials to find a final volume measurement.

step 6

6. For rectangular objects, use metric units for measuring the length, width, and height. Record the measurements in your data table.

7. For irregular objects, fill the graduated cylinder about half full with water. Record the exact volume of water in the cylinder. **Note:** The surface of the liquid will be curved in the graduated cylinder. Read the volume of the liquid at the bottom of the curve called the meniscus.

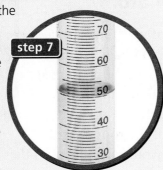

step 7

8. Carefully place the object you are measuring into the cylinder. The object must be completely under the water. Record the exact volume of water in the cylinder containing the object by reading the meniscus.

▶ Observe and Analyze

Write It Up

1. **RECORD OBSERVATIONS** Make sure you have filled out your data table completely.

2. **INTERPRET** For each object, explain why you chose a particular method for measuring the volume.

▶ Conclude

Write It Up

1. **IDENTIFY LIMITS** Which sources of error might have affected your measurements?

2. **APPLY** Doctors need to know the mass of a patient before deciding how much of a medication to prescribe. Why is it important to measure each patient's mass before prescribing medicine?

3. **APPLY** Scientists in the United States work closely with scientists in other countries to develop new technology. What are the advantages of having a single system of measurement?

▶ INVESTIGATE Further

CHALLENGE Measuring cups and spoons used in cooking often include both customary and metric units. Convert the measurements in a favorite recipe into metric units. Convert the amounts of solid ingredients to grams, and liquid ingredients to milliliters or liters. If possible, use the new measurements to follow the recipe and prepare the food. Were your conversions accurate?

Mass and Volume
Observe and Analyze
Table 1. Masses of Various Objects

Object	Mass (g)			Average
	Trial 1	Trial 2	Trial 3	
rock				
5 pennies				
sponge				
tissue box				

Table 2. Volumes of Various Objects

Object	Method Used	Volume (cm³ or mL)			
		Trial 1	Trial 2	Trial 3	Average
rock					
5 pennies					
sponge					
tissue box					

Matter is made of atoms.

 BEFORE, you learned

- Matter has mass
- Matter has volume

NOW, you will learn

- About the smallest particles of matter
- How atoms combine into molecules
- How atoms and molecules move

VOCABULARY

atom p. 16
molecule p. 18

THINK ABOUT

How small is an atom?

All matter is made up of very tiny particles called atoms. It is hard to imagine exactly how small these particles are. Suppose that each of the particles making up the pin shown in the photograph on the right were actually the size of the round head on the pin. How large would the pin be in that case? If you could stick such a pin in the ground, it would cover about 90 square miles—about one-seventh the area of London, England. It would also be about 80 miles high—almost 15 times the height of Mount Everest.

Atoms are extremely small.

VOCABULARY
Make a four square diagram for *atom* that includes details that will help you remember the term.

How small can things get? If you break a stone wall into smaller and smaller pieces, you would have a pile of smaller stones. If you could break the smaller stones into the smallest pieces possible, you would have a pile of atoms. An **atom** is the smallest basic unit of matter.

The idea that all matter is made of extremely tiny particles dates back to the fifth century B.C., when Greek philosophers proposed the first atomic theory of matter. All matter, they said, was made of only a few different types of tiny particles called atoms. The different arrangements of atoms explained the differences among the substances that make up the world. Although the modern view of the atom is different from the ancient view, the idea of atoms as basic building blocks has been confirmed. Today scientists have identified more than 100 different types of atoms.

 CHECK YOUR READING What are atoms? How are they like building blocks?

Atoms

It is hard to imagine that visible matter is composed of particles too tiny to see. Although you cannot see an individual atom, you are constantly seeing large collections of them. You are a collection of atoms. So are your textbook, a desk, and all the other matter around you. Matter is not something that contains atoms; matter is atoms. A desk, for example, is a collection of atoms and the empty space between those atoms. Without the atoms, there would be no desk—just empty space.

Atoms are so small that they cannot be seen even with very strong optical microscopes. Try to imagine the size of an atom by considering that a single teaspoonful of water contains approximately 500,000,000,000,000,000,000,000 atoms. Although atoms are extremely small, they do have a mass. The mass of a single teaspoonful of water is about 5 grams. This mass is equal to the mass of all the atoms that the water is made of added together.

READING TiP

The word *atom* comes from the Greek word *atomos*, meaning "indivisible," or "cannot be divided."

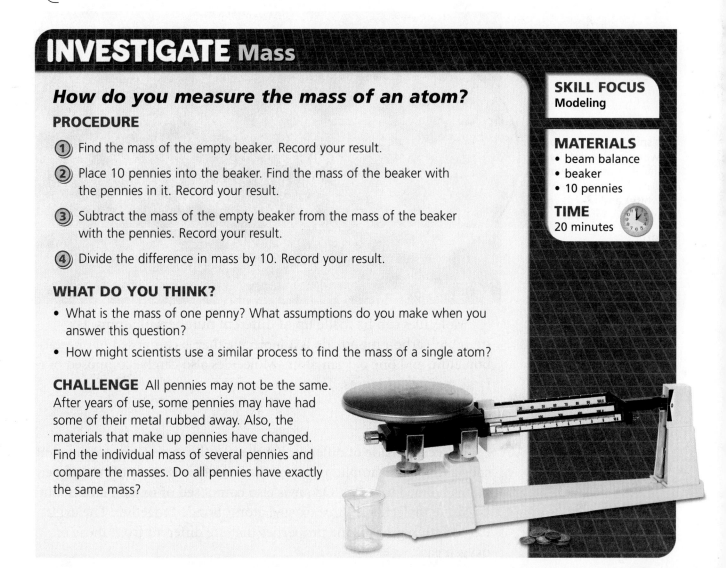

INVESTIGATE Mass

How do you measure the mass of an atom?

PROCEDURE

1. Find the mass of the empty beaker. Record your result.

2. Place 10 pennies into the beaker. Find the mass of the beaker with the pennies in it. Record your result.

3. Subtract the mass of the empty beaker from the mass of the beaker with the pennies. Record your result.

4. Divide the difference in mass by 10. Record your result.

WHAT DO YOU THINK?

- What is the mass of one penny? What assumptions do you make when you answer this question?

- How might scientists use a similar process to find the mass of a single atom?

CHALLENGE All pennies may not be the same. After years of use, some pennies may have had some of their metal rubbed away. Also, the materials that make up pennies have changed. Find the individual mass of several pennies and compare the masses. Do all pennies have exactly the same mass?

SKILL FOCUS
Modeling

MATERIALS
- beam balance
- beaker
- 10 pennies

TIME
20 minutes

Molecules

When two or more atoms bond together, or combine, they make a particle called a **molecule.** A molecule can be made of atoms that are different or atoms that are alike. A molecule of water, for example, is a combination of different atoms—two hydrogen atoms and one oxygen atom (also written as H_2O). Hydrogen gas molecules are made of the same atom—two hydrogen atoms bonded together.

A molecule is the smallest amount of a substance made of combined atoms that is considered to be that substance. Think about what would happen if you tried to divide water to find its smallest part. Ultimately you would reach a single molecule of water. What would you have if you divided this molecule into its individual atoms of hydrogen and oxygen? If you break up a water molecule, it is no longer water. Instead, you would have hydrogen and oxygen, two different substances.

CHECK YOUR READING How is a molecule related to an atom?

READING TiP

Not all atoms and molecules have color. In this book atoms and molecules are given colors to make them easier to identify.

The droplets of water in this spider web are made of water molecules. Each molecule contains two hydrogen atoms (shown in white) and one oxygen atom (shown in red).

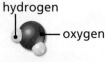

hydrogen

oxygen

water

Molecules can be made up of different numbers of atoms. For example, carbon monoxide is a molecule that is composed of one carbon atom and one oxygen atom. Molecules also can be composed of a large number of atoms. The most common type of vitamin E molecule, for example, contains 29 carbon atoms, 50 hydrogen atoms, and 2 oxygen atoms.

Molecules made of different numbers of the same atom are different substances. For example, an oxygen gas molecule is made of two oxygen atoms bonded together. Ozone is also composed of oxygen atoms, but an ozone molecule is three oxygen atoms bonded together. The extra oxygen atom gives ozone properties that are different from those of oxygen gas.

oxygen   **ozone**

This photograph shows the interior of Grand Central Terminal in New York City. Light from the window reflects off dust particles that are being moved by the motion of the molecules in air.

Atoms and molecules are always in motion.

If you have ever looked at a bright beam of sunlight, you may have seen dust particles floating in the air. If you were to watch carefully, you might notice that the dust does not fall toward the floor but instead seems to dart about in all different directions. Molecules in air are constantly moving and hitting the dust particles. Because the molecules are moving in many directions, they collide with the dust particles from different directions. This action causes the darting motion of the dust that you observe.

Atoms and molecules are always in motion. Sometimes this motion is easy to observe, such as when you see evidence of molecules in air bouncing dust particles around. Water molecules move too. When you place a drop of food coloring into water, the motion of the water molecules eventually causes the food coloring to spread throughout the water.

The motion of individual atoms and molecules is hard to observe in solid objects, such as a table. The atoms and molecules in a table cannot move about freely like the ones in water and air. However, the atoms and molecules in a table are constantly moving—by shaking back and forth, or by twisting—even if they stay in the same place.

1.2 Review

KEY CONCEPTS

1. What are atoms?
2. What is the smallest particle of a substance that is still considered to be that substance?
3. Why do dust particles in the air appear to be moving in different directions?

CRITICAL THINKING

4. **Apply** How does tea flavor spread from a tea bag throughout a cup of hot water?
5. **Infer** If a water molecule (H_2O) has two hydrogen atoms and one oxygen atom, how would you describe the make-up of a carbon dioxide molecule (CO_2)?

◆ CHALLENGE

6. **Synthesize** Assume that a water balloon has the same number of water molecules as a helium balloon has helium atoms. If the mass of the water is 4.5 times greater than the mass of the helium, how does the mass of a water molecule compare with the mass of a helium atom?

Particles Too Small to See

Atoms are so small that you cannot see them through an ordinary microscope. In fact, millions of them could fit in the period at the end of this sentence. Scientists can make images of atoms, however, using an instrument called a scanning tunneling microscope (STM).

Bumps on a Surface

The needle of the scanning tunneling microscope has a very sharp tip that is only one atom wide. The tip is brought close to the surface of the material being observed, and an electric current is applied to the tip. The microscope measures the interaction between the electrically charged needle tip and the nearest atom on the surface of the material. An image of the surface is created by moving the needle just above the surface. The image appears as a series of bumps that shows where the atoms are located. The result is similar to a contour map.

Moving Atoms

Scientists also can use the tip of the STM needle to move atoms on a surface. The large image at left is an STM image of a structure made by pushing individual atoms into place on a very smooth metal surface. This structure was designed as a corral to trap individual atoms inside.

Scientists can manipulate individual atoms to build structures, such as this one made of iron atoms.

Tiny Pieces of Matter

- Images of atoms did not exist until 1970.

- Atoms are so small that a single rain-drop contains more than 500 billion trillion atoms.

- If each atom were the size of a pea, your fingerprint would be larger than Alaska.

- In the space between stars, matter is so spread out that a volume of one liter contains only about 1000 atoms.

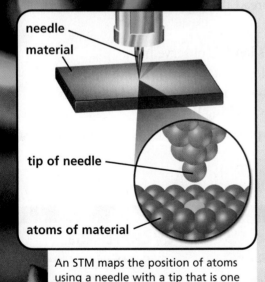

needle
material

tip of needle

atoms of material

An STM maps the position of atoms using a needle with a tip that is one atom wide.

EXPLORE

1. **INFER** Why must the tip of a scanning tunneling microscope be only one atom wide to make an image of atoms on a surface?

2. **CHALLENGE** Find out more about images of atoms on the Internet. How are STM images used in research to design better materials?

RESOURCE CENTER
CLASSZONE.COM
Find more images from scanning tunneling microscopes.

KEY CONCEPT

1.3 Matter combines to form different substances.

BEFORE, you learned

- Matter is made of tiny particles called atoms
- Atoms combine to form molecules

NOW, you will learn

- How pure matter and mixed matter are different
- How atoms and elements are related
- How atoms form compounds

VOCABULARY

element p. 22
compound p. 23
mixture p. 23

EXPLORE Mixed Substances

What happens when substances are mixed?

PROCEDURE

1. Observe and describe a teaspoon of cornstarch and a teaspoon of water.

2. Mix the two substances together in the cup. Observe and describe the result.

WHAT DO YOU THINK?

- After you mixed the substances, could you still see each substance?
- How was the new substance different from the original substances?

MATERIALS

- cornstarch
- water
- small cup
- spoon

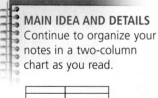

MAIN IDEA AND DETAILS
Continue to organize your notes in a two-column chart as you read.

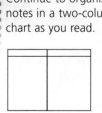

Matter can be pure or mixed.

Matter can be pure, or it can be two or more substances mixed together. Most of the substances you see around you are mixed, although you can't always tell that by looking at them. For example, the air you breathe is a combination of several substances. Wood, paper, steel, and lemonade are all mixed substances.

You might think that the water that you drink from a bottle or from the tap is a pure substance. However, drinking water has minerals dissolved in it and chemicals added to it that you cannot see. Often the difference between pure and mixed substances is apparent only on the atomic or molecular level.

A pure substance has only one type of component. For example, pure water contains only water molecules. Pure silver contains only silver atoms. Coins and jewelry that look like silver are often made of silver in combination with other metals.

REMINDER

A molecule consists of two or more atoms that are bonded together.

If you could look at the atoms in a bar of pure gold, you would find only gold atoms. If you looked at the atoms in a container of pure water, you would find water molecules, which are a combination of hydrogen and oxygen atoms. Does the presence of two types of atoms mean that water is not really a pure substance after all?

A substance is considered pure if it contains only a single type of atom, such as gold, or a single combination of atoms that are bonded together, such as a water molecule. Because the hydrogen and oxygen atoms are bonded together as molecules, water that has nothing else in it is considered a pure substance.

Elements

One type of pure substance is an element. An **element** is a substance that contains only a single type of atom. The number of atoms is not important as long as all the atoms are of the same type. You cannot separate an element into other substances.

You are probably familiar with many elements, such as silver, oxygen, hydrogen, helium, and aluminum. There are as many elements as there are types of atoms—more than 100. You can see the orderly arrangement of atoms in the element gold, on the left below.

CHECK YOUR READING   Why is an element considered to be a pure substance?

Element: Gold

The atoms in gold are all the same type of atom. Therefore, gold is an element.

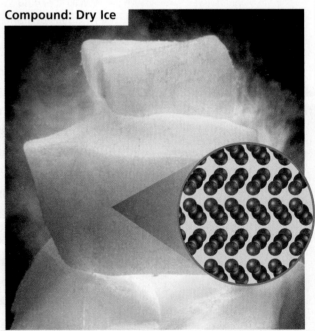

Compound: Dry Ice

Dry ice is frozen carbon dioxide, a compound. Each molecule is made of one carbon atom and two oxygen atoms.

Compounds

A **compound** is a substance that consists of two or more different types of atoms bonded together. A large variety of substances can be made by combining different types of atoms to make different compounds. Some types of compounds are made of molecules, such as water and carbon dioxide, shown on page 22. Other compounds are made of atoms that are bonded together in a different way. Table salt is an example.

A compound can have very different properties from the individual elements that make up that compound. Pure table salt is a common compound that is a combination of sodium and chlorine. Although table salt is safe to eat, the individual elements that go into making it—sodium and chlorine—are poisonous.

 CHECK YOUR READING What is the relationship between atoms and a compound?

Mixtures

Most of the matter around you is a mixture of different substances. Seawater, for instance, contains water, salt, and other minerals mixed together. Your blood is a mixture of blood cells and plasma. Plasma is also a mixture, made up of water, sugar, fat, protein, salts, and minerals.

A **mixture** is a combination of different substances that remain the same individual substances and can be separated by physical means. For example, if you mix apples, oranges, and bananas to make a fruit salad, you do not change the different fruits into a new kind of fruit. Mixtures do not always contain the same amount of the various substances. For example, depending on how the salad is made, the amount of each type of fruit it contains will vary.

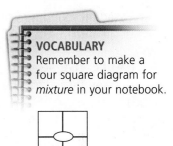

VOCABULARY
Remember to make a four square diagram for *mixture* in your notebook.

APPLY In what ways can a city population be considered a mixture?

INVESTIGATE Mixtures

How well do oil and water mix?

SKILL FOCUS
Inferring

MATERIALS
- food coloring
- beaker of water
- jar with lid
- vegetable oil
for Challenge:
- dish soap

TIME
20 minutes

PROCEDURE

1. Add a few drops of food coloring to the water in the beaker. Swirl the water around in the beaker until the water is evenly colored throughout.

2. Pour the colored water from the beaker into the jar until the jar is about one-fourth full.

3. Add the same amount of vegetable oil to the jar. Screw the lid tightly on the jar.

4. Carefully shake the jar several times with your hand over the cover, and then set it on the table. Observe and record what happens to the liquids in the jar.

5. Turn the jar upside down and hold it that way. Observe what happens to the liquids and record your observations.

WHAT DO YOU THINK?

- Does water mix with food coloring? What evidence supports your answer?
- Do water and oil mix? What evidence supports your answer?
- What happened when you turned the jar upside down?
- Based on your observations, what can you infer about the ability of different liquids to mix?

CHALLENGE To clean greasy dishes, you add soap to the dishwater. Try adding soap to your mixture. What does the soap do?

OIL

Comparing Mixtures and Compounds

RESOURCE CENTER
CLASSZONE.COM

Find out more about mixtures.

Although mixtures and compounds may seem similar, they are very different. Consider how mixtures and compounds compare with each other.

- The substances in mixtures remain the same substances. Compounds are new substances formed by atoms that bond together.

- Mixtures can be separated by physical means. Compounds can be separated only by breaking the bonds between atoms.

- The proportions of different substances in a mixture can vary throughout the mixture or from mixture to mixture. The proportions of different substances in a compound are fixed because the type and number of atoms that make up a basic unit of the compound are always the same.

CHECK YOUR READING How is a mixture different from a compound?

Parts of mixtures can be the same or different throughout.

It is obvious that something is a mixture when you can see the different substances in it. For example, if you scoop up a handful of soil, you might see that it contains dirt, small rocks, leaves, and even insects. You can separate the soil into its different parts.

Exactly what you see depends on what part of the soil you scoop up. One handful of soil might have more pebbles or insects in it than another handful would. There are many mixtures, such as soil, that have different properties in different areas of the mixture. Such a mixture is called a hetero-geneous (HEHT-uhr-uh-JEE-nee-uhs) mixture.

In some types of mixtures, however, you cannot see the individual substances. For example, if you mix sugar into a cup of water and stir it well, the sugar seems to disappear. You can tell that the sugar is still there because the water tastes sweet, but you cannot see the sugar or easily separate it out again.

When substances are evenly spread throughout a mixture, you cannot tell one part of the mixture from another part. For instance, one drop of sugar water will be almost exactly like any other drop. Such a mixture is called a homogeneous (HOH-muh-JEE-nee-uhs) mixture. Homogenized milk is processed so that it becomes a homogeneous mixture of water and milk fat. Milk that has not been homogenized will separate—most of the milk fat will float to the top as cream while leaving the rest of the milk low in fat.

READING TIP

The prefix *hetero* means "different," and the prefix *homo* means "same." The Greek root *genos* means "kind."

1.3 Review

KEY CONCEPTS

1. What is the difference between pure and mixed matter?

2. How are atoms and elements related?

3. How are compounds different from mixtures?

CRITICAL THINKING

4. **Infer** What can you infer about the size of sugar particles that are dissolved in a mixture of sugar and water?

5. **Infer** Why is it easier to remove the ice cubes from cold lemonade than it is to remove the sugar?

⬤ CHALLENGE

6. **Apply** A unit of sulfuric acid is a molecule of 2 atoms of hydrogen, 1 atom of sulfur, and 4 atoms of oxygen. How many of each type of atom are there in 2 molecules of sulfuric acid?

MATH TUTORIAL
CLASSZONE.COM

Click on Math Tutorial for more help with circle graphs.

A Mixture of Spices

Two different mixtures of spices may contain the exact same ingredients but have very different flavors. For example, a mixture of cumin, nutmeg, and ginger powder can be made using more cumin than ginger, or it can be made using more ginger than cumin.

One way to show how much of each substance a mixture contains is to use a circle graph. A circle graph is a visual way to show how a quantity is divided into different parts. A circle graph represents quantities as parts of a whole.

Example

Make a circle graph to represent a spice mixture that is 1/2 cumin, 1/3 nutmeg, and 1/6 ginger.

(1) To find the angle measure for each sector of the circle graph, multiply each fraction in your mixture by 360°.

Cumin: $\frac{1}{2} \cdot 360° = 180°$

Nutmeg: $\frac{1}{3} \cdot 360° = 120°$

Ginger: $\frac{1}{6} \cdot 360° = 60°$

(2) Use a compass to draw a circle. Use a protractor to draw the angle for each sector.

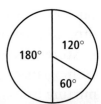

(3) Label each sector and give your graph a title.

ANSWER

Spice Mixture

cumin · nutmeg · ginger

Answer the following questions.

1. Draw a circle graph representing a spice mixture that is 1/2 ginger, 1/4 cumin, and 1/4 crushed red pepper.

2. A jeweler creates a ring that is 3/4 gold, 3/16 silver, and 1/16 copper. Draw a circle graph representing the mixture of metals in the ring.

3. Draw a circle graph representing a mixture that is 1/5 sand, 2/5 water, and 2/5 salt.

CHALLENGE Dry air is a mixture of about 78 percent nitrogen, 21 percent oxygen, and 1 percent other elements. Create a circle graph representing the elements found in air.

1.4

KEY CONCEPT
Matter exists in different physical states.

 BEFORE, you learned

- Matter has mass
- Matter is made of atoms
- Atoms and molecules in matter are always moving

 NOW, you will learn

- About the different states of matter
- How the different states of matter behave

VOCABULARY

states of matter p. 27
solid p. 28
liquid p. 28
gas p. 28

EXPLORE Solids and Liquids

How do solids and liquids compare?

PROCEDURE

① Observe the water, ice, and marble. Pick them up and feel them. Can you change their shape? their volume?

② Record your observations. Compare and contrast each object with the other two.

WHAT DO YOU THINK?

- How are the ice and the water in the cup similar? How are they different?
- How are the ice and the marble similar? How are they different?

MATERIALS
- water in a cup
- ice cube
- marble
- pie tin

Particle arrangement and motion determine the state of matter.

When you put water in a freezer, the water freezes into a solid (ice). When you place an ice cube on a warm plate, the ice melts into liquid water again. If you leave the plate in the sun, the water becomes water vapor. Ice, water, and water vapor are made of exactly the same type of molecule—a molecule of two hydrogen atoms and one oxygen atom. What, then, makes them different?

Ice, water, and water vapor are different states of water. **States of matter** are the different forms in which matter can exist. The three familiar states are solid, liquid, and gas. When a substance changes from one state to another, the molecules in the substance do not change. However, the arrangement of the molecules does change, giving each state of matter its own characteristics.

Solid, liquid, and gas are common states of matter.

MAIN IDEA AND DETAILS
Remember to organize your
notes in a two-column chart
as you read.

A substance can exist as a solid, a liquid, or a gas. The state of a substance depends on the space between its particles and on the way in which the particles move. The illustration on page 29 shows how particles are arranged in the three different states.

❶ A **solid** is a substance that has a fixed volume and a fixed shape. In a solid, the particles are close together and usually form a regular pattern. Particles in a solid can vibrate but are fixed in one place. Because each particle is attached to several others, individual particles cannot move from one location to another, and the solid is rigid.

❷ A **liquid** has a fixed volume but does not have a fixed shape. Liquids take on the shape of the container they are in. The particles in a liquid are attracted to one another and are close together. However, particles in a liquid are not fixed in place and can move from one place to another.

❸ A **gas** has no fixed volume or shape. A gas can take on both the shape and the volume of a container. Gas particles are not close to one another and can move easily in any direction. There is much more space between gas particles than there is between particles in a liquid or a solid. The space between gas particles can increase or decrease with changes in temperature and pressure.

 Describe two differences between a solid and a gas.

The particles in a solid are usually closer together than the particles in a liquid. For example, the particles in solid steel are closer together than the particles in molten—or melted—steel. However, water is an important exception. The molecules that make up ice actually have more space between them than the molecules in liquid water do.

The fact that the molecules in ice are farther apart than the molecules in liquid water has important consequences for life on Earth. Because there is more space between its molecules, ice floats on liquid water. By contrast, a piece of solid steel would not float in molten steel but would sink to the bottom.

Because ice floats, it remains on the surface of rivers and lakes when they freeze. The ice layer helps insulate the water and slow down the freezing process. Animals living in rivers and lakes can survive in the liquid water layer below the ice layer.

States of Matter

Matter can exist in different states. The state of matter depends on the arrangement and motion of the particles.

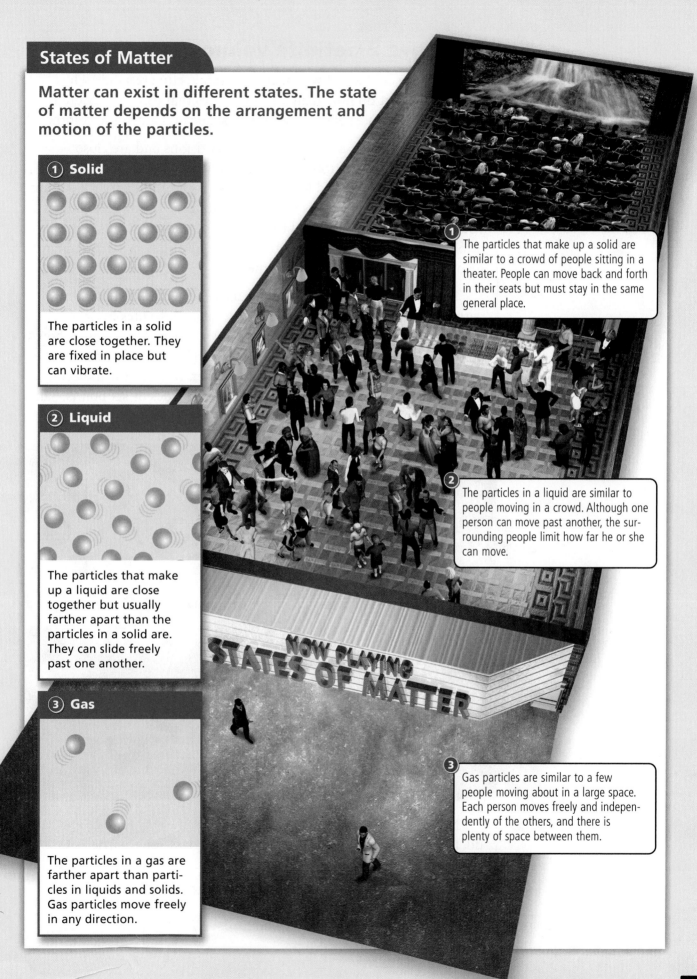

① Solid

The particles in a solid are close together. They are fixed in place but can vibrate.

② Liquid

The particles that make up a liquid are close together but usually farther apart than the particles in a solid are. They can slide freely past one another.

③ Gas

The particles in a gas are farther apart than particles in liquids and solids. Gas particles move freely in any direction.

① The particles that make up a solid are similar to a crowd of people sitting in a theater. People can move back and forth in their seats but must stay in the same general place.

② The particles in a liquid are similar to people moving in a crowd. Although one person can move past another, the surrounding people limit how far he or she can move.

③ Gas particles are similar to a few people moving about in a large space. Each person moves freely and independently of the others, and there is plenty of space between them.

NOW PLAYING
STATES OF MATTER

Solids have a definite volume and shape.

REMINDER

Volume is the amount of space that an object occupies.

A piece of ice, a block of wood, and a ceramic cup are solids. They have shapes that do not change and volumes that can be measured. Any matter that is a solid has a definite shape and a definite volume.

The molecules in a solid are in fixed positions and are close together. Although the molecules can still vibrate, they cannot move from one part of the solid to another part. As a result, a solid does not easily change its shape or its volume. If you force the molecules apart, you can change the shape and the volume of a solid by breaking it into pieces. However, each of those pieces will still be a solid and have its own particular shape and volume.

The particles in some solids, such as ice or table salt, occur in a very regular pattern. The pattern of the water molecules in ice, for example, can be seen when you look at a snowflake like the one shown below. The water molecules in a snowflake are arranged in hexagonal shapes that are layered on top of one another. Because the molecular pattern has six sides, snowflakes form with six sides or six points. Salt also has a regular structure, although it takes a different shape.

The particles in many solids, such as the water molecules in this snowflake, have a regular pattern.

Not all solids have regular shapes in the same way that ice and salt do, however. Some solids, such as plastic or glass, have particles that are not arranged in a regular pattern.

CHECK YOUR READING
What two characteristics are needed for a substance to be a solid?

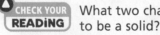

Liquids have a definite volume but no definite shape.

Water, milk, and oil are liquids. A liquid has a definite volume but does not have a definite shape. The volume of a certain amount of oil can be measured, but the shape that the oil takes depends on what container it is in. If the oil is in a tall, thin container, it has a tall, thin shape. If it is in a short, wide container, it has a short, wide shape. Liquids take the shape of their containers.

The molecules in a liquid are close together, but they are not tightly attached to one another as the molecules in a solid are. Instead, molecules in liquids can move independently. As a result, liquids can flow. Instead of having a rigid form, the molecules in a liquid move and fill the bottom of the container they are in.

MAIN IDEA AND DETAILS
As you read, organize the headings and details in a two-column chart.

 CHECK YOUR READING How is a liquid different from a solid?

INVESTIGATE Liquids

How do different liquids behave?

PROCEDURE

1. Using the graduated cylinder, measure 5 mL of colored water. Add it to the test tube.

2. Measure 5 mL of vegetable oil. Pour the oil into the test tube. Record your observations.

3. Pour a small amount of corn syrup directly into the test tube. Record what happens to all three liquids.

4. Add 10 mL more of colored water to the test tube and record what happens.

5. Add 5 mL more of vegetable oil and record what happens.

WHAT DO YOU THINK?

- How did the layers change as more liquid was added?
- What are some behaviors of each of the liquids in this experiment that can be used to tell them apart?
- What would happen if you changed the order in which you added the liquids?

CHALLENGE Think of a liquid you are familiar with that was not used in this experiment. What do you think would happen if you added that liquid to your test tube? Explain.

SKILL FOCUS
Measuring

MATERIALS
- graduated cylinder
- colored water
- test tube
- test-tube rack
- vegetable oil
- corn syrup

TIME
20 minutes

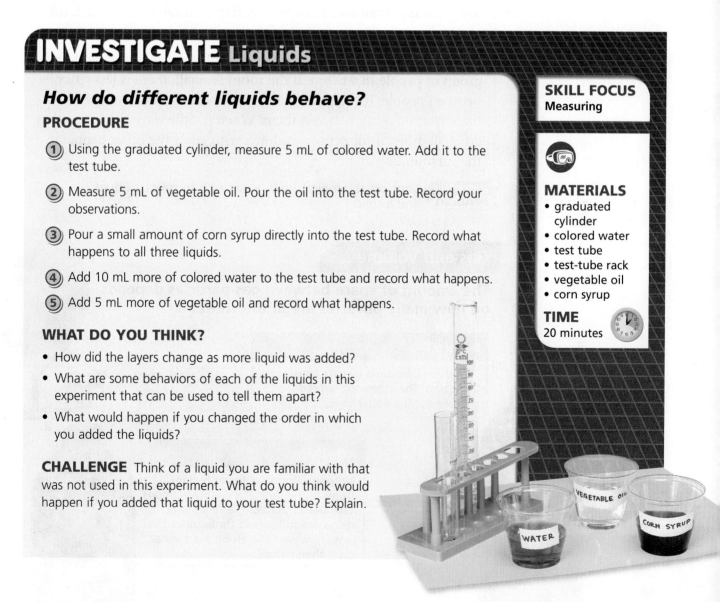

Gases have no definite volume or shape.

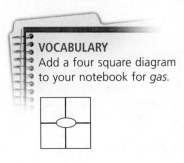

VOCABULARY
Add a four square diagram to your notebook for *gas*.

The air that you breathe, the helium in a balloon, and the neon inside the tube in a neon light are gases. A gas is a substance with no definite volume and no definite shape. Solids and liquids have volumes that do not change easily. If you have a container filled with one liter of a liquid that you pour into a two-liter container, the liquid will occupy only half of the new container. A gas, on the other hand, has a volume that changes to match the volume of its container.

Gas Composition

The molecules in a gas are very far apart compared with the molecules in a solid or a liquid. The amount of space between the molecules in a gas can change easily. If a rigid container—one that cannot change its shape—has a certain amount of air and more air is pumped in, the volume of the gas does not change. However, there is less space between the molecules than there was before. If the container is opened, the molecules spread out and mix with the air in the atmosphere.

As you saw, gas molecules in a container can be compared to a group of people in a room. If the room is small, there is less space between people. If the room is large, people can spread out so that there is more space between them. When people leave the room, they go in all different directions and mix with all of the other people in the surrounding area.

 CHECK YOUR READING Contrast the molecules in a gas with those of a liquid and a solid.

Gas and Volume

The amount of space between gas particles depends on how many particles are in the container.

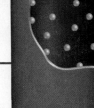

Before Use

The atoms of helium gas are constantly in motion. The atoms are spread throughout the entire tank.

After Use

Although there are fewer helium atoms in the tank after many balloons have been inflated, the remaining atoms are still spread throughout the tank. However, the atoms are farther apart than before.

Gas Behavior

Because gas molecules are always in motion, they are continually hitting one another and the sides of any container they may be in. As the molecules bounce off one another and the surfaces of the container, they apply a pressure against the container. You can feel the effects of gas pressure if you pump air into a bicycle tire. The more air you put into the tire, the harder it feels because more gas molecules are pressing the tire outward.

SIMULATION
CLASSZONE.COM

Explore the behavior of a gas.

The speed at which gas molecules move depends on the temperature of the gas. Gas molecules move faster at higher temperatures than at lower temperatures. The volume, pressure, and temperature of a gas are related to one another, and changing one can change the others.

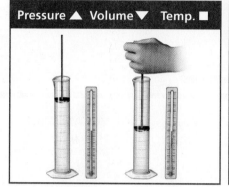

Pressure ▲ Volume ▼ Temp. ■

If the temperature of a gas stays the same, increasing the pressure of the gas decreases its volume.

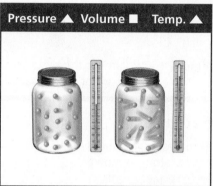

Pressure ▲ Volume ■ Temp. ▲

If the volume of a gas stays the same, increasing the temperature of the gas also increases the pressure.

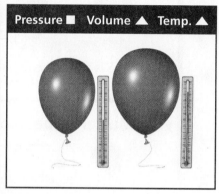

Pressure ■ Volume ▲ Temp. ▲

If the pressure of a gas stays the same, increasing the temperature of the gas also increases the volume.

In nature, volume, pressure, and temperature may all be changing at the same time. By studying how gas behaves when one property is kept constant, scientists can predict how gas will behave when all three properties change.

1.4 Review

KEY CONCEPTS

1. What are the characteristics of the three familiar states of matter?

2. How can you change the shape and volume of a liquid?

3. How does gas behave inside a closed container?

CRITICAL THINKING

4. **Infer** What happens to a liquid that is not in a container?

5. **Synthesize** What is the relationship between the temperature and the volume of a gas?

⚫ CHALLENGE

6. **Synthesize** Can an oxygen canister ever be half empty? Explain.

Chapter Review

the BIG idea

Everything that has mass and takes up space is matter.

CONTENT REVIEW
CLASSZONE.COM

◀ KEY CONCEPTS SUMMARY

 1.1 Matter has mass and volume.

Mass is a measure of how much matter an object contains.

Volume is the measure of the amount of space matter occupies.

VOCABULARY
matter p. 9
mass p. 10
weight p. 11
volume p. 11

 1.2 Matter is made of atoms.

An atom is the smallest basic unit of matter. Two or more atoms bonded together form a molecule. Atoms and molecules are always in motion.

VOCABULARY
atom p. 16
molecule p. 18

1.3 Matter combines to form different substances.

Matter can be pure, such as an element (gold), or a compound (water).

Matter can be a mixture. Mixtures contain two or more pure substances.

VOCABULARY
element p. 22
compound p. 23
mixture p. 23

1.4 Matter exists in different physical states.

Solids have a fixed volume and a fixed shape.

Liquids have a fixed volume but no fixed shape.

Gases have no fixed volume and no fixed shape.

VOCABULARY
states of matter p. 27
solid p. 28
liquid p. 28
gas p. 28

Reviewing Vocabulary

Copy and complete the chart below. If the right column is blank, give a brief description or definition. If the left column is blank, give the correct term.

Term	Description
1.	the downward pull of gravity on an object
2. liquid	
3.	the smallest basic unit of matter
4. solid	
5.	state of matter with no fixed volume and no fixed shape
6.	a combination of different substances that remain individual substances
7. matter	
8.	a measure of how much matter an object contains
9. element	
10.	a particle made of two or more atoms bonded together
11. compound	

Reviewing Key Concepts

Multiple Choice *Choose the letter of the best answer.*

12. The standard unit for measuring mass is the
   a. kilogram
   b. gram per cubic centimeter
   c. milliliter
   d. milliliter per cubic centimeter

13. A unit for measuring the volume of a liquid is the
   a. kilogram
   b. gram per cubic centimeter
   c. milliliter
   d. milliliter per cubic centimeter

14. The weight of an object is measured by using a scale that
   a. compares the mass of the object with a standard unit of mass
   b. shows the amount of space the object occupies
   c. indicates how much water is displaced by the object
   d. tells how hard the object is pushing or pulling on it

15. To find the volume of a rectangular box,
   a. divide the length by the height
   b. multiply the length, width, and height
   c. subtract the mass from the weight
   d. multiply one atom's mass by the total

16. Compounds can be separated only by
   a. breaking the atoms into smaller pieces
   b. breaking the bonds between the atoms
   c. using a magnet to attract certain atoms
   d. evaporating the liquid that contains the atoms

17. Whether a substance is a solid, a liquid, or a gas depends on how close its atoms are to one another and
   a. the volume of each atom
   b. how much matter the atoms have
   c. how free the atoms are to move
   d. the size of the container

18. A liquid has
   a. a fixed volume and a fixed shape
   b. no fixed volume and a fixed shape
   c. a fixed volume and no fixed shape
   d. no fixed volume and no fixed shape

Short Answer *Answer each of the following questions in a sentence or two.*

19. Describe the movement of particles in a solid, a liquid, and a gas.

20. In bright sunlight, dust particles in the air appear to dart about. What causes this effect?

21. Why is the volume of a rectangular object measured in cubic units?

22. Describe how the molecules in the air behave when you pump air into a bicycle tire.

Thinking Critically

23. **CLASSIFY** Write the headings *Matter* and *Not Matter* on your paper. Place each of these terms in the correct category: wood, water, metal, air, light, sound.

24. **INFER** If you could break up a carbon dioxide molecule, would you still have carbon dioxide? Explain your answer.

25. **MODEL** In what ways is sand in a bowl like a liquid? In what ways is it different?

26. **INFER** If you cut a hole in a basketball, what happens to the gas inside?

27. **COMPARE AND CONTRAST** Create a Venn diagram that shows how mixtures and compounds are alike and different.

28. **ANALYZE** If you place a solid rubber ball into a box, why doesn't the ball change its shape to fit the container?

29. **CALCULATE** What is the volume of an aquarium that is 120 cm long, 60 cm wide, and 100 cm high?

30. **CALCULATE** A truck whose bed is 2.5 m long, 1.5 m wide, and 1 m high is delivering sand for a sand-sculpture competition. How many trips must the truck make to deliver 7 cubic meters of sand?

Use the information in the photograph below to answer the next three questions.

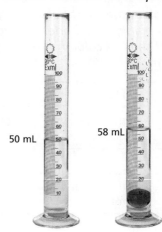

50 mL   58 mL

31. **INFER** One way to find the volume of a marble is by displacement. To determine a marble's volume, add 50 mL of water to a graduated cylinder and place the marble in the cylinder. Why does the water level change when you put the marble in the cylinder?

32. **CALCULATE** What is the volume of the marble?

33. **PREDICT** If you carefully removed the marble and let all of the water on it drain back into the cylinder, what would the volume of the water be? Explain.

the BIG idea

34. **SYNTHESIZE** Look back at the photograph on pages 6–7. Describe the picture in terms of states of matter.

35. **WRITE** Make a list of all the matter in a two-meter radius around you. Classify each as a solid, liquid, or gas.

UNIT PROJECTS

If you are doing a unit project, make a folder for your project. Include in your folder a list of the resources you will need, the date on which the project is due, and a schedule to track your progress. Begin gathering data.

Interpreting Graphs

The graph below shows the changing volume of a gas as it was slowly heated, with the pressure held constant.

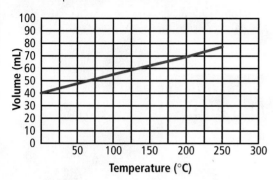

Use the graph to answer the questions.

1. As the temperature of the gas rises, what happens to its volume?

    a. It increases.

    b. It stays the same.

    c. It decreases.

    d. It changes without pattern.

2. What is the volume of the gas at 250°C as compared with the volume at 0°C?

    a. about three times greater

    b. about double

    c. about one-half

    d. about the same

3. What happens to a gas as it is cooled below 0°C?

    a. The volume would increase.

    b. The volume would continue to decrease.

    c. The volume would remain at 40 mL.

    d. A gas cannot be cooled below 0°C.

4. If you raised the temperature of this gas to 300°C, what would be its approximate volume?

    a. 70 mL   **c.** 80 mL

    b. 75 mL   **d.** 85 mL

5. If the volume of the gas at 0°C was 80 mL instead of 40 mL, what would you expect the volume to be at 200°C?

    a. 35 mL   **c.** 80 mL

    b. 70 mL   **d.** 140 mL

Extended Response

Answer the two questions below in detail. Include some of the terms from the word box. Underline each term you use in your answer.

gravity	mass	molecule
states of matter	weight	

6. An astronaut's helmet, measured on a balance, has the same number of kilograms on both Earth and the Moon. On a spring scale, though, it registers more newtons on Earth than on the Moon. Why?

7. Explain how water changes as it moves from a solid to a liquid and then to a gas.

CHAPTER

2 Properties of Matter

> **What properties could help you identify this sculpture as sugar?**

the **BIG** idea

Matter has properties that can be changed by physical and chemical processes.

Key Concepts

SECTION

2.1 Matter has observable properties.
Learn how to recognize physical and chemical properties.

SECTION

2.2 Changes of state are physical changes.
Learn how energy is related to changes of state.

SECTION

2.3 Properties are used to identify substances.
Learn how the properties of substances can be used to identify them and to separate mixtures.

Internet Preview

CLASSZONE.COM

Chapter 2 online resources: Content Review, Simulation, three Resource Centers, Math Tutorial, Test Practice

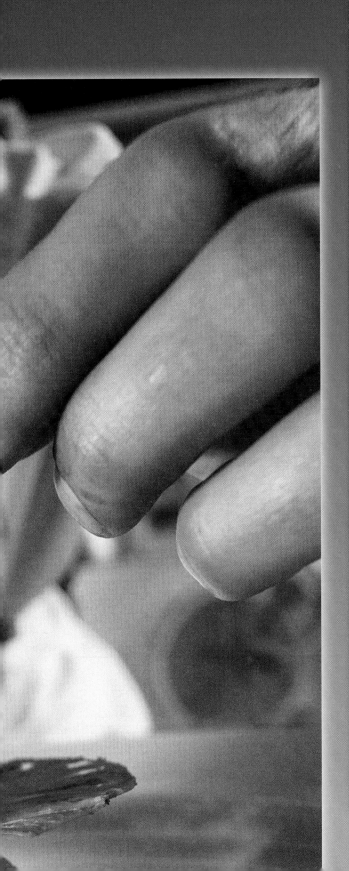

EXPLORE (the BIG idea)

Float or Sink

Form a piece of clay into a solid ball or cube. Place it in a bowl of water. Notice if it floats or sinks. Then mold the clay into a boatlike shape. Notice if this new object floats or sinks.

Observe and Think What did you change about the clay? What didn't you change? What would happen if you filled the boat with water?

Hot Chocolate

Place two candy-coated chocolates on a paper towel. Place two more in your hand and close your hand. Wait three minutes. Break open the candies and examine the chocolate.

Observe and Think What happened to the chocolate in your hand? on the towel? What do you think accounts for any differences you see?

Internet Activity: Physical and Chemical Changes

Go to **ClassZone.com** to see how materials can go through physical and chemical changes.

Observe and Think Think about each change. What can you infer about the difference between a physical change and a chemical change?

NSTA
scilinks.org
SCI LINKS

Physical Properties of Matter **Code: MDL062**

Getting Ready to Learn

◀ CONCEPT REVIEW

- Everything is made of matter.
- Matter has mass and volume.
- Atoms combine to form molecules.

◀ VOCABULARY REVIEW

mass p. 10

volume p. 11

molecule p. 18

states of matter p. 27

 CONTENT REVIEW
CLASSZONE.COM
Review concepts and vocabulary.

▶ TAKING NOTES

MAIN IDEA WEB

Write each new blue heading in a box. Then write notes in boxes around the center box that give important terms and details about that heading.

VOCABULARY STRATEGY

Think about a vocabulary term as a **magnet word** diagram. Write related terms and ideas in boxes around it.

See the Note-Taking Handbook on pages R45–R51.

SCIENCE NOTEBOOK

color, shape, size, texture, volume, mass	melting point, boiling point

Physical properties describe a substance.

density: a measure of the amount of matter in a given volume	

CHEMICAL CHANGE

burning — change in temperature

rusting — change in color

tarnishing — formation of bubbles

KEY CONCEPT

Matter has observable properties.

A

◀ **BEFORE**, you learned

- Matter has mass and volume
- Matter is made of atoms
- Matter exists in different states

▶ **NOW**, you will learn

- About physical and chemical properties
- About physical changes
- About chemical changes

VOCABULARY

physical property p. 41
density p. 43
physical change p. 44
chemical property p. 46
chemical change p. 46

EXPLORE Physical Properties

How can a substance be changed?

PROCEDURE

MATERIAL
rectangular piece of clay

① Observe the clay. Note its physical characteristics, such as color, shape, texture, and size.

② Change the shape of the clay. Note which characteristics changed and which ones stayed the same.

WHAT DO YOU THINK?
- How did reshaping the clay change its physical characteristics?
- How were the mass and the volume of the clay affected?

Physical properties describe a substance.

What words would you use to describe a table? a chair? the sandwich you ate for lunch? You would probably say something about the shape, color, and size of each item. Next you might consider whether it is hard or soft, smooth or rough to the touch. Normally, when describing an object, you identify the characteristics of the object that you can observe without changing the identity of the object.

The characteristics of a substance that can be observed without changing the identity of the substance are called **physical properties.** In science, observation can include measuring and handling a substance. All of your senses can be used to detect physical properties. Color, shape, size, texture, volume, and mass are a few of the physical properties you probably have encountered.

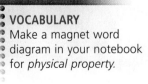

VOCABULARY
Make a magnet word diagram in your notebook for *physical property*.

 Describe some of the physical properties of your desk.

Physical Properties

How do you know which characteristics are physical properties? Just ask yourself whether observing the property involves changing the substance to a different substance. For example, you can stretch a rubber band. Does stretching the rubber band change what it is made of? No. The rubber band is still a rubber band before and after it is stretched. It may look a little different, but it is still a rubber band.

Mass and volume are two physical properties. Measuring these properties does not change the identity of a substance. For example, a lump of clay might have a mass of 200 grams (g) and a volume of 100 cubic centimeters (cm^3). If you were to break the clay in half, you would have two 100 g pieces of clay, each with a volume of 50 cm^3. You can bend and shape the clay too. Even if you were to mold a realistic model of a car out of the clay, it still would be a piece of clay. Although you have changed some of the properties of the object, such as its shape and volume, you have not changed the fact that the substance you are observing is clay.

REMINDER

Because all formulas for volume involve the multiplication of three measurements, volume has a unit that is cubed (such as cm^3).

CHECK YOUR READING Which physical properties listed above are found by taking measurements? Which are not?

Physical Properties

Physical properties of clay—such as volume, mass, color, texture, and shape—can be observed without changing the fact that the substance is clay.

Block of Clay

Shaped Clay

READING VISUALS COMPARE AND CONTRAST Which physical properties do the two pieces of clay have in common? Which are different?

Density

The relationship between the mass and the volume of a substance is another important physical property. For any substance, the amount of mass in a unit of volume is constant. For different substances, the amount of mass in a unit of volume may differ. This relationship explains why you can easily lift a shoebox full of feathers but not one filled with pennies, even though both are the same size. A volume of pennies contains more mass than an equal volume of feathers. The relationship between mass and volume is called density.

Density is a measure of the amount of matter present in a given volume of a substance. Density is normally expressed in units of grams per cubic centimeter (g/cm^3). In other words, density is the mass in grams divided by the volume in cubic centimeters.

$$\text{Density} = \frac{\text{mass}}{\text{Volume}} \qquad D = \frac{m}{V}$$

How would you find the density of 200 g of clay with a volume of 100 cm^3? You calculate that the clay has a density of 200 g divided by 100 cm^3, or 2 g/cm^3. If you divide the clay in half and find the density of one piece of clay, it will be 100 g/50 cm^3, or 2 g/cm^3—the same as the original piece. Notice that density is a property of a substance that remains the same no matter how much of the substance you have.

READING TiP

The density of solids is usually measured in grams per cubic centimeter (g/cm^3). The density of liquids is usually measured in grams per milliliter (g/mL). Recall that 1 mL = 1 cm^3.

Calculating Density

Sample Problem

A glass marble has a volume of 5 cm^3 and a mass of 13 g. What is the density of glass?

What do you know?	Volume = 5 cm^3, mass = 13 g
What do you want to find out?	Density
Write the formula:	$D = \dfrac{m}{V}$
Substitute into the formula:	$D = \dfrac{13\ g}{5\ cm^3}$
Calculate and simplify:	$D = 2.6\ g/cm^3$
Check that your units agree:	Unit is g/cm^3. Unit of density is g/cm^3. Units agree.
Answer:	$D = 2.6\ g/cm^3$

Practice the Math

1. A lead sinker has a mass of 227 g and a volume of 20 cm^3. What is the density of lead?
2. A glass of milk has a volume of 100 mL. If the milk has a mass of 103 g, what is the density of milk?

Physical Changes

MAIN IDEA WEB
As you read, organize your notes in a web.

You have read that a physical property is any property that can be observed without changing the identity of the substance. What then would be a physical change? A **physical change** is a change in any physical property of a substance, not in the substance itself. Breaking a piece of clay in half is a physical change because it changes only the size and shape of the clay. Stretching a rubber band is a physical change because the size of the rubber band changes. The color of the rubber band sometimes can change as well when it is stretched. However, the material that the rubber band is made of does not change. The rubber band is still rubber.

What happens when water changes from a liquid into water vapor or ice? Is this a physical change? Remember to ask yourself what has changed about the material. Ice is a solid and water is a liquid, but both are the same substance—both are composed of H_2O molecules. As you will read in more detail in the next section, a change in a substance's state of matter is a physical change.

 How is a physical change related to a substance's physical properties?

A substance can go through many different physical changes and still remain the same substance. Consider, for example, the changes that happen to the wool that ultimately becomes a sweater.

1. Wool is sheared from the sheep. The wool is then cleaned and placed into a machine that separates the wool fibers from one another. Shearing and separating the fibers are physical changes that change the shape, volume, and texture of the wool.

2. The wool fibers are spun into yarn. Again, the shape and volume of the wool change. The fibers are twisted so that they are packed more closely together and are intertwined with one another.

3. The yarn is dyed. The dye changes the color of the wool, but it does not change the wool into another substance. This type of color change is a physical change.

4. Knitting the yarn into a sweater also does not change the wool into another substance. A wool sweater is still wool, even though it no longer resembles the wool on a sheep.

It can be difficult to determine if a specific change is a physical change or not. Some changes, such as a change in color, also can occur when new substances are formed during the change. When deciding whether a change is a physical change or not, ask yourself whether you have the same substance you started with. If the substance is the same, then the changes it underwent were all physical changes.

Physical Changes

The process of turning wool into a sweater requires that the wool undergo physical changes. Changes in shape, volume, texture, and color occur as raw wool is turned into a colorful sweater.

① Shearing

Preparing the wool produces physical changes. The wool is removed from the sheep and then cleaned before the wool fibers are separated.

② Spinning

Further physical changes occur as a machine twists the wool fibers into a long, thin rope of yarn.

③ Dyeing

Dyeing produces color changes but does not change the basic substance of the wool.

④ The final product, a wool sweater, is still wool.

READING VISUALS How does the yarn in the sweater differ from the wool on the sheep?

Chemical properties describe how substances form new substances.

RESOURCE CENTER
CLASSZONE.COM

Learn about the chemical properties of matter.

If you wanted to keep a campfire burning, would you add a piece of wood or a piece of iron? You would add wood, of course, because you know that wood burns but iron does not. Is the ability to burn a physical property of the wood? The ability to burn seems to be quite different from physical properties such as color, density, and shape. More important, after the wood burns, all that is left is a pile of ashes and some new substances in the air. The wood has obviously changed into something else. The ability to burn, therefore, must describe another kind of property that substances have—not a physical property but a chemical property.

Chemical Properties and Changes

Chemical properties describe how substances can form new substances. Combustibility, for example, describes how well an object can burn. Wood burns well and turns into ashes and other substances. Can you think of a chemical property for the metal iron? Especially when left outdoors in wet weather, iron rusts. The ability to rust is a chemical property of iron. The metal silver does not rust, but eventually a darker substance called tarnish forms on its surface. You may have noticed a layer of tarnish on some silver spoons or jewelry.

INFER The bust of Abraham Lincoln is made of bronze. Why is the nose a different color from the rest of the head?

The chemical properties of copper cause it to become a blue-green color when it is exposed to air. A famous example of tarnished copper is the Statue of Liberty. The chemical properties of bronze are different. Some bronze objects tarnish to a dark brown color, like the bust of Abraham Lincoln in the photograph on the left.

Chemical properties can be identified by the changes they produce. The change of one substance into another substance is called a **chemical change.** A piece of wood burning, an iron fence rusting, and a silver spoon tarnishing are all examples of chemical changes. A chemical change affects the substances involved in the change. During a chemical change, combinations of atoms in the original substances are rearranged to make new substances. For example, when rust forms on iron, the iron atoms combine with oxygen atoms in the air to form a new substance that is made of both iron and oxygen.

A chemical change is also involved when an antacid tablet is dropped into a glass of water. As the tablet dissolves, bubbles of gas appear. The water and the substances in the tablet react to form new substances. One of these substances is carbon dioxide gas, which forms the bubbles that you see.

Not all chemical changes are as destructive as burning, rusting, or tarnishing. Chemical changes are also involved in cooking. When you boil an egg, for example, the substances in the raw egg change into new substances as energy is added to the egg. When you eat the egg, further chemical changes take place as your body digests the egg. The process forms new molecules that your body then can use to function.

CHECK YOUR READING Give three examples of chemical changes.

The only true indication of a chemical change is that a new substance has been formed. Sometimes, however, it is difficult to tell whether new substances have been formed or not. In many cases you have to judge which type of change has occurred only on the basis of your observations of the change and your previous experience. However, some common signs can suggest that a chemical change has occurred. You can use these signs to guide you as you try to classify a change that you are observing.

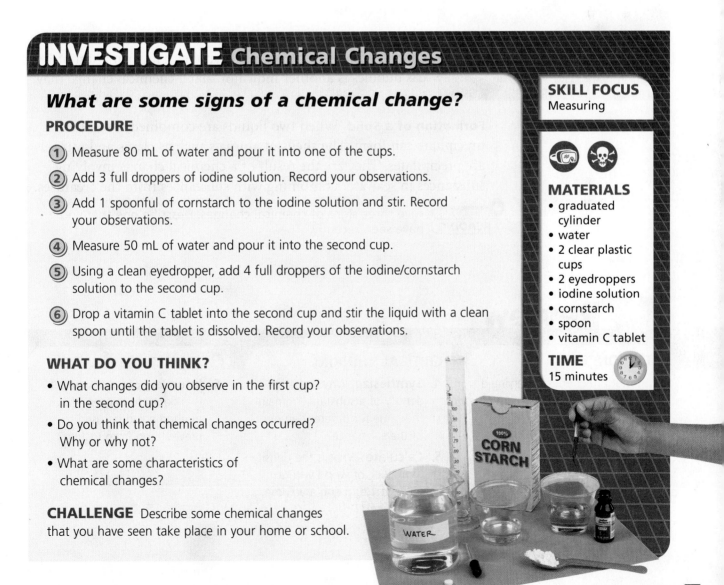

INVESTIGATE Chemical Changes

What are some signs of a chemical change?

PROCEDURE

1. Measure 80 mL of water and pour it into one of the cups.
2. Add 3 full droppers of iodine solution. Record your observations.
3. Add 1 spoonful of cornstarch to the iodine solution and stir. Record your observations.
4. Measure 50 mL of water and pour it into the second cup.
5. Using a clean eyedropper, add 4 full droppers of the iodine/cornstarch solution to the second cup.
6. Drop a vitamin C tablet into the second cup and stir the liquid with a clean spoon until the tablet is dissolved. Record your observations.

WHAT DO YOU THINK?

- What changes did you observe in the first cup? in the second cup?
- Do you think that chemical changes occurred? Why or why not?
- What are some characteristics of chemical changes?

CHALLENGE Describe some chemical changes that you have seen take place in your home or school.

SKILL FOCUS
Measuring

MATERIALS
- graduated cylinder
- water
- 2 clear plastic cups
- 2 eyedroppers
- iodine solution
- cornstarch
- spoon
- vitamin C tablet

TIME
15 minutes

Signs of a Chemical Change

Carbon dioxide bubbles form as substances in the tablet react with water.

You may not be able to see that any new substances have formed during a change. Below are some signs that a chemical change may have occurred. If you observe two or more of these signs during a change, you most likely are observing a chemical change.

Production of an Odor Some chemical changes produce new smells. The chemical change that occurs when an egg is rotting produces the smell of sulfur. If you go outdoors after a thunderstorm, you may detect an unusual odor in the air. The odor is an indication that lightning has caused a chemical change in the air.

Change in Temperature Chemical changes often are accompanied by a change in temperature. You may have noticed that the temperature is higher near logs burning in a campfire.

Change in Color A change in color is often an indication of a chemical change. For example, fruit may change color when it ripens.

Formation of Bubbles When an antacid tablet makes contact with water, it begins to bubble. The formation of gas bubbles is another indicator that a chemical change may have occurred.

Formation of a Solid When two liquids are combined, a solid called a precipitate can form. The shells of animals such as clams and mussels are precipitates. They are the result of a chemical change involving substances in seawater combining with substances from the creatures.

 CHECK YOUR READING Give three signs of chemical changes. Describe one that you have seen recently.

2.1 Review

KEY CONCEPTS

1. What effect does observing a substance's physical properties have on the substance?

2. Describe how a physical property such as mass or texture can change without causing a change in the substance.

3. Explain why burning is a chemical change in wood.

CRITICAL THINKING

4. **Synthesize** Why does the density of a substance remain the same for different amounts of the substance?

5. **Calculate** What is the density of a block of wood with a mass of 120 g and a volume of 200 cm^3?

⬥ CHALLENGE

6. **Infer** Iron can rust when it is exposed to oxygen. What method could be used to prevent iron from rusting?

MATH TUTORIAL
CLASSZONE.COM

Click on Math Tutorial for more help with solving proportions.

Density of Materials

Two statues are made of the same type of marble. One is larger than the other. However, they both have the same density because they are made of the same material. Recall the formula for density.

$$\text{Density} = \frac{\text{mass}}{\text{Volume}}$$

Because the density is the same, you know that the mass of one statue divided by its volume is the same as the mass of the other statue divided by its volume. You can set this up and solve it as a proportion.

Example

A small marble statue has a mass of 2.5 kg and a volume of 1000 cm^3. A large marble statue with the same density has a mass of 10 kg. What is the volume of the large statue?

(1) Write the information as an equation showing the proportion.

$$\frac{\text{mass of small statue}}{\text{volume of small statue}} = \frac{\text{mass of large statue}}{\text{volume of large statue}}$$

(2) Insert the known values into your equation.

$$\frac{2.5 \text{ kg}}{1000 \text{ cm}^3} = \frac{10 \text{ kg}}{\text{volume of large statue}}$$

(3) Compare the numerators: 10 kg is 4 times greater than 2.5 kg.

(4) The denominators of the fractions are related in the same way. Therefore, the volume of the large statue is 4 times the volume of the small one.

volume of large statue = 4 • 1000 cm^3 = 4000 cm^3

ANSWER The volume of the large statue is 4000 cm^3.

Answer the following questions.

1. A lump of gold has a volume of 10 cm^3 and a mass of 193 g. Another lump of gold has a mass of 96.5 g. What is the volume of the second lump of gold?

2. A carpenter saws a wooden beam into two pieces. One piece has a mass of 600 g and a volume of 1000 cm^3. What is the mass of the second piece if its volume is 250 cm^3?

3. A 200 mL bottle is completely filled with cooking oil. The oil has a mass of 180 g. If 150 mL of the oil is poured into a pot, what is the mass of the poured oil?

CHALLENGE You have two spheres made of the same material. One has a diameter that is twice as large as the other. How do their masses compare?

If the marble statue and the marble bust both have the same density, their masses are proportional to their volumes.

Changes of state are physical changes.

 BEFORE, you learned

- Substances have physical and chemical properties
- Physical changes do not change a substance into a new substance
- Chemical changes result in new substances

 NOW, you will learn

- How liquids can become solids, and solids can become liquids
- How liquids can become gases, and gases can become liquids
- How energy is related to changes of state

VOCABULARY

melting p. 51
melting point p. 51
freezing p. 52
freezing point p. 52
evaporation p. 53
sublimation p. 53
boiling p. 54
boiling point p. 54
condensation p. 55

THINK ABOUT

Where does dew come from?

On a cool morning, droplets of dew cover the grass. Where does this water come from? You might think it had rained recently. However, dew forms even if it has not rained. Air is made of a mixture of different gases, including water vapor. Some of the water vapor condenses—or becomes a liquid—on the cool grass and forms drops of liquid water.

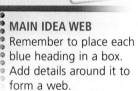

MAIN IDEA WEB
Remember to place each blue heading in a box. Add details around it to form a web.

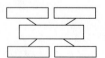

Matter can change from one state to another.

Matter is commonly found in three states: solid, liquid, and gas. A solid has a fixed volume and a fixed shape. A liquid also has a fixed volume but takes the shape of its container. A gas has neither a fixed volume nor a fixed shape. Matter always exists in one of these states, but it can change from one state to another.

When matter changes from one state to another, the substance itself does not change. Water, ice, and water vapor are all the same basic substance. As water turns into ice or water vapor, the water molecules themselves do not change. What changes are the arrangement of the molecules and the amount of space between them. Changes in state are physical changes because changes in state do not change the basic substance.

 CHECK YOUR READING Why is a change in state a physical change rather than a chemical change?

Solids can become liquids, and liquids can become solids.

If you leave an ice cube on a kitchen counter, it changes to the liquid form of water. Water changes to the solid form of water, ice, when it is placed in a freezer. In a similar way, if a bar of iron is heated to a high enough temperature, it will become liquid iron. As the liquid iron cools, it becomes solid iron again.

Melting

Melting is the process by which a solid becomes a liquid. Different solids melt at different temperatures. The lowest temperature at which a substance begins to melt is called its **melting point.** Although the melting point of ice is 0°C (32°F), iron must be heated to a much higher temperature before it will melt.

Remember that particles are always in motion, even in a solid. Because the particles in a solid are bound together, they do not move from place to place—but they do vibrate. As a solid heats up, its particles gain energy and vibrate faster. If the vibrations are fast enough, the particles break loose and slide past one another. In other words, the solid melts and becomes a liquid.

Some substances have a well-defined melting point. If you are melting ice, for example, you can predict that when the temperature reaches 0°C, the ice will start to melt. Substances with an orderly structure start melting when they reach a specific temperature.

VOCABULARY
Add magnet word diagrams for *melting* and *melting point* to your notebook.

Melting a Solid

Steel melts at very high temperatures. Liquid steel can be poured into molds to form the beams that are used in bridges like the one shown on the left.

READING VISUALS What would happen to the steel in this bridge if it became as hot as the steel in the bucket?

Other substances, such as plastic and chocolate, do not have a well-defined melting point. Chocolate becomes soft when the temperature is high enough, but it still maintains its shape. Eventually, the chocolate becomes a liquid, but there is no specific temperature at which you can say the change happened. Instead, the melting happens gradually over a range of temperatures.

CHECK YOUR READING Describe the movement of molecules in a substance that is at its melting point.

Icicles grow as water drips down them, freezes, and sticks to the ice that is already there. On a warm day, the frozen icicles melt again.

Freezing

READING TiP

On the Celsius temperature scale, under normal conditions, water freezes at 0°C and boils at 100°C. On the Fahrenheit scale, water freezes at 32°F and boils at 212°F.

Freezing is the process by which a liquid becomes a solid. Although you may think of cold temperatures when you hear the word *freezing*, many substances are solid, or frozen, at room temperature and above. Think about a soda can and a candle. The can and the candle are frozen at temperatures you would find in a classroom.

As the temperature of a liquid is lowered, its particles lose energy. As a result, the particles move more slowly. Eventually, the particles move slowly enough that the attractions among them cause the liquid to become a solid. The temperature at which a specific liquid becomes a solid is called the **freezing point** of the substance.

The freezing point of a substance is the same as that substance's melting point. At this particular temperature, the substance can exist as either a solid or a liquid. At temperatures below the freezing/ melting point, the substance is a solid. At temperatures above the freezing/melting point, the substance is a liquid.

CHECK YOUR READING What is the relationship between a substance's melting point and freezing point?

Liquids can become gases, and gases can become liquids.

Suppose you spill water on a picnic table on a warm day. You might notice that the water eventually disappears from the table. What has happened to the water molecules? The liquid water has become water vapor, a gas. The water vapor mixes with the surrounding air. At the same picnic, you might also notice that a cold can of soda has beads of water forming on it. The water vapor in the air has become the liquid water found on the soda can.

Evaporation

Evaporation is a process by which a liquid becomes a gas. It usually occurs at the surface of a liquid. Although all particles in a liquid move, they do not all move at the same speed. Some particles move faster than others. The fastest moving particles at the surface of the liquid can break away from the liquid and escape to become gas particles.

As the temperature increases, the energy in the liquid increases. More particles can escape from the surface of the liquid. As a result, the liquid evaporates more quickly. This is why spilled water will evaporate faster in hot weather than in cold weather.

READING TIP

The root of the word *evaporation* is *vapor,* a Latin word meaning "steam."

CHECK YOUR READING Describe the movement of particles in a liquid as it evaporates.

It is interesting to note that under certain conditions, solids can lose particles through a process similar to evaporation. When a solid changes directly to a gas, the process is called **sublimation.** You may have seen dry ice being used in a cooler to keep foods cold. Dry ice is frozen carbon dioxide that sublimates in normal atmospheric conditions.

Evaporation

During evaporation, fast-moving particles escape from the surface of a liquid and become gas particles.

Boiling

RESOURCE CENTER
CLASSZONE.COM

Explore melting points
and boiling points.

Boiling is another process by which a liquid becomes a gas. Unlike evaporation, boiling produces bubbles. If you heat a pot of water on the stove, you will notice that after a while tiny bubbles begin to form. These bubbles contain dissolved air that is escaping from the liquid. As you continue to heat the water, large bubbles suddenly form and rise to the surface. These bubbles contain energetic water molecules that have escaped from the liquid water to form a gas. This process is boiling.

Boiling can occur only when the liquid reaches a certain temperature, called the **boiling point** of the liquid. Liquids evaporate over a wide range of temperatures. Boiling, however, occurs at a specific temperature for each liquid. Water, for example, has a boiling point of 100°C (212°F) at normal atmospheric pressure.

In the mountains, water boils at a temperature lower than 100°C. For example, in Leadville, Colorado, which has an elevation of 3094 m (10,152 ft) above sea level, water boils at 89°C (192°F). This happens because at high elevations the air pressure is much lower than at sea level. Because less pressure is pushing down on the surface of the water, bubbles can form inside the liquid at a lower temperature. Less energetic water molecules are needed to expand the bubbles under these conditions. The lower boiling point of water means that foods cooked in water, such as pasta, require a longer time to prepare.

Different substances boil at different temperatures. Helium, which is a gas at room temperature, boils at –270°C (–454°F). Aluminum, on the other hand, boils at 2519°C (4566°F). This fact explains why some substances usually are found as gases but others are not.

Boiling

Bubbles of vapor form inside the boiling water.

Tiny droplets of water form on a window as water vapor from the air condenses into liquid water.

Condensation

The process by which a gas changes its state to become a liquid is called **condensation.** You probably have seen an example of condensation when you enjoyed a cold drink on a warm day. The beads of water that formed on the glass or can were water vapor that condensed from the surrounding air.

The cold can or glass cooled the air surrounding it. When you cool a gas, it loses energy. As the particles move more slowly, the attractions among them cause droplets of liquid to form. Condensed water often forms when warm air containing water vapor comes into contact with a cold surface, such as a glass of ice or ground that has cooled during the night.

As with evaporation, condensation can occur over a wide range of temperatures. Like the particles in liquids, the individual particles in a gas are moving at many different speeds. Slowly moving particles near the cool surface condense as they lose energy. The faster moving particles also slow down but continue to move too fast to stick to the other particles in the liquid that is forming. However, if you cool a gas to a temperature below its boiling point, almost all of the gas will condense.

READING TiP

The root of the word *condensation* is *condense,* which comes from a Latin word meaning "to thicken."

2.2 Review

KEY CONCEPTS

1. Describe three ways in which matter can change from one state to another.

2. Compare and contrast the processes of evaporation and condensation.

3. How does adding energy to matter by heating it affect the energy of its particles?

CRITICAL THINKING

4. **Synthesize** Explain how water can exist as both a solid and a liquid at 0°C.

5. **Apply** Explain how a pat of butter at room temperature can be considered to be frozen.

⬥ CHALLENGE

6. **Infer** You know that water vapor condenses from air when the air temperature is lowered. Should it be possible to condense oxygen from air? What would have to happen?

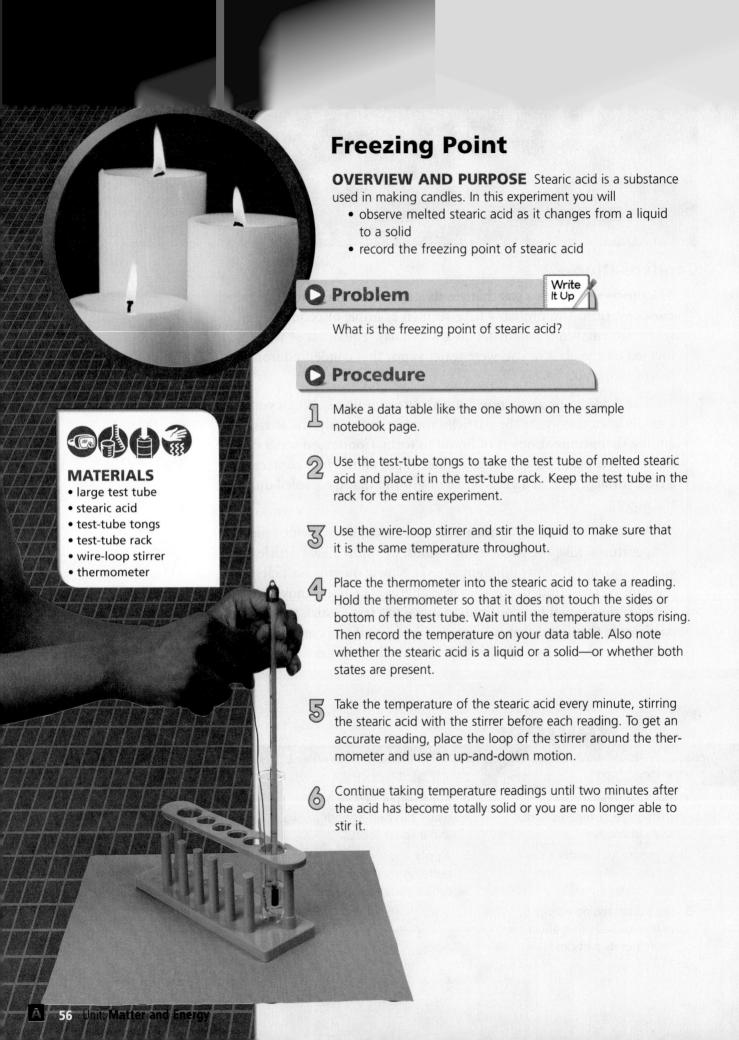

Freezing Point

OVERVIEW AND PURPOSE Stearic acid is a substance used in making candles. In this experiment you will
- observe melted stearic acid as it changes from a liquid to a solid
- record the freezing point of stearic acid

▶ Problem

Write It Up

What is the freezing point of stearic acid?

▶ Procedure

1. Make a data table like the one shown on the sample notebook page.

2. Use the test-tube tongs to take the test tube of melted stearic acid and place it in the test-tube rack. Keep the test tube in the rack for the entire experiment.

3. Use the wire-loop stirrer and stir the liquid to make sure that it is the same temperature throughout.

4. Place the thermometer into the stearic acid to take a reading. Hold the thermometer so that it does not touch the sides or bottom of the test tube. Wait until the temperature stops rising. Then record the temperature on your data table. Also note whether the stearic acid is a liquid or a solid—or whether both states are present.

5. Take the temperature of the stearic acid every minute, stirring the stearic acid with the stirrer before each reading. To get an accurate reading, place the loop of the stirrer around the thermometer and use an up-and-down motion.

6. Continue taking temperature readings until two minutes after the acid has become totally solid or you are no longer able to stir it.

MATERIALS
- large test tube
- stearic acid
- test-tube tongs
- test-tube rack
- wire-loop stirrer
- thermometer

7. Make a note of the temperature on your data table when the first signs of a solid formation appear.

8. Make a note of the temperature on your data table when the stearic acid is completely solid.

9. Leave the thermometer and stirrer in the test tube and carry it carefully in the test-tube rack to your teacher.

▶ Observe and Analyze
Write It Up

1. **RECORD OBSERVATIONS** Make a line graph showing the freezing curve of stearic acid. Label the vertical axis **Temperature** and the horizontal axis **Time**.

2. **RECORD OBSERVATIONS** Label your graph to show when the stearic acid was a liquid, when it was a solid, and when it was present in both states.

3. **ANALYZE** Explain how your graph tells you the freezing point of stearic acid.

▶ Conclude
Write It Up

1. **INTERPRET** Answer the question in the problem.

2. **IDENTIFY** How does the freezing point of stearic acid compare with the freezing point of water?

3. **INFER** What happened to the energy of the molecules as the stearic acid changed from a liquid to a solid?

4. **INFER** From your observations, infer the melting point of stearic acid. How is the melting point of stearic acid related to its freezing point?

5. **APPLY** Why do you think stearic acid is used as an ingredient in bar soaps but not in liquid soaps?

▶ INVESTIGATE Further

CHALLENGE What do you think would happen if you mixed in another substance with the stearic acid? How would that affect the freezing point? What experiment would you perform to find the answer?

Freezing Point
Problem What is the freezing point of stearic acid?
Observe and Analyze
Table 1. Freezing Point of Stearic Acid

Time (min)	Temperature (°C)	Liquid	Solid	Both
0.0				
1.0				
2.0				
3.0				
4.0				
5.0				
6.0				
7.0				

KEY CONCEPT
2.3 Properties are used to identify substances.

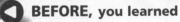

BEFORE, you learned	NOW, you will learn
• Matter can change from one state to another	• How properties can help you identify substances
• Changes in state require energy changes	• How properties of substances can be used to separate substances

---

EXPLORE Identifying Substances

How can properties help you identify a substance?

PROCEDURE

1. Place some of substance A into one cup and some of substance B into the other cup. Label the cups.

2. Carefully add some water to each cup. Observe and record what happens.

WHAT DO YOU THINK?

• Which result was a physical change? a chemical change? Explain.

• The substances are baking soda and baking powder. Baking powder and water produce carbon dioxide gas. Which substance is baking powder?

MATERIALS
• substance A
• substance B
• 2 cups
• water

Substances have characteristic properties.

MAIN IDEA WEB
As you read, place each blue heading in a box. Add details around it to form a web.

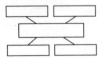

You often use the properties of a substance to identify it. For example, when you reach into your pocket, you can tell the difference between a ticket stub and a folded piece of tissue because one is stiff and smooth and the other is soft. You can identify nickels, dimes, and quarters without looking at them by feeling their shapes and comparing their sizes. To tell the difference between a nickel and a subway token, however, you might have to use another property, such as color. Texture, shape, and color are physical properties that you use all the time to identify and sort objects.

 How can physical properties be used to identify a substance?

Identifying Unknown Substances

Suppose you have a glass of an unknown liquid that you want to identify. It looks like milk, but you cannot be sure. How could you determine what it is? Of course, you would not taste an unknown substance, but there are many properties other than taste that you could use to identify the substance safely.

To proceed scientifically, you could measure several properties of the unknown liquid and compare them with the properties of known substances. You might observe and measure such properties as color, odor, texture, density, boiling point, and freezing point. A few of these properties might be enough to tell you that your white liquid is glue rather than milk.

To determine the difference among several colorless liquids, scientists would use additional tests. Their tests, however, would rely on the same idea of measuring and comparing the properties of an unknown with something that is already known.

Properties Used for Identifying Substances

You are already familiar with the most common physical properties of matter. Some of these properties, such as mass and volume, depend upon the specific object in question. You cannot use mass to tell one substance from another because two very different objects can have the same mass—a kilogram of feathers has the same mass as a kilogram of peanut butter, for example.

aerogel

Other properties, such as density, can be used to identify substances. They do not vary from one sample of the same substance to another. For example, you could see a difference between a kilogram of liquid soap and a kilogram of honey by measuring their densities.

The physical properties described below can be used to identify a substance.

Density The densities of wood, plastic, and steel are all different. Scientists already have determined the densities of many substances. As a result, you can conveniently compare the density of an unknown substance with the densities of known substances. Finding any matching densities will give you information about the possible identity of the unknown substance. However, it is possible for two different substances to have the same density. In that case, in order to identify the substance positively, you would need additional data.

Aerogel, an extremely lightweight material used in the space program, has such a low density that it can float on soap bubbles.

CHECK YOUR READING   Why can't you identify a substance on the basis of density alone?

These fibers act as heat insulators to keep the inside of the sleeping bag warm.

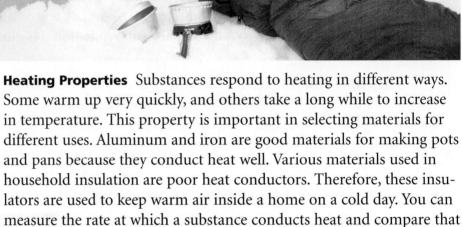

READING TiP

The root of the word *solubility* is the Latin word *solvere,* which means "to loosen."

Iron filings are attracted by the magnet. The wood chips, however, are not.

Heating Properties Substances respond to heating in different ways. Some warm up very quickly, and others take a long while to increase in temperature. This property is important in selecting materials for different uses. Aluminum and iron are good materials for making pots and pans because they conduct heat well. Various materials used in household insulation are poor heat conductors. Therefore, these insulators are used to keep warm air inside a home on a cold day. You can measure the rate at which a substance conducts heat and compare that rate with the heat conduction rates of other substances.

Solubility Solubility is a measure of how much of a substance dissolves in a given volume of a liquid. Sugar and dirt, for instance, have very different solubilities in water. If you put a spoonful of sugar into a cup of water and stir, the sugar dissolves in the water very rapidly. If you put a spoonful of dirt into water and stir, most of the dirt settles to the bottom as soon as you stop stirring.

Electric Properties Some substances conduct electricity better than others. This means that they allow electric charge to move through them easily. Copper wire is used to carry electricity because it is a good conductor. Materials that do not conduct easily, such as rubber and plastics, are used to block the flow of charge. With the proper equipment, scientists can test the electric conductivity of an unknown substance.

Magnetic Properties Some substances are attracted to magnets, but others are not. You can use a magnet to pick up a paper clip but not a plastic button or a wooden match. The elements iron, cobalt, and nickel are magnetic—meaning they respond to magnets—but copper, aluminum, and zinc are not. Steel, which contains iron, is also magnetic.

Mixtures can be separated by using the properties of the substances in them.

Suppose you have a bag of cans that you want to recycle. The recycling center accepts only aluminum cans. You know that some of your cans contain steel. You would probably find it difficult to tell aluminum cans from steel ones just by looking at them. How could you separate the cans? Aluminum and steel may look similar, but they have different magnetic properties. You could use a magnet to test each can. If the magnet sticks to the can, the can contains steel. Recycling centers often use magnets to separate aluminum cans from steel cans.

Some mixtures contain solids mixed with liquids. A filter can be used to separate the solid from the liquid. One example of this is a tea bag. The paper filter allows the liquid water to mix with the tea, because water molecules are small enough to pass through the filter. The large pieces of tea, however, cannot pass through the filter and remain inside the tea bag.

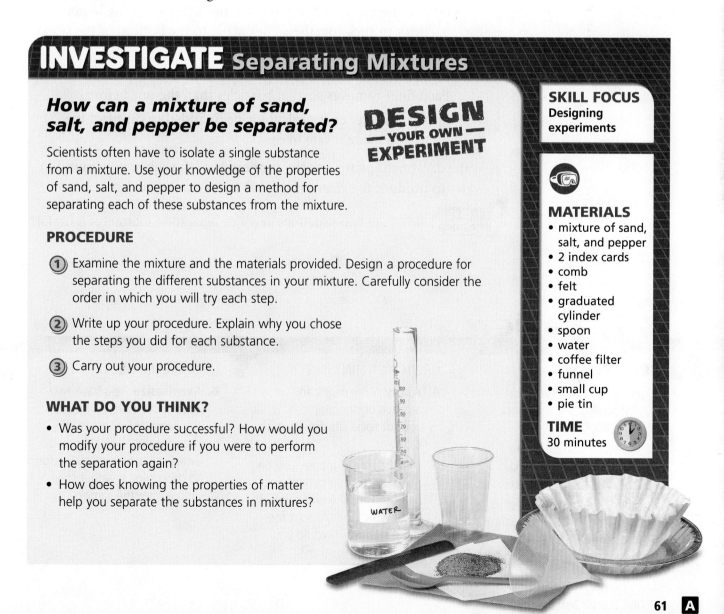

INVESTIGATE Separating Mixtures

How can a mixture of sand, salt, and pepper be separated?

DESIGN —YOUR OWN— EXPERIMENT

Scientists often have to isolate a single substance from a mixture. Use your knowledge of the properties of sand, salt, and pepper to design a method for separating each of these substances from the mixture.

PROCEDURE

(1) Examine the mixture and the materials provided. Design a procedure for separating the different substances in your mixture. Carefully consider the order in which you will try each step.

(2) Write up your procedure. Explain why you chose the steps you did for each substance.

(3) Carry out your procedure.

WHAT DO YOU THINK?

- Was your procedure successful? How would you modify your procedure if you were to perform the separation again?

- How does knowing the properties of matter help you separate the substances in mixtures?

WATER

SKILL FOCUS
Designing experiments

MATERIALS
- mixture of sand, salt, and pepper
- 2 index cards
- comb
- felt
- graduated cylinder
- spoon
- water
- coffee filter
- funnel
- small cup
- pie tin

TIME
30 minutes

Some mixtures are more difficult to separate than others. For example, if you stir sugar into water, the sugar dissolves and breaks up into individual molecules that are too tiny to filter out. In this case, you can take advantage of the fact that water is a liquid and will evaporate from an open dish. Sugar, however, does not evaporate. The mixture can be heated to speed the evaporation of the water, leaving the sugar behind.

There are many important reasons for separating substances. One reason is to make a substance safe to consume, such as drinking water. In order to produce drinking water, workers at a water-treatment plant must separate many of the substances that are mixed in with the water.

This water-treatment plant separates harmful substances from the water.

The process in water-treatment plants generally includes these steps:

- First, a chemical is added to the water that causes the larger particles to stick together. They settle to the bottom of the water, where they can be removed.
- Next, the water is run through a series of special molecular filters. Each filter removes smaller particles than the one before.
- Finally, another chemical, chlorine, is added to disinfect the water and make it safe to drink.

Water-treatment plants use the properties of the substances found in water to produce the clean water that flows from your tap.

 CHECK YOUR READING What are two situations in which separating substances is useful?

2.3 Review

KEY CONCEPTS

1. How can properties help you distinguish one substance from another?

2. What are two physical properties that can help you identify a substance?

3. How can understanding properties help you separate substances from a mixture?

CRITICAL THINKING

4. **Apply** Why might an archaeologist digging in ancient ruins sift dirt through a screen?

5. **Synthesize** Suppose you had a mixture of iron pellets, pebbles, and small wood spheres, all of which were about the same size. How would you separate this mixture?

⚠ CHALLENGE

6. **Synthesize** You have two solid substances that look the same. What measurements would you take and which tests would you perform to determine whether they actually are the same?

Separating Minerals

A few minerals, such as rock salt, occur in large deposits that can be mined in a form that is ready to use. Most minerals, however, are combined with other materials, so they need to be separated from the mixtures of which they are a part. Scientists and miners use the differences in physical properties to analyze samples and to separate the materials removed from a mine.

Appearance

Gemstones are prized because of their obvious physical properties, such as color, shininess, and hardness. Particularly valuable minerals, such as diamonds and emeralds, are often located by digging underground and noting the differences between the gemstone and the surrounding dirt and rock.

Density

When gold deposits wash into a streambed, tiny particles of gold mix with the sand. It is hard to separate them by appearance because the pieces are so small. In the 1800s, as prospectors swirled this sand around in a pan, the lighter particles of sand washed away with the water. The denser gold particles collected in the bottom of the pan. Some modern gold mines use the same principle in machines that handle tons of material, washing away the lighter dirt and rock to leave bits of gold.

Magnetism

Machines called magnetic separators divide a mixture into magnetic and nonmagnetic materials. In order to separate iron from other materials, rocks are crushed and carried past a strong magnet. Particles that contain iron are drawn toward the magnet and fall into one bin, while the nonmagnetic materials fall into another bin.

Melting Point

Thousands of years ago, people discovered that when some minerals are placed in a very hot fire, metals—such as copper, tin, and zinc— can be separated from the rock around them. When the ores reach a certain temperature, the metal melts and can be collected as a liquid.

EXPLORE

1. **INFER** At a copper ore mine in Chile, one of the world's largest magnets is used to remove pieces of iron from the ore. What can you infer about the copper ore?

2. **CHALLENGE** Electrostatic precipitators are important tools for protecting the environment from pollution. Use the Internet to learn how they are used in power plants and other factories that burn fuels.

Workers can identify garnets in a mine because their physical properties are different from the physical properties of their surroundings.

RESOURCE CENTER
CLASSZONE.COM

Find out more about separating materials from mixtures.

the BIG idea

Matter has properties that can be changed by physical and chemical processes.

CONTENT REVIEW
CLASSZONE.COM

◀ KEY CONCEPTS SUMMARY

2.1 Matter has observable properties.

- Physical properties can be observed without changing the substance.
- Physical changes can change some physical properties but do not change the substance.

- Chemical properties describe how substances form new substances.
- Chemical changes create new substances.

VOCABULARY
physical property p. 41
density p. 43
physical change p. 44
chemical property p. 46
chemical change p. 46

2.2 Changes of states are physical changes.

Matter is commonly found in three states: solid, liquid, and gas.

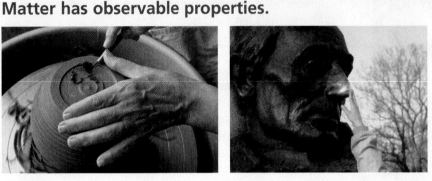

freezing
Solid   Liquid
melting

condensation
Liquid   Gas
evaporation, boiling

VOCABULARY
melting p. 51
melting point p. 51
freezing p. 52
freezing point p. 52
evaporation p. 53
sublimation p. 53
boiling p. 54
boiling point p. 54
condensation p. 55

2.3 Properties are used to identify substances.

Physical properties that can be used to identify substances include:

- density
- heating properties
- solubility
- electric properties
- magnetic properties

Mixtures can be separated by using the properties of the substances they contain.

Reviewing Vocabulary

Describe how the terms in the following sets of terms are related.

1. physical property, physical change

2. chemical property, chemical change

3. density, matter

4. melting, melting point, freezing point

5. boiling, boiling point, liquid

6. evaporation, condensation

7. sublimation, solid

Reviewing Key Concepts

Multiple Choice *Choose the letter of the best answer.*

8. Color, shape, size, and texture are
   a. physical properties
   b. chemical properties
   c. physical changes
   d. chemical changes

9. Density describes the relationship between a substance's
   a. matter and mass
   b. mass and volume
   c. volume and area
   d. temperature and mass

10. Dissolving sugar in water is an example of a
    a. physical change
    b. chemical change
    c. change in state
    d. pressure change

11. An electric current can be used to decompose, or break down, water into oxygen gas and hydrogen gas. This is an example of a
    a. physical change
    b. chemical change
    c. change in state
    d. pressure change

12. The formation of rust on iron is a chemical change because
    a. the color and shape have changed
    b. the mass and volume have changed
    c. the substance remains the same
    d. a new substance has been formed

13. The process by which a solid becomes a liquid is called
    a. boiling
    b. freezing
    c. melting
    d. evaporating

14. The process by which a liquid becomes a solid is called
    a. boiling
    b. freezing
    c. melting
    d. evaporating

15. Two processes by which a liquid can become a gas are
    a. evaporation and boiling
    b. melting and freezing
    c. sublimation and condensation
    d. evaporation and condensation

Short Answer *Answer each of the following questions in a sentence or two.*

16. When a sculptor shapes marble to make a statue, is this a physical or a chemical change? Explain your answer.

17. Describe and identify various physical changes that water can undergo.

18. Why does dew often form on grass on a cool morning, even if there has been no rain?

19. Describe the difference between evaporation and boiling in terms of the movement of the liquid's particles in each case.

20. What effect does altitude have on the boiling point of water?

21. **ANALYZE** Whole milk is a mixture. When bacteria in the milk digest part of the mixture, changes occur. Lactic acid is produced, and the milk tastes sour. Explain why this process is a chemical change.

22. **INFER** Sharpening a pencil leaves behind pencil shavings. Why is sharpening a pencil a physical change instead of a chemical change?

23. **ANALYZE** Dumping cooked spaghetti and water into a colander separates the two substances because the liquid water can run through the holes in the colander but the solid spaghetti cannot. Explain how this is an example of separating a mixture based on the physical properties of its components.

24. **INFER** The density of water is 1.0 g/mL. Anything with a density less than 1.0 g/mL will float in water. The density of a fresh egg is about 1.2 g/mL. The density of a spoiled egg is about 0.9 g/mL. If you place an egg in water and it floats, what does that tell you about the egg?

Use the photograph below to answer the next three questions.

25. **COMPARE** Which physical properties of the puddle change as the water evaporates? Which physical properties remain the same?

26. **ANALYZE** Can water evaporate from this puddle on a cold day? Explain your answer.

27. **PREDICT** What would happen to any minerals and salts in the water if the water completely evaporated?

Use the chart below to answer the next two questions.

Densities Measured at 20°C

Material	Density (g/cm^3)
gold	19.3
lead	11.3
silver	10.5
copper	9.0
iron	7.9

28. **PREDICT** Suppose you measure the mass and the volume of a shiny metal object and find that its density is 10.5 g/mL. Could you make a reasonable guess as to what material the object is made of? What factor or factors might affect your guess?

29. **CALCULATE** A solid nickel bar has a mass of 2.75 kg and a volume of 308.71 cm^3. Between which two materials would nickel fall on the chart?

the BIG idea

30. **PREDICT** Look again at the photograph on pages 38–39. The chef has melted sugar to make a sculpture. Describe how the sugar has changed in terms of its physical and chemical properties. Predict what will happen to the sculpture over time.

31. **RESEARCH** Think of a question you have about the properties of matter that is still unanswered. For example, there may be a specific type of matter about which you are curious. What information do you need in order to answer your question? How might you find the information?

UNIT PROJECTS

Check your schedule for your unit project. How are you doing? Be sure that you have placed data or notes from your research in your project folder.

Analyzing Experiments

Read the following description of an experiment together with the chart.
Then answer the questions that follow.

Archimedes was a Greek mathematician and scientist who lived in the third century B.C. He figured out that any object placed in a liquid displaced a volume of that liquid equal to its own volume. He used this knowledge to solve a problem.

The king of Syracuse had been given a crown of gold. But he was not sure whether the crown was pure gold. Archimedes solved the king's problem by testing the crown's density.

He immersed the crown in water and measured the volume of water it displaced. Archimedes compared the amount of water displaced by the crown with the amount of water displaced by a bar of pure gold with the same mass. The comparison told him whether the crown was all gold or a mixture of gold and another element.

Element	Density (g/cm^3)
copper	8.96
gold	19.30
iron	7.86
lead	11.34
silver	10.50
tin	7.31

1. Which problem was Archimedes trying to solve?
   a. what the density of gold was
   b. what the crown was made of
   c. what the mass of the crown was
   d. how much water the crown displaced

2. Archimedes used the method that he did because a crown has an irregular shape and the volume of such an object cannot be measured in any other way. Which one of the following objects would also require this method?
   a. a square wooden box
   b. a cylindrical tin can
   c. a small bronze statue
   d. a rectangular piece of glass

3. Suppose Archimedes found that the crown had a mass of 772 grams and displaced 40 milliliters of water. Using the formula $D = m/V$, what would you determine the crown to be made of?
   a. pure gold
   b. half gold and half another element
   c. some other element with gold plating
   d. cannot be determined from the data

4. Using the formula, compare how much water a gold crown would displace if it had a mass of 579 grams.
   a. 10 mL   **c.** 30 mL
   b. 20 mL   **d.** 193 mL

5. If you had crowns made of each element in the chart that were the same mass, which would displace more water than a gold crown of that mass?
   a. all   **c.** tin only
   b. lead only   **d.** none

Extended Response

Answer the two questions below in detail.

6. What is the difference between a physical change and a chemical change? Include examples of each type in your explanation.

7. Why does someone cooking spaghetti at a high elevation need to boil it longer than someone cooking spaghetti at a lower elevation?

CHAPTER
3 Energy

the **BIG** idea

Energy has different forms, but it is always conserved.

Key Concepts

SECTION
3.1 Energy exists in different forms.
Learn about several different forms of energy.

SECTION
3.2 Energy can change forms but is never lost.
Learn about the law of conservation of energy.

SECTION
3.3 Technology improves the ways people use energy.
Learn how technology can be used to make energy conversions more efficient.

Internet Preview

CLASSZONE.COM

Chapter 3 online resources: Content Review, Simulation, Visualization, three Resource Centers, Math Tutorial, Test Practice

What different forms of energy are shown in this photograph?

A Penny for Your Energy

Chill an empty glass bottle. Immediately complete the following steps: Rub a drop of cooking oil around the rim of the bottle. Place a coin on the rim so the oil forms a seal between the coin and the bottle. Wrap your hands around the bottle.

Observe and Think What happened to the coin? What do you think caused this to happen?

Hot Dog!

Cover a piece of cardboard with aluminum foil, and bend it into the shape of a U. Poke a wooden skewer through a hot dog, and through each side of the cardboard. Push corks over both ends of the skewer so the cardboard does not flatten out. Place your setup in direct sunlight for 30 minutes.

Observe and Think What happened to the hot dog? Were there any changes you had to make while the hot dog was in sunlight?

Internet Activity: Energy

Go to **ClassZone.com** to investigate the relationship between potential energy and kinetic energy.

Observe and Think How did you change potential energy? How do these changes affect kinetic energy?

NSTA
scilinks.org
SCLINKS

Forms of Energy Code: MDL063

Getting Ready to Learn

CONCEPT REVIEW

- Matter has mass and is made of tiny particles.
- Matter can be changed physically or chemically.
- A change in the state of matter is a physical change.

VOCABULARY REVIEW

matter p. 9

mass p. 10

atom p. 16

physical change p. 44

chemical change p. 46

CONTENT REVIEW
CLASSZONE.COM
Review concepts and vocabulary.

TAKING NOTES

MIND MAP

Write each main idea, or blue heading, in an oval; then write details that relate to each other and to the main idea. Organize the details so that each spoke of the web has notes about one part of the main idea.

VOCABULARY STRATEGY

Write each new vocabulary term in the center of a **frame game** diagram. Decide what information to frame it with. Use examples, descriptions, parts, sentences that use the term in context, or pictures. You can change the frame to fit each term.

See the Note-Taking Handbook on pages R45–R51.

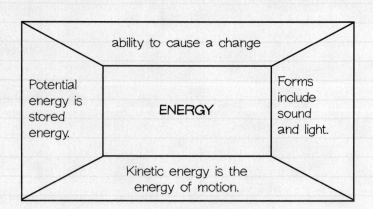

SCIENCE NOTEBOOK

ability to cause a change

different changes from different forms

DIFFERENT FORMS OF ENERGY HAVE DIFFERENT USES.

sunlight — electromagnetic energy

motion — mechanical energy

food — chemical energy

ability to cause a change

Potential energy is stored energy.

ENERGY

Forms include sound and light.

Kinetic energy is the energy of motion.

Energy exists in different forms.

◀ BEFORE, you learned	▶ NOW, you will learn
• All substances are made of matter	• How energy causes change
• Matter has both physical and chemical properties	• About common forms of energy
• Matter can exist in different physical states	• About kinetic energy and potential energy

VOCABULARY

energy p. 72
kinetic energy p. 74
potential energy p. 75

EXPLORE Energy

How can you demonstrate energy?

PROCEDURE

① Fill the bowl halfway with sand. Place the bowl on the floor as shown. Make sure the sand is level.

② Place a pebble and a rock near the edge of a table above the bowl of sand.

③ Gently push the pebble off the table into the sand. Record your observations.

④ Remove the pebble, and make sure the sand is level. Gently push the rock off the table into the sand. Record your observations.

WHAT DO YOU THINK?

• What happened to the sand when you dropped the pebble? when you dropped the rock?

• How can you explain any differences you observed?

MATERIALS

• large plastic bowl
• sand
• pebble
• rock

Different forms of energy have different uses.

Energy takes many different forms and has many different effects. Just about everything you see happening around you involves energy. Lamps and other appliances in your home operate on electrical energy. Plants use energy from the Sun to grow. You use energy provided by the food you eat to carry out all of your everyday activities—eating, exercising, reading, and even sitting and thinking. In this chapter, you will learn what these and other forms of energy have in common.

Energy

All forms of energy have one important point in common—they cause changes to occur. The flow of electrical energy through a wire causes a cool, dark bulb to get hot and glow. The energy of the wind causes a flag to flutter.

You are a source of energy that makes changes in your environment. For example, when you pick up a tennis racquet or a paintbrush, you change the position of that object. When you hit a tennis ball or smooth paint on a canvas, you cause further changes. Energy is involved in every one of these actions. At its most basic level, **energy** is the ability to cause change.

 CHECK YOUR READING Provide your own example of energy and how it causes a change.

The photograph below shows a city street. All of the activities that take place on every street in any city require energy, so there are many changes taking place in the picture. Consider one of the cars. A person's energy is used to turn the key that starts the car. The key's movement starts the car's engine and gasoline begins burning. Gasoline provides the energy for the car to move. The person's hand, the turning key, and the burning gasoline all contain energy that causes change.

VOCABULARY
Remember to use a frame game diagram for *energy* and other vocabulary terms.

The motion of the cars and the glow of the streetlights are changes produced by energy.

Forms of Energy

Scientists classify energy into many forms, each of which causes change in a different way. Some of these forms are described below.

Mechanical Energy The energy that moves objects is mechanical energy. The energy that you use to put a book on a shelf is mechanical energy, as is energy that a person uses to turn a car key.

Sound Energy Sound results from the vibration of particles in a solid, liquid, or gas. People and other animals are able to detect these tiny vibrations with structures in their ears that vibrate due to the sound. So, when you hear a car drive past, you are detecting vibrations in the air produced by sound energy. Sound cannot travel through empty space. If there were no air or other substance between you and the car, you would not hear sounds from the car.

Chemical Energy Energy that is stored in the chemical composition of matter is chemical energy. The amount of chemical energy in a substance depends on the types and arrangement of atoms in the substance. When wood or gasoline burns, chemical energy produces heat. The energy used by the cells in your body comes from chemical energy stored in the foods you eat.

Thermal Energy The total amount of energy from the movement of particles in matter is thermal energy. Recall that matter is made of atoms, and atoms combined in molecules. The atoms and molecules in matter are always moving. The energy of this motion in an object is the object's thermal energy. You will learn more about thermal energy in the next chapter.

Electromagnetic Energy Electromagnetic (ih-LEHK-troh-mag-NEHT-ihk) energy is transmitted through space in the form of electromagnetic waves. Unlike sound, electromagnetic waves can travel through empty space. These waves include visible light, x-rays, and microwaves. X-rays are high energy waves used by doctors and dentists to look at your bones and teeth. Microwaves can be used to cook food or to transmit cellular telephone calls but contain far less energy than x-rays. The Sun releases a large amount of electromagnetic energy, some of which is absorbed by Earth.

Nuclear Energy The center of an atom—its nucleus—is the source of nuclear energy. A large amount of energy in the nucleus holds the nuclear particles together. When a heavy atom's nucleus breaks apart, or when the nuclei (NOO-klee-EYE) of two small atoms join together, energy is released. Nuclear energy released from the fusing of small nuclei to form larger nuclei keeps the Sun burning.

CHECK YOUR READING How does chemical energy cause a change? What about electromagnetic energy?

APPLY Where in this photograph can you find chemical, sound, and mechanical energy?

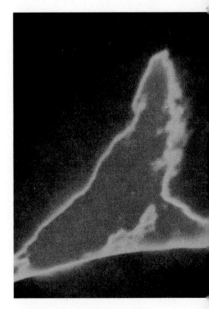

This solar flare releases electromagnetic energy and thermal energy produced by nuclear energy in the Sun.

Kinetic energy and potential energy are the two general types of energy.

RESOURCE CENTER
CLASSZONE.COM

Learn more about kinetic energy and potential energy.

All of the forms of energy can be described in terms of two general types of energy—kinetic energy and potential energy. Anything that is moving, such as a car that is being driven or an atom in the air, has kinetic energy. All matter also has potential energy, or energy that is stored and can be released at a later time.

Kinetic Energy

READING TiP

Kinetic means "related to motion."

The energy of motion is called **kinetic energy.** It depends on both an object's mass and the speed at which the object is moving.

All objects are made of matter, and matter has mass. The more matter an object contains, the greater its mass. If you held a bowling ball in one hand and a soccer ball in the other, you could feel that the bowling ball has more mass than the soccer ball.

- **Kinetic energy increases as mass increases.** If the bowling ball and the soccer ball were moving at the same speed, the bowling ball would have more kinetic energy because of its greater mass.

- **Kinetic energy increases as speed increases.** If two identical bowling balls were rolling along at different speeds, the faster one would have more kinetic energy because of its greater speed. The speed skater in the photographs below has more kinetic energy when he is racing than he does when he is moving slowly.

High Speed

This skater has a large amount of kinetic energy when moving at a high speed.

Low Speed

When the same skater is moving more slowly, he has less kinetic energy.

READING VISUALS **APPLY** How could a skater with less mass than another skater have more kinetic energy?

Potential Energy

Suppose you are holding a soccer ball in your hands. Even if the ball is not moving, it has energy because it has the potential to fall. **Potential energy** is the stored energy that an object has due to its position or chemical composition. The ball's position above the ground gives it potential energy.

The most obvious form of potential energy is potential energy that results from gravity. Gravity is the force that pulls objects toward Earth's surface. The giant boulder on the right has potential energy because of its position above the ground. The mass of the boulder and its height above the ground determine how much potential energy it has due to gravity.

It is easy to know whether an object has kinetic energy because the object is moving. It is not so easy to know how much and what form of potential energy an object has, because objects can have potential energy from several sources. For example, in addition to potential energy from gravity, substances contain potential energy due to their chemical composition—the atoms they contain.

Because the boulder could fall, it has potential energy from gravity.

 CHECK YOUR READING How can you tell kinetic energy and potential energy apart?

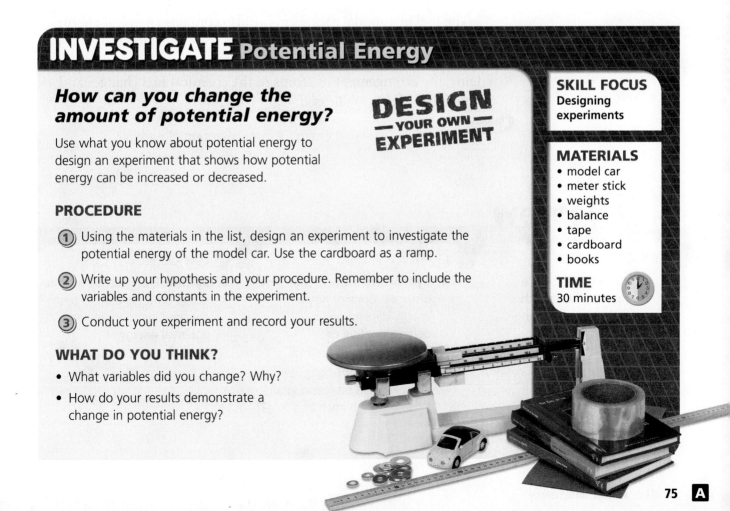

INVESTIGATE Potential Energy

How can you change the amount of potential energy?

DESIGN — YOUR OWN — EXPERIMENT

Use what you know about potential energy to design an experiment that shows how potential energy can be increased or decreased.

PROCEDURE

1. Using the materials in the list, design an experiment to investigate the potential energy of the model car. Use the cardboard as a ramp.

2. Write up your hypothesis and your procedure. Remember to include the variables and constants in the experiment.

3. Conduct your experiment and record your results.

WHAT DO YOU THINK?

- What variables did you change? Why?
- How do your results demonstrate a change in potential energy?

SKILL FOCUS
Designing experiments

MATERIALS
- model car
- meter stick
- weights
- balance
- tape
- cardboard
- books

TIME
30 minutes

Another form of potential energy related to an object's position comes from stretching or compressing an object. Think about the spring that is pushed down in a jack-in-the-box. The spring's potential energy increases when the spring is compressed and decreases when it is released. Look at the bow that is being bent in the photograph on the left. When the bowstring is pulled, the bow bends and stores energy. When the string is released, both the string and the bow return to their normal shape. Stored energy is released as the bow and the string straighten out and the arrow is pushed forward.

Pulling the string, which bends the bow, gives the bow potential energy.

When a rock falls or a bow straightens, potential energy is released. In fact, in these examples, the potential energy produced either by gravity or by bending is changed into kinetic energy.

Chemical energy, such as the energy stored in food, is less visible, but it is also a form of potential energy. This form of potential energy depends on chemical composition rather than position. It is the result of the atoms, and the bonds between atoms, that make up the molecules in food. When these molecules are broken apart, and their atoms rearranged through a series of chemical changes, energy is released.

Chemical energy in the fuel of a model rocket engine is potential energy.

The fuel in a model rocket engine also contains chemical energy. Like the molecules that provide energy in your body, the molecules in the fuel store potential energy. When the fuel ignites in the rocket engine, the arrangement of atoms in the chemical fuel changes and its potential energy is released.

 CHECK YOUR READING   Why is chemical energy a form of potential energy?

3.1 Review

KEY CONCEPTS

1. List three ways you use energy. How does each example involve a change?

2. What are some changes that can be caused by sound energy? by electromagnetic energy?

3. What two factors determine an object's kinetic energy?

CRITICAL THINKING

4. **Synthesize** How do the different forms of potential energy depend on an object's position or chemical composition?

5. **Infer** What forms of potential energy would be found in an apple on the branch of a tree? Explain.

CHALLENGE

6. **Synthesize** Describe a stone falling off a tabletop in terms of both kinetic energy and potential energy.

Gasoline or Electric?

Cars use a significant amount of the world's energy. Most cars get their energy from the chemical energy of gasoline, a fossil fuel. Cars can also get their energy from sources other than gasoline. For many years, engineers have been working to design cars that run only on electricity. The goals of developing these new cars include reducing air pollution and decreasing the use of fossil fuels. So why have electric cars not replaced gasoline-powered cars?

❯ Advantages of Electric Cars

- Electric motors are more simple than gasoline engines.
- Electric cars use energy more efficiently than gasoline-powered cars, so they are cheaper to operate.
- Controlling pollution at power plants that produce electricity is easier than controlling pollution from cars.
- Electric motors are quieter than gasoline engines.
- Electric cars do not produce smog, which is a major health concern in large cities.

❯ Disadvantages of Electric Cars

- At this time, electric cars can travel only about 120 miles on a single battery charge.
- It takes several hours to recharge the batteries of an electric car using today's charging systems.
- The batteries of an electric car need to be replaced after being recharged about 600 times.
- An electric car's range is decreased by heating or cooling the inside of the car because, unlike batteries in gasoline-powered cars, its batteries are not recharged during driving.

❯ Finding Solutions

As a Group

What technology would need to be improved for electric cars to replace gasoline-powered cars? What facilities that do not exist today would be needed to serve electric cars?

As a Class

Compare your group's solutions to those of other groups. Use the Internet to research hybrid vehicles. How would these vehicles solve some of the problems that you identified?

RESOURCE CENTER
CLASSZONE.COM
Find out more about electric cars.

3.2 Energy can change forms but is never lost.

 BEFORE, you learned

- Energy causes change
- Energy has different forms
- Kinetic energy and potential energy are the two general types of energy

 **NOW, you will learn**

- How energy can be converted from one form to another
- About the law of conservation of energy
- How energy conversions may be inefficient

VOCABULARY

law of conservation of energy p. 82
energy efficiency p. 83

THINK ABOUT

How does energy change form?

Potential energy is stored in the chemicals on the head of a match. The flame of a burning match releases that energy as light and heat. Where does the energy to strike the match come from in the first place?

MIND MAP
Use a mind map to take notes about how energy changes forms.

Energy changes forms.

A match may not appear to have any energy by itself, but it does contain potential energy that can be released. The chemical energy stored in a match can be changed into light and heat. Before the chemical energy in the match changes forms, however, other energy conversions must take place.

Plants convert energy from the Sun into chemical energy, which is stored in the form of sugars in their cells. When a person eats food that comes from plants—or from animals that have eaten plants—the person's cells can release this chemical energy. Some of this chemical energy is converted into the kinetic energy that a person uses to rub the match over a rough surface to strike it. The friction between the match and the striking surface produces heat. The heat provides the energy needed to start the chemical changes that produce the flame. From the Sun to the flame, at least five energy conversions have taken place.

 CHECK YOUR READING How is a person's chemical energy changed into another form of energy in the lighting of a match?

Conversions Between Potential Energy and Kinetic Energy

The results of some energy conversions are obvious, such as when electrical energy in a light bulb is changed into light and heat. Other energy conversions are not so obvious. The examples below and on page 80 explore, step by step, some ways in which energy conversions occur in the world around you.

Potential energy can be changed into kinetic energy and back into potential energy. Look at the illustrations and photograph of the ski jumper shown below.

① At first, the ski jumper is at the top of the hill. This position gives him potential energy (PE) due to gravity.

② As the ski jumper starts moving downhill, some of his potential energy changes into kinetic energy (KE). Kinetic energy moves him down the slope to the ramp.

③ When the ski jumper takes off from the ramp, some of his kinetic energy is changed back into potential energy as he rises in the air.

When the ski jumper descends to the ground, his potential energy once again changes into kinetic energy. After the ski jumper lands and stops moving, how might he regain the potential energy that he had at the top of the hill? The kinetic energy of a ski lift can move the ski jumper back up the mountain and give him potential energy again.

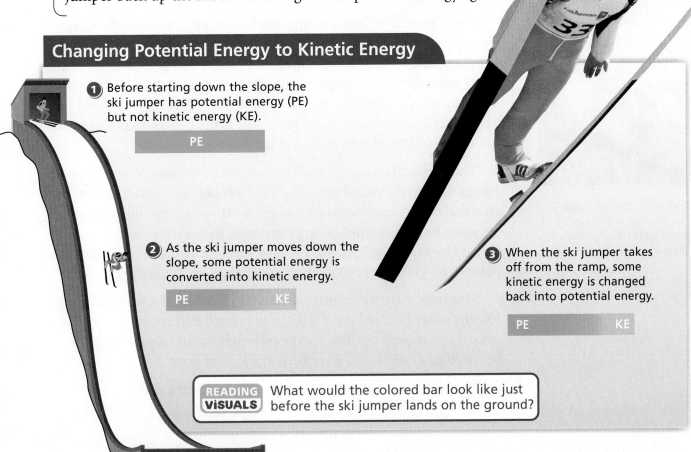

Changing Potential Energy to Kinetic Energy

① Before starting down the slope, the ski jumper has potential energy (PE) but not kinetic energy (KE).

PE

② As the ski jumper moves down the slope, some potential energy is converted into kinetic energy.

PE   KE

③ When the ski jumper takes off from the ramp, some kinetic energy is changed back into potential energy.

PE   KE

READING VISUALS   What would the colored bar look like just before the ski jumper lands on the ground?

Using Energy Conversions

People have developed ways to convert energy from one form to another for many purposes. Read about the energy conversion process below, and follow that process in the illustrations on page 81 to see how energy in water that is stored behind a dam is changed into electrical energy.

READING TiP

As you read about the process for producing electrical energy, follow the steps on page 81.

1 The water held behind the dam has potential energy because of its position.

2 Some of the water is allowed to flow through a tunnel within the dam. The potential energy in the stored water changes into kinetic energy when the water moves through the tunnel.

3 The kinetic energy of the moving water turns turbines within the dam. The water's kinetic energy becomes kinetic energy in the turbines. The kinetic energy of the turning turbines is converted into electrical energy by electrical generators.

4 Electrical energy is transported away from the dam through wires. The electrical energy is converted into many different forms of energy and is used in many different ways. For example, at a concert or a play, electrical energy is converted into light and heat by lighting systems and into sound energy by sound systems.

As you can see, several energy conversions occur in order to produce a usable form of energy—potential energy becomes kinetic energy, and kinetic energy becomes electrical energy.

Other sources of useful energy begin with electromagnetic energy from the Sun. In fact, almost all of the energy on Earth began as electromagnetic energy from the Sun. This energy can be converted into many other forms of energy. Plants convert the electromagnetic energy of sunlight into chemical energy as they grow. This energy, stored by plants hundreds of millions of years ago, is the energy found in fossil fuels, such as petroleum, coal, and natural gas.

The chemical energy in fossil fuels is converted into other forms of energy for specific uses. In power plants, people burn coal to convert its chemical energy into electrical energy. In homes, people burn natural gas to convert its chemical energy into heat that warms them and cooks their food. In car engines, people burn gasoline, which is made from petroleum, to convert its chemical energy into kinetic energy.

One important difference between fossil fuels and sources of energy like the water held behind a dam, is that fossil fuels cannot be replaced once they are used up. The energy of moving water, by contrast, is renewable as long as the river behind the dam flows.

Hoover Dam produces a large amount of electrical energy for California, Nevada, and Arizona.

CHECK YOUR READING How can potential energy be changed into a usable form of energy?

Converting Energy

Energy is often converted from one form to another in order to meet everyday needs.

① Water held behind the dam has **potential energy.**

④ **Electrical energy** is transmitted through wires, and then converted into many other forms of energy.

② **Potential energy** is converted to **kinetic energy** when the water moves through the tunnel.

③ **Kinetic energy** is used to turn turbines. This **mechanical energy** is converted into **electrical energy** by generators.

Potential Energy to Kinetic Energy

The potential energy of water behind the dam becomes the kinetic energy of moving water.

Kinetic Energy to Electrical Energy

The kinetic energy of turning turbines becomes electrical energy in these generators.

READING ViSUALS How many different energy conversions are described in this diagram?

Energy is always conserved.

When you observe energy conversions in your daily life, it may seem that energy constantly disappears. After all, if you give a soccer ball kinetic energy by kicking it along the ground, it will roll for a while but eventually stop. Consider what might have happened to the ball's kinetic energy.

As the ball rolls, it rubs against the ground. Some kinetic energy changes into heat as a result of friction. Some of the ball's energy also changes into sound energy that you can hear as the ball moves. Although the ball loses kinetic energy, the overall amount of energy in the universe does not decrease. The photograph below shows how the soccer ball's kinetic energy decreases.

The soccer ball's kinetic energy decreases as that energy is changed into sound energy and heat.

kinetic energy converted to heat

kinetic energy converted to sound

In the soccer ball example, the ball loses energy, but this energy is transferred to other parts of the universe. Energy is conserved. The **law of conservation of energy** states that energy can neither be created nor destroyed. Conservation of energy is called a law because this rule is true in all known cases. Although in many instances it may appear that energy is gained or lost, it is really only changed in form.

READING TiP

Conservation refers to a total that does not change.

CHECK YOUR READING Explain what is meant by the law of conservation of energy.

Conservation of energy is a balance of energy in the universe. When a soccer ball is kicked, a certain amount of energy is transferred by the kick. The ball gains an equal amount of energy, mostly in the form of kinetic energy. However, the ball's kinetic energy decreases as some of that energy is converted into sound energy and heat from the friction between the ball and the ground.

According to the law of conservation of energy, the amount of energy that a soccer player gives to the ball by kicking it is equal to the energy the ball gains. The energy the ball loses, in turn, is equal to the amount of energy that is transferred to the universe as sound energy and heat as the ball slows down.

Energy conversions may produce unwanted forms of energy.

When energy changes forms, the total amount of energy is conserved. However, the amount of useful energy is almost always less than the total amount of energy. For example, consider the energy used by an electric fan. The amount of electrical energy used is greater than the kinetic energy of the moving fan blades. Because energy is always conserved, some of the electrical energy flowing into the fan's motor is obviously changed into unusable or unwanted forms.

Some electrical energy is converted into unwanted sound energy.

Some electrical energy is converted into kinetic energy of the fan blades.

Some electrical energy is converted into unwanted heat.

The fan converts a significant portion of the electrical energy into the kinetic energy of the fan blades. At the same time, some electrical energy changes into heat in the fan's motor. If the fan shakes, some of the electrical energy is being turned into unwanted kinetic energy. The more efficiently the fan uses electrical energy, though, the more energy will be transformed into kinetic energy that moves the air.

Energy efficiency is a measurement of usable energy after an energy conversion. You may be familiar with energy-efficient household appliances. These appliances convert a greater percentage of energy into the desired form than inefficient ones. The more energy-efficient a fan is, the more electrical energy it turns into kinetic energy in the moving blades. Less electrical energy is needed to operate appliances that are energy efficient.

CHECK YOUR READING   What does it mean when an energy conversion is efficient?

3.2 Review

KEY CONCEPTS

1. Describe an energy conversion you have observed in your own life.

2. Explain the law of conservation of energy in your own words.

3. Give an example of an energy conversion that produces unwanted forms of energy.

CRITICAL THINKING

4. **Synthesize** Suppose you are jumping on a trampoline. Describe the conversions that occur between kinetic energy and potential energy.

5. **Infer** Look at the ski jumper on page 79. Has all of his potential energy likely been changed into kinetic energy at the moment he lands? Explain.

CHALLENGE

6. **Communicate** Draw and label a diagram that shows at least three different energy conversions that might occur when a light bulb is turned on.

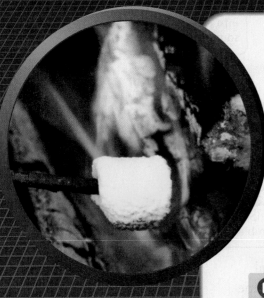

Energy Conversions

OVERVIEW AND PURPOSE All foods contain stored chemical energy, but some foods contain more chemical energy than others. People need this chemical energy for all of their activities. The amount of chemical energy stored in foods like marshmallows can be measured by burning the foods. In this investigation, you will

- construct an apparatus to investigate the amount of energy in samples of food
- calculate the amount of energy released when the foods are burned

▶ Problem

Write It Up

How much energy is stored in different types of food?

▶ Hypothesize

Write It Up

Write a hypothesis to explain which type of food contains a greater amount of chemical energy. Your hypothesis should take the form of an "If . . . , then . . . , because . . ." statement.

▶ Procedure

MATERIALS

- can opener
- empty aluminum can
- dowel rod
- water
- graduated cylinder
- ring stand with ring
- thermometer
- aluminum pie plate
- aluminum foil
- tape
- large paper clip
- cork
- modeling clay
- crouton
- caramel rice cake
- balance
- wooden matches

1. Create a data table similar to the one shown on the sample notebook page.

2. Using the can opener, punch two holes directly opposite each other near the top of the can. Slide the dowel rod through the holes as shown in the photograph to the left.

3. Measure 50 mL of water with a graduated cylinder, and pour the water into the can. Record the mass of the water. (**Hint:** 1 mL of water = 1 gram)

4. Rest the ends of the dowel rod on the ring in the ring stand to hold the can in the air. Carefully place the thermometer in the can. Measure and record the initial temperature (T1) of the water in the can.

5. Make a collar of aluminum foil and tape it around the can as shown. Leave enough room to insert the burner platform and food sample.

6 Construct the burner platform as follows: Open up the paper clip. Push the straightened end into a cork, and push the bottom of the cork into the clay. Push the burner onto the pie plate so it will not move. Put the pie plate under the ring.

step 6

7 Find and record the mass of the crouton. Place the crouton on the flattened end of the burner platform. Adjust the height of the ring so the bottom of the can is about 4 cm above the crouton.

8 Use a match to ignite the crouton. Allow the crouton to burn completely. Measure and record the final temperature (T2) of the water.

9 Empty the water from the can and repeat steps 3–8 with a caramel rice cake. The mass of the rice cake should equal the mass of the crouton.

▶ Observe and Analyze   Write It Up

1. **RECORD OBSERVATIONS** Make sure to record all measurements in the data table.

2. **CALCULATE** Find the energy released from the food samples by following the next two steps.

   Calculate and record the change in temperature.
   change in temperature = T2 – T1

   Calculate and record the energy released in calories. One calorie is the energy needed to raise the temperature of 1 g of water by 1°C.
   energy released = (mass of water · change in temperature · 1 cal/g°C)

3. **GRAPH** Make a bar graph showing the number of calories in each food sample. Which type of food contains a greater amount of chemical energy?

▶ Conclude   Write It Up

1. **INTERPRET** Answer the question posed in the problem.

2. **INFER** Did your results support your hypothesis? Explain.

3. **EVALUATE** What happens to any energy released by the burning food that is not captured by the water? How could you change the setup for a more accurate measurement?

4. **APPLY** Find out how much fat and carbohydrate the different foods contain. Explain the relationship between this information and the number of calories in the foods.

▶ INVESTIGATE Further

CHALLENGE The Calories listed in foods are equal to 1000 calories (1 kilocalorie). Calculate the amount of energy in your food samples in terms of Calories per gram of food (Calories/g). Using a balance, find the mass of any ash that remains after burning the food. Subtract that mass from the original mass of the sample to calculate mass burned. Divide total calories by mass burned, then divide that value by 1000 to find Calories/g. Compare your results to those given on the product labels.

Energy Conversions
Problem How much energy is stored in different types of food?
Hypothesize
Observe and Analyze
Table 1. Energy in Food

	Sample 1	Sample 2
Mass of water (g)		
Initial water temp. (T1) (°C)		
Final water temp. (T2) (°C)		
Mass of food (g)		
Change in temp. (T2 – T1) (°C)		
Energy released (mass·change in temp.·cal/g°C)		

Conclude

Technology improves the ways people use energy.

 BEFORE, you learned

- Energy can change forms
- When energy changes forms, the overall amount of energy remains the same
- Energy conversions usually produce unwanted forms of energy

NOW, you will learn

- How technology can improve energy conversions
- About advantages and disadvantages of different types of energy conversions
- How technology can improve the use of natural resources

VOCABULARY

solar cell p. 88

EXPLORE Solar Cells

Why does a solar calculator need a large solar cell?

PROCEDURE

 1. Measure the area of the calculator's solar cell. (**Hint:** area = length • width)

2. Turn the calculator on. Make sure that there is enough light for the calculator to work.

3. Gradually cover the solar cell with the index card. Observe the calculator's display as you cover more of the cell.

4. Measure the uncovered area of the solar cell when the calculator no longer works.

MATERIALS
- solar calculator without backup battery
- ruler
- index card

WHAT DO YOU THINK?
- How much of the solar cell is needed to keep the calculator working?
- Why might a solar calculator have a solar cell that is larger than necessary?

 MIND MAP
Use a mind map to take notes about technology that improves energy conversions.

Technology improves energy conversions.

In many common energy conversions, most of the wasted energy is released as heat. One example is the common incandescent light bulb. Amazingly, only about 5 percent of the electrical energy that enters an incandescent light bulb is converted into light. That means that 95 percent of the electrical energy turns into unwanted forms of energy. Most is released as heat and ends up in the form of thermal energy in the surrounding air. To decrease this amount of wasted energy, scientists have investigated several more efficient types of lights.

Efficient Lights

Research to replace light bulbs with a more energy-efficient source of light has resulted in the light-emitting diode, or LED. LEDs have the advantage of converting almost all of the electrical energy they use into light.

The first LEDs were not nearly as bright as typical light bulbs, but over time scientists and engineers have been able to produce brighter LEDs. LEDs have many uses, including television remote controls, computer displays, outdoor signs, giant video boards in stadiums, and traffic signals. LEDs are also used to transmit information through fiber optic cables that connect home audio and visual systems.

 READING How are LEDs more efficient than incandescent lights?

LEDs that produce infrared light are used in remote controls.

Efficient Cars

Another common but inefficient energy conversion is the burning of gasoline in cars. A large percentage of gasoline's chemical energy is not converted into the car's kinetic energy. Some of the kinetic energy is then wasted as heat from the car's engine, tires, and brakes. Here, too, efficiency can be improved through advances in technology.

Fuel injectors, common in cars since the 1980s, have improved the efficiency of engines. These devices carefully monitor and control the amount of gasoline that is fed into a car's engine. This precise control of fuel provides a significant increase in the distance a car can travel on a tank of gasoline. More recently, hybrid cars have been developed. These cars use both gasoline and electrical energy from batteries. These cars are very fuel efficient. Even better, some of the kinetic energy lost during braking in hybrid cars is used to generate electrical energy to recharge the car's batteries.

Hybrid cars may look very similar to typical gasoline-powered cars, but their engines are different.

Technology improves the use of energy resources.

Much of the energy used on Earth comes from fossil fuels such as coal, petroleum, and natural gas. However, the supply of fossil fuels is limited. So, scientists and engineers are exploring the use of several alternative energy sources. Today, for example, both solar energy and wind energy are used on a small scale to generate electrical energy.

Solar energy and wind energy have several advantages compared to fossil fuels. Their supply is not limited, and they do not produce the same harmful waste products that fossil fuels do. However, there are also many obstacles that must be overcome before solar energy and wind energy, among other alternative energy sources, are as widely used as fossil fuels.

CHECK YOUR READING What are the advantages of solar energy and wind energy as compared to fossil fuels?

Solar Energy

VISUALIZATION
CLASSZONE.COM

Observe how solar cells produce electricity.

Solar cells are important in today's solar energy technology. Modern **solar cells** are made of several layers of light-sensitive materials, which convert sunlight directly into electrical energy. Solar cells provide the electrical energy for such things as satellites in orbit around Earth, hand-held calculators, and, as shown below, experimental cars.

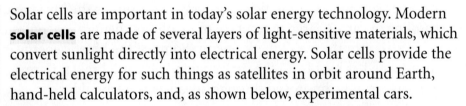

Solar Energy for Electricity

Solar cells can produce electricity to run a car.

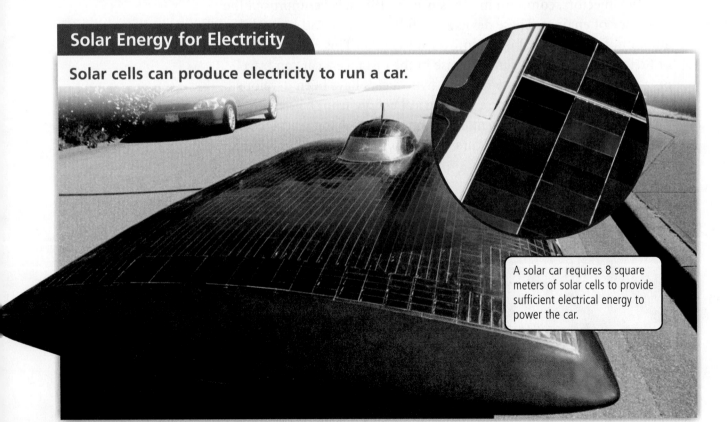

A solar car requires 8 square meters of solar cells to provide sufficient electrical energy to power the car.

Solar cells produce electrical energy quietly and cleanly. However, they are not yet commonly used because the materials used to make them are very expensive. What's more, solar cells are not very efficient in producing electrical energy. Large numbers of solar cells produce only a relatively small amount of electrical energy. Typical solar cells convert only about 12 to 15 percent of the sunlight that reaches them into electrical energy. However, solar cells currently being developed could have efficiencies close to 40 percent.

Solar energy can be used in homes to provide heat and electrical energy.

In addition to converting the Sun's light directly into electrical energy, people have used the Sun's radiation for heating. In ancient Rome, glass was used to trap solar energy indoors so that plants could be grown in the winter. Today radiation from the Sun is still used to grow plants in greenhouses and to warm buildings. The photograph above shows a house that uses solar energy in both ways. The solar cells on the roof provide electrical energy, and the large windows help to trap the warmth. In fact, some solar power systems also use that warmth to produce additional electrical energy.

CHECK YOUR READING How can energy from the Sun be used by people?

INVESTIGATE Solar Energy

What improves the collection of solar energy?

PROCEDURE

1. Cover the top of one cup with white plastic, and cover the top of the other cup with black plastic. Secure the plastic with a rubber band.

2. Use the scissors to make a small hole in the center of each cup's plastic lid. Insert a thermometer through each opening.

3. Place the cups in direct sunlight, and record their temperatures every minute for 10 minutes.

WHAT DO YOU THINK?

- Which cup showed a greater temperature change? Why do you think this happened?

- Make a line graph of your results to show the change in temperature in each cup.

CHALLENGE Try the experiment again, using aluminum foil instead of white plastic. How do the results differ with the aluminum foil? Why might this be the case?

SKILL FOCUS
Observing

MATERIALS
- 2 plastic cups
- white plastic
- black plastic
- 2 rubber bands
- scissors
- 2 thermometers
- stopwatch
for Challenge:
- aluminum foil

TIME
20 minutes

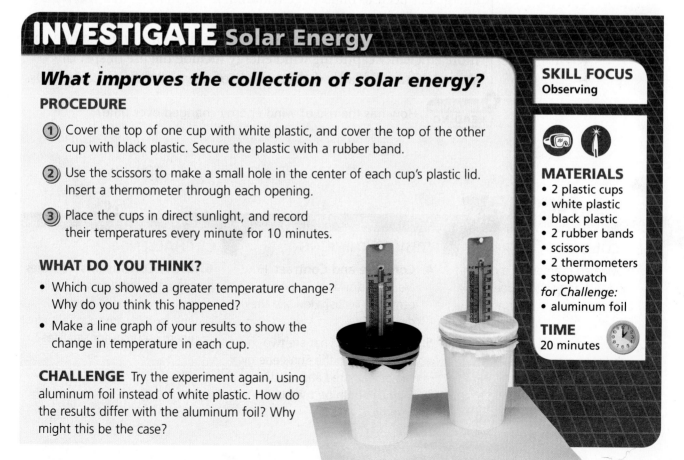

INFER Why might so many windmills be needed at a windfarm?

RESOURCE CENTER
CLASSZONE.COM

Find out more about alternative energy sources.

Wind Energy

For many centuries, people have used the kinetic energy of wind to sail ships, and, by using windmills, to grind grain and pump water. More recently, windmills have been used to generate electrical energy. In the early 1900s, for example, windmills were already being used to produce electrical energy in rural areas of the United States.

Like the technological advances in the use of solar energy, advances in capturing and using wind energy have helped to improve its efficiency and usefulness. One way to better capture the wind's energy has been to build huge windmill farms in areas that receive a consistent amount of wind. Windmill farms are found in several states, including Texas, California, and Washington. Other methods of more efficiently capturing wind energy include the use of specially shaped windmill blades that are made of new, more flexible materials.

 How has the use of wind energy changed over time?

3.3 Review

KEY CONCEPTS

1. Provide an example of a common technology that does not efficiently convert energy. Explain.

2. Describe two ways in which hybrid cars are more energy-efficient than gasoline-powered cars.

3. List two advantages and two disadvantages of solar power.

CRITICAL THINKING

4. **Compare and Contrast** How are LEDs similar to incandescent light bulbs? How are they different?

5. **Synthesize** What are two ways in which the Sun's energy can be captured and used? How can both be used in a home?

CHALLENGE

6. **Draw Conclusions** Satellites orbiting Earth use solar cells as their source of electrical energy. Why are solar cells ideal energy sources for satellites?

MATH TUTORIAL
CLASSZONE.COM

Click on Math Tutorial
for more help with rates.

Cool Efficiency

Energy efficiency is important because energy supplies are limited. The energy used by appliances such as air conditioners is measured in British thermal units, or BTUs. One BTU warms one pound of water by 1°F. The cooling ability of an air conditioner is measured by the number of BTUs it can move. Consider the number of BTUs that an air conditioning system must move in an ice rink.

An air conditioner typically has an energy efficiency ratio (EER) rating. The EER measures how efficiently a cooling system operates when the outdoor temperature is 95°F. The EER is the ratio of cooling per hour to the amount of electricity used, which is measured in watts. The higher the EER, the more energy efficient the air conditioner is.

$$EER = \frac{BTUs/hr}{watts\ used}$$

Example

Suppose an air conditioner uses 750 watts of electricity to cool 6000 BTUs per hour at 95°F. Calculate the air conditioner's EER.

(1) Use the formula above to calculate the EER.

$$EER = \frac{BTUs/hr}{watts\ used}$$

(2) Enter the known values into the formula.

$$EER = \frac{6000\ BTUs/hr}{750\ watts\ used}$$

(3) Solve the formula for the unknown value.

$$EER = \frac{6000\ BTUs/hr}{750\ watts\ used} = 8$$

ANSWER EER = 8 BTUs/hr per watt used

Answer the following questions.

1. What is the EER of a cooling system that uses 500 watts of electricity to move 6000 BTUs per hour at 95°F?

2. What is the EER of a cooling system that uses 1500 watts of electricity to move 12,000 BTUs per hour at 95°F?

3. Which air conditioner in the two questions above is more efficient?

CHALLENGE How many BTUs per hour would an air conditioner move at 95°F if it had an EER of 10 and used 1200 watts of electricity?

Indoor ice rinks require cooling systems that can keep ice frozen even when the outdoor temperature is 95°F.

Chapter Review

the **BIG** idea

Energy has different forms, but it is always conserved.

CONTENT REVIEW
CLASSZONE.COM

KEY CONCEPTS SUMMARY

 Energy exists in different forms.

- Energy is the ability to cause a change.
- Different forms of energy produce changes in different ways.
- Kinetic energy depends on mass and speed.

Potential energy depends on position and chemical composition.

VOCABULARY
energy p. 72
kinetic energy p. 74
potential energy p. 75

 Energy can change forms but is never lost.

- Energy often needs to be transformed in order to produce a useful form of energy.
- The law of conservation of energy states that energy is never created or destroyed.

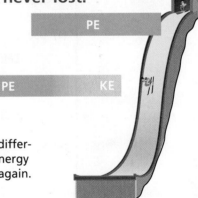

Energy can be transformed in many different ways, including from potential energy (PE) to kinetic energy (KE) and back again.

VOCABULARY
law of conservation of energy p. 82
energy efficiency p. 83

 Technology improves the ways people use energy.

- Different forms of technology are being developed and used to improve the efficiency of energy conversions.
- Solar cells convert sunlight into electrical energy.

New solar cells convert light into electrical energy more efficiently than those in the past.

VOCABULARY
solar cell p. 88

Reviewing Vocabulary

Review vocabulary terms by making a four square diagram for each term as shown in the example below. Include a definition, characteristics, examples from real life, and, if possible, nonexamples of the term.

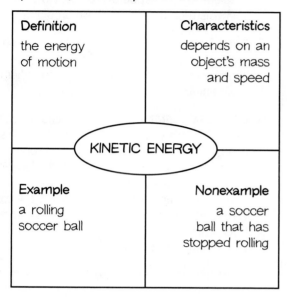

Definition	Characteristics
the energy of motion	depends on an object's mass and speed

KINETIC ENERGY

Example	Nonexample
a rolling soccer ball	a soccer ball that has stopped rolling

1. energy

2. potential energy

3. conservation of energy

4. energy efficiency

Reviewing Key Concepts

Multiple Choice *Choose the letter of the best answer.*

5. All forms of energy are a combination of
   a. mechanical energy and chemical energy
   b. chemical energy and kinetic energy
   c. potential energy and thermal energy
   d. potential energy and kinetic energy

6. Which type of energy is transmitted by vibrations of air?
   a. electromagnetic   **c.** nuclear
   b. sound   **d.** chemical

7. When energy is converted from one form to another, what is usually produced?
   a. chemical energy   **c.** heat
   b. gravity   **d.** nuclear energy

8. An object's kinetic energy is determined by its
   a. position and composition
   b. speed and position
   c. mass and speed
   d. height and width

9. Which of the following is a conversion from chemical energy to mechanical energy?
   a. a dark light bulb starting to glow
   b. food being heated in an oven
   c. a ball rolling down a hill
   d. a person lifting a weight

10. An energy-efficient electric fan converts a large portion of the electrical energy that enters it into
   a. an unwanted form of energy
   b. kinetic energy of the fan blades
   c. thermal energy in the fan's motor
   d. sound energy in the fan's motor

11. The energy in wind used to generate electricity is
   a. chemical energy
   b. sound energy
   c. potential energy
   d. kinetic energy

12. A skier on a hill has potential energy due to
   a. speed   **c.** compression
   b. energy efficiency **d.** position

Short Answer *Write a short answer to each question.*

13. Explain how the law of conservation of energy might apply to an energy conversion that you observe in your daily life.

14. Describe a situation in which chemical energy is converted into mechanical energy. Explain each step of the energy conversion process.

Thinking Critically

The illustrations below show an in-line skater on a ramp. Use the illustrations to answer the next five questions.

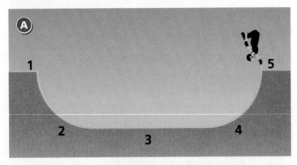

15. OBSERVE At what point in the illustrations would the skater have the most potential energy? the most kinetic energy? Explain.

16. SYNTHESIZE At what point in illustration B will the skater's kinetic energy begin to be changed back into potential energy? Explain.

17. INFER When the skater's kinetic energy is changed back into potential energy, will this amount of potential energy likely be equal to the skater's potential energy in illustration A? Why or why not?

18. PREDICT Describe how energy may appear to decrease in the example shown above. What energy conversions that produce unwanted forms of energy are occurring? Explain.

19. SYNTHESIZE Draw colored bars that might represent the potential energy and kinetic energy of the skater at each of the five labeled points on illustration A. Explain why you drew the bars the way you did. (**Hint:** See the illustration on p. 79.)

20. SYNTHESIZE How are plants and solar cells similar? How are the ways in which they capture sunlight and convert it into other forms of energy different? Explain.

21. COMPARE Explain how energy sources such as solar energy and wind energy have similar problems that must be overcome. How have scientists tried to address these problems?

22. INFER Suppose that one air conditioner becomes very hot when it is working but another air conditioner does not. Which air conditioner is more energy efficient? How can you tell?

23. DRAW CONCLUSIONS Suppose a vacuum cleaner uses 100 units of electrical energy. All of this energy is converted into thermal and sound energy (from the motor), and into the kinetic energy of air being pulled into the vacuum cleaner. If 60 units of electrical energy are converted into thermal energy and sound energy, how much electrical energy is converted into the desired form of energy? How do you know?

24. COMMUNICATE Describe a process in which energy changes forms at least twice. Draw and label a diagram that shows these energy conversions.

the **BIG** idea

25. APPLY Look again at the photograph on pages 68 and 69 and consider the opening question. How might your answer have changed after reading the chapter?

26. COMMUNICATE How have your ideas about energy and its different forms changed after reading the chapter? Provide an example from your life to describe how you would have thought of energy compared to how you might think about it now.

UNIT PROJECTS

If you need to do an experiment for your unit project, gather the materials. Be sure to allow enough time to observe results before the project is due.

Interpreting Graphs

Study the graph below. Then answer the first five questions.

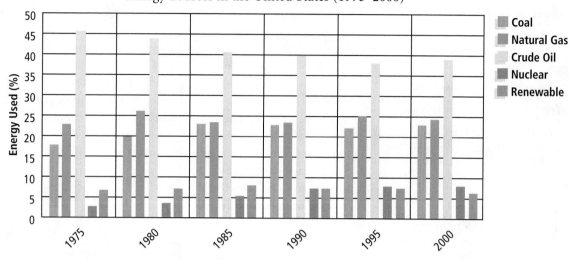

Energy Sources in the United States (1975–2000)

Source: U.S. Energy Information Administration,
Monthly Energy Review (June 2003)

1. In which year did the greatest percentage of energy used in the United States come from crude oil?

a. 1975   **c.** 1995

b. 1980   **d.** 2000

2. What three sources of energy account for about 80 percent of all energy used in each year shown?

a. coal, crude oil, nuclear

b. natural gas, crude oil, renewable

c. coal, natural gas, crude oil

d. crude oil, nuclear, renewable

3. Which sources of energy show a greater percentage in 2000 as compared to 1980?

a. crude oil, renewable   **c.** coal, nuclear

b. natural gas, crude oil   **d.** coal, crude oil

4. The use of which energy source tended to decrease between 1975 and 2000?

a. coal   **c.** crude oil

b. natural gas   **d.** nuclear

5. The use of which source of energy steadily increased between 1975 and 1995?

a. coal   **c.** nuclear

b. crude oil   **d.** renewable

Extended Response

Answer the questions in detail. Include some of the terms from the word box on the right. Underline each term you use in your answers.

chemical energy	potential energy
electrical energy	sound energy
mechanical energy	thermal energy

6. When gasoline is burned in a moving car's engine, which forms of energy are being used? Which forms of energy are produced? Explain.

7. Name two appliances in your home that you believe are inefficient. What about them indicates that they may be inefficient?

TIMELINES in Science

ABOUT TEMPERATURE AND HEAT

Most likely, the first fires early people saw were caused by lightning. Eventually, people realized that fire provided warmth and light, and they learned how to make it themselves. During the Stone Age 25,000 years ago, people used firewood to cook food as well as to warm and light their shelters. Wood was the first fuel.

This timeline shows a few of the many steps on the path toward understanding temperature and heat. Notice how the observations and ideas of previous thinkers sparked new theories by later scientists. The boxes below the timeline show how technology has led to new insights and to applications related to temperature and heat.

445 B.C.

Four Basic Substances Named

Greek philosopher Empedocles says that everything on Earth is made of some combination of four basic substances: earth, air, fire, and water. Different types of matter have different qualities depending on how they combine these substances.

350 B.C.

Aristotle Expands Theory of Matter

Greek philosopher Aristotle names four basic qualities of matter: dryness, wetness, hotness, and coldness. Each of the four basic substances has two of these qualities.

EVENTS

| 480 B.C. | 440 B.C. | 400 B.C. | 360 B.C. | 320 B.C. |

APPLICATIONS AND TECHNOLOGY

People have been trying to understand and control heat since early times.

A.D. 1617

Heat Is Motion

English philosopher Francis Bacon uses observation and experimentation to demonstrate that heat is a form of motion. Most people remain unconvinced. They consider heat to be a fluid, which they call caloric.

1762

Calorimetry Founded

Scottish chemist Joseph Black founds the science of calorimetry, which describes the amount of energy as heat a substance can hold. His research in boiling and evaporation is valuable to his friend James Watt, who is making improvements to the steam engine.

1724

Mercury Used for Thermometer

Gabriel Fahrenheit, a German instrument maker, reports that mercury works well for measuring temperature. It expands evenly as temperature rises, and its silvery appearance makes it easy to see inside a glass tube. On Fahrenheit's scale, the boiling point of pure water is 212 degrees and the freezing point is 32 degrees.

1742

New Temperature Scale Used

Swedish astronomer Anders Celsius devises a scale for measuring temperature in which the freezing point of water is 0 degrees. The boiling point of pure water is 100 degrees. He calls this the Centigrade scale, from Latin words meaning "one hundred steps."

| A.D. 1600 | 1640 | 1680 | 1720 | 1760 |

APPLICATION

Alchemy: The Quest to Create Gold

Alchemists, who hoped to turn less valuable metals into gold, took up the Greeks' theory of the four basic substances. They thought they could convert one substance into another by changing the balance of the four basic substances. Their ideas spread to the Byzantine Empire after A.D. 641, where these concepts were combined with advances in techniques for manipulating heat. Alchemy spread to Western Europe during the 1100s and 1200s.

Alchemists used chemical processes such as heating in furnaces, boiling in pots or cauldrons, distillation, pounding, and grinding. Because it was difficult to control the temperature, and thermometers had not yet been invented, alchemists usually had many different kinds of furnaces. Although alchemy is not considered a true science today, it did contribute methods and processes still used by chemists. It remained popular until around 1700.

1798
Heat and Friction Linked
While observing cannons at a weapons factory, American-born scientist Benjamin Thompson (Count Rumford) notices that friction between the cutting tools and the metal cannon barrels generates large amounts of heat. He concludes that friction is an unending source of heat. This observation helps put an end to the theory that heat is a fluid.

1906
Absolute Zero Identified
German physicist Walther Nernst suggests that absolute zero is the temperature at which the individual particles in an object would be practically motionless. Absolute zero, equivalent to −273°C, is the lowest temperature any object can reach. This limit was identified by British physicist Lord Kelvin in 1848. However, this temperature can never actually be reached by any real object.

1824
Heat Moves from Warmer to Cooler Objects
French physicist Nicolas Sadi Carnot shows that heat is a flow of energy from an object with a higher temperature to an object with a lower temperature. This explains why ice placed in a hot liquid melts and becomes a liquid rather than the liquid becoming ice.

1845
Various Energies Produce Heat
British physicist James Joule shows that mechanical energy can be converted to heat. Using a paddle-wheel device, he shows that the various forms of energy, such as mechanical and thermal, are basically the same and can change from one form to another. Joule also states that a given amount of energy of whatever form always yields that same amount of heat.

1800   **1840**   **1880**   **1920**

TECHNOLOGY
Keeping Heat In or Out
In 1892 Scottish physicist James Dewar invented the vacuum flask—a container in which warm fluids could be kept warm and cool fluids cool. A vacuum between the inner and outer walls of the container reduced conduction, which is the transfer of heat between two objects that are touching each other. Because a vacuum contains no matter, it does not conduct heat. Dewar's flask had silver walls to reflect radiated energy. As long as the flask was sealed, the vacuum was maintained and the temperature of a liquid inside the flask did not change much. A variation on Dewar's flask was produced in the early 1900s under the trade name Thermos. Today we call any vacuum container used for keeping beverages hot or cold a thermos.

This cutaway shows the inside of one of Dewar's experimental flasks.

2003

Wasps Stay Cool

Scientists in Israel have found evidence that some wasps have an internal air-conditioning system. Like a refrigerator, the wasp uses energy to stay cooler than the air around it. The energy may come from several sources, such as the energy generated by an electric current produced when the wasp's shell is exposed to sunlight. This ability to stay cool allows wasps to hunt for food even on very hot days.

SPOTLIGHT on
DAVID CROSTHWAIT

David Crosthwait (1898–1976) was a leader in the United States in the field of heat transfer. He received 39 U.S. patents for his inventions related to heating, ventilating, and air-conditioning. He was an expert on methods of heating and cooling with water.

In the 1920s and 1930s, huge skyscrapers were being built. Crosthwait was hired to design the heating system for Radio City Music Hall in New York City's Rockefeller Center.

Crosthwait's inventions improved heating systems in large buildings. His innovations include an improved boiler, a new thermostat control, and a new vacuum pump. Crosthwait's influence lives on, as steam is still used to heat and cool many skyscrapers in the United States.

RESOURCE CENTER
CLASSZONE.COM

Learn about current temperature and heat research.

1960 2000

APPLICATION

Using Thermal Energy from Ponds

Ponds can be used to store solar energy. The goal is to turn the solar energy into energy people can use. Salt must be added to the ponds, however, so that the water at the bottom is denser than the water at the top. This prevents thermal energy stored on the bottom from moving up to the surface, where it would be lost to the air through evaporation. A net on the surface helps prevent wind from mixing the water layers.

ACTIVITIES

Design a Procedure

Many people claim that it is possible to determine the temperature by listening to the chirping of crickets. Crickets are sensitive to changes in air temperature and chirp more quickly when the temperature rises. To calculate the temperature in degrees Celsius, count the number of chirps in 7 seconds and add 5.

Write a procedure for an experiment that would test this claim. What factors would you consider testing? What range of temperatures would you test?

Writing About Science

Alchemy has fascinated people for centuries. Research its influence on both the technology and procedures of modern chemistry. Write a short report.

Temperature and Heat

the BIG idea

Heat is a flow of energy due to temperature differences.

How does heat from the Sun increase this giraffe's temperature?

Key Concepts

SECTION

4.1 Temperature depends on particle movement.
Learn how kinetic energy is the basis of temperature.

SECTION

4.2 Energy flows from warmer to cooler objects.
Learn about differences between temperature and heat, and how temperature changes in different substances.

SECTION

4.3 The transfer of energy as heat can be controlled.
Learn how energy is transferred through heat, and how that transfer can be controlled.

Internet Preview

CLASSZONE.COM

Chapter 4 online resources: Content Review, two Simulations, two Resource Centers, Math Tutorial, Test Practice

EXPLORE (the **BIG** idea)

Moving Colors

Fill a clear plastic cup halfway with cold water. Fill another cup halfway with hot water. Using an eyedropper, place a drop of food coloring at the very bottom of each cup. Observe.

Observe and Think What happened to the drop of food coloring in cold water? in hot water? Why might this have happened?

Does It Chill?

Place an outdoor thermometer in an empty paper cup, and place the cup in the freezer. Check the thermometer every minute and record the time it takes for the temperature to reach 0°C (32°F). Remove the cup from the freezer. After it returns to room temperature, fill the cup with soil and repeat the experiment.

Observe and Think How long did it take for the temperature to reach 0°C each time? Why might there have been a difference?

Internet Activity: Kinetic Theory

Go to **ClassZone.com** to explore how temperature affects the speed of particles. Examine the effects of particle size as well.

Observe and Think What is the relationship between temperature and kinetic energy? How does particle mass affect temperature?

NSTA scilinks.org
SCI LINKS

Kinetic Theory **Code: MDL064**

Getting Ready to Learn

◀ CONCEPT REVIEW

- Matter is made of particles too small to see.
- Matter can be solid, liquid, or gas.
- Energy is the ability to cause a change.
- There are different forms of energy.

◀ VOCABULARY REVIEW

matter p. 9

energy p. 72

kinetic energy p. 74

 CONTENT REVIEW
CLASSZONE.COM
Review concepts and vocabulary.

▶ TAKING NOTES

CHOOSE YOUR OWN STRATEGY

Take notes using one or more of the strategies from earlier chapters—**main idea and detail notes, main idea web,** or **mind map.** Feel free to mix and match the strategies, or use an entirely different note-taking strategy.

VOCABULARY STRATEGY

Place each vocabulary term at the center of a **description wheel** diagram. Write some words describing it on the spokes.

See the Note-Taking Handbook on pages R45–R51.

SCIENCE NOTEBOOK

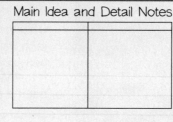

Main Idea and Detail Notes   Mind Map

Main Idea Web

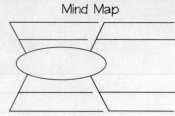

solids, liquids, gases / temperature / KINETIC THEORY OF MATTER / kinetic energy / particle movement

Temperature depends on particle movement.

◀ **BEFORE, you learned**

- All matter is made of particles
- Kinetic energy is the energy of motion
- Energy can be transferred or changed but is never created or destroyed

▶ **NOW, you will learn**

- How temperature depends on kinetic energy
- How temperature is measured
- How changes in temperature can affect matter

VOCABULARY

kinetic theory of matter p. 104
temperature p. 105
degree p. 106
thermometer p. 107

EXPLORE Temperature

What can cause a change in temperature?

PROCEDURE

① Work with a partner. Hold the rubber band with both hands. Without stretching it, hold it to the underside of your partner's wrist.

② Move the rubber band away, then quickly stretch it once and keep it stretched. Hold it to the underside of your partner's wrist.

③ Move the rubber band away and quickly let it return to its normal size. Hold it to the underside of your partner's wrist.

MATERIALS

large rubber band

WHAT DO YOU THINK?

- What effect did stretching the rubber band have on the temperature of the rubber band?
- What may have caused this change to occur?

All matter is made of moving particles.

NOTE-TAKING STRATEGY
You could take notes on the movement of particles in matter by using a main idea web.

You have read that any object in motion has kinetic energy. All the moving objects you see around you—from cars to planes to butterflies—have kinetic energy. Even objects so small that you cannot see them, such as atoms, are in motion and have kinetic energy.

You might think that a large unmoving object, such as a house or a wooden chair, does not have any kinetic energy. However, all matter is made of atoms, and atoms are always in motion, even if the objects themselves do not change their position. The motion of these tiny particles gives the object energy. The chair you are sitting on has some amount of energy. You also have energy, even when you are not moving.

The Kinetic Theory of Matter

▼ REMINDER

Kinetic energy is the energy of motion.

Physical properties and physical changes are the result of how particles of matter behave. The **kinetic theory of matter** states that all of the particles that make up matter are constantly in motion. As a result, all particles in matter have kinetic energy. The kinetic theory of matter helps explain the different states of matter—solid, liquid, and gas.

① The particles in a solid, such as concrete, are not free to move around very much. They vibrate back and forth in the same position and are held tightly together by forces of attraction.

② The particles in a liquid, such as water in a pool, move much more freely than particles in a solid. They are constantly sliding around and tumbling over each other as they move.

③ In a gas, such as the air around you or in a bubble in water, particles are far apart and move around at high speeds. Particles might collide with one another, but otherwise they do not interact much.

READING **TiP**

In illustrations of particle movement, more motion lines mean a greater speed.

Particles do not always move at the same speed. Within any group of particles, some are moving faster than others. A fast-moving particle might collide with another particle and lose some of its speed. A slow-moving particle might be struck by a faster one and start moving faster. Particles have a wide range of speeds and often change speeds.

⬭ CHECK YOUR READING What is the kinetic theory of matter?

Matter in Motion

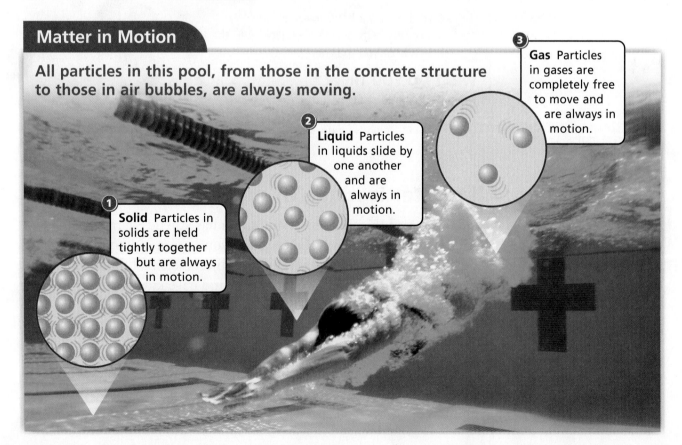

All particles in this pool, from those in the concrete structure to those in air bubbles, are always moving.

③ **Gas** Particles in gases are completely free to move and are always in motion.

② **Liquid** Particles in liquids slide by one another and are always in motion.

① **Solid** Particles in solids are held tightly together but are always in motion.

Temperature and Kinetic Energy

Particles of matter moving at different speeds have different kinetic energies because kinetic energy depends on speed. It is not possible to know the kinetic energy of each particle in an object. However, the average kinetic energy of all the particles in an object can be determined.

Temperature is a measure of the average kinetic energy of all the particles in an object. If a liquid, such as hot cocoa, has a high temperature, the particles in the liquid are moving very fast and have a high average kinetic energy. The cocoa feels hot. If a drink, such as a fruit smoothie, has a low temperature, the particles in the liquid are moving more slowly and have a lower average kinetic energy. The smoothie feels cold.

VOCABULARY
Remember to make a description wheel diagram for *temperature* and other vocabulary terms.

hot liquid   cold liquid

You experience the connection between temperature and the kinetic energy of particles every day. For example, to raise the temperature of your hands on a cold day—to warm your hands—you have to add energy, perhaps by putting your hands near a fire or a hot stove. The added energy makes the particles in your hands move faster. If you let a hot bowl sit on a table for a while, the particles in the bowl slow down due to collisions with particles in the air and in the table. The temperature of the bowl decreases, and it becomes cooler.

Temperature is the measurement of the average kinetic energy of particles, not just their speed. Recall that kinetic energy depends on mass as well as speed. Particles in a metal doorknob do not move as fast as particles in air. However, the particles in a doorknob have more mass and they can have the same amount of kinetic energy as particles in air. As a result, the doorknob and the air can have equal temperatures.

 CHECK YOUR READING How does temperature change when kinetic energy increases?

Temperature can be measured.

RESOURCE CENTER
CLASSZONE.COM
Find out more about
temperature and
temperature scales.

You have read that a warmer temperature means a greater average kinetic energy. How is temperature measured and what does that measurement mean? Suppose you hear on the radio that the temperature outside is 30 degrees. Do you need to wear a warm coat to spend the day outside? The answer depends on the temperature scale being used. There are two common temperature scales, both of which measure the average kinetic energy of particles. However, 30 degrees on one scale is quite different from 30 degrees on the other scale.

Temperature Scales

To establish a temperature scale, two known values and the number of units between the values are needed. The freezing and boiling points of pure water are often used as the standard values. These points are always the same under the same conditions and they are easy to reproduce. In the two common scales, temperature is measured in units called **degrees** (°), which are equally spaced units between two points.

The scale used most commonly in the United States for measuring temperature—in uses ranging from cooking directions to weather reports—is the Fahrenheit (FAR-uhn-HYT) scale (°F). It was developed in the early 1700s by Gabriel Fahrenheit. On the Fahrenheit scale, pure water freezes at 32°F and boils at 212°F. Thus, there are 180 degrees—180 equal units—between the freezing point and the boiling point of water.

During a summer day in Death Valley, California, the temperature can reach 49°C (120°F).

The temperature scale most commonly used in the rest of the world, and also used more often in science, is the Celsius (SEHL-see-uhs) scale (°C). This scale was developed in the 1740s by Anders Celsius. On the Celsius scale, pure water freezes at 0°C and boils at 100°C, so there are 100 degrees—100 equal units—between these two temperatures.

Recall the question asked in the first paragraph of this page. If the outside temperature is 30 degrees, do you need to wear a warm coat? If the temperature is 30°F, the answer is yes, because that temperature is colder than the freezing point of water. If the temperature is 30°C, the answer is no—it is a nice warm day (86°F).

 How are the Fahrenheit and Celsius temperature scales different? How are they similar?

Thermometers

Temperature is measured by using a device called a thermometer. A **thermometer** measures temperature through the regular variation of some physical property of the material inside the thermometer. A mercury or alcohol thermometer, for example, can measure temperature because the liquid inside the thermometer always expands or contracts by a certain amount in response to a change in temperature.

Liquid-filled thermometers measure how much the liquid expands in a narrow tube as the temperature increases. The distances along the tube are marked so that the temperature can be read. At one time, thermometers were filled with liquid mercury because it expands or contracts evenly at both high and low temperatures. This means that mercury expands or contracts by the same amount in response to a given change in temperature. However, mercury is dangerous to handle, so many thermometers today are filled with alcohol instead.

Some thermometers work in a different way—they use a material whose electrical properties change when the temperature changes. These thermometers can be read by computers. Some show the temperature on a display panel and are often used in cars and in homes.

 CHECK YOUR READING How do liquid-filled thermometers work?

INVESTIGATE Temperature Measurements

How does a thermometer work?

PROCEDURE

1. To make your own thermometer, fill the bottle halfway with the alcohol solution. Add a small amount of food coloring and mix thoroughly.

2. Place the straw into the bottle. Use clay to suspend the straw above the bottom of the bottle and to seal the bottle's mouth completely.

3. Pour ice water into the bowl and place the bottle into the ice water. Record your observations, and then empty the bowl.

4. Pour hot water into the bowl and place the bottle into the hot water. Record your observations.

WHAT DO YOU THINK?

- What happened to the level of the alcohol solution in the straw when the bottle was put into the ice water? into the hot water?

- Why do you think these changes happened?

CHALLENGE How could you modify your thermometer so that you could use it to measure a temperature?

SKILL FOCUS
Modeling

MATERIALS
- plastic bottle
- alcohol solution
- food coloring
- clear plastic straw
- clay
- bowl
- ice water
- hot tap water

TIME
30 minutes

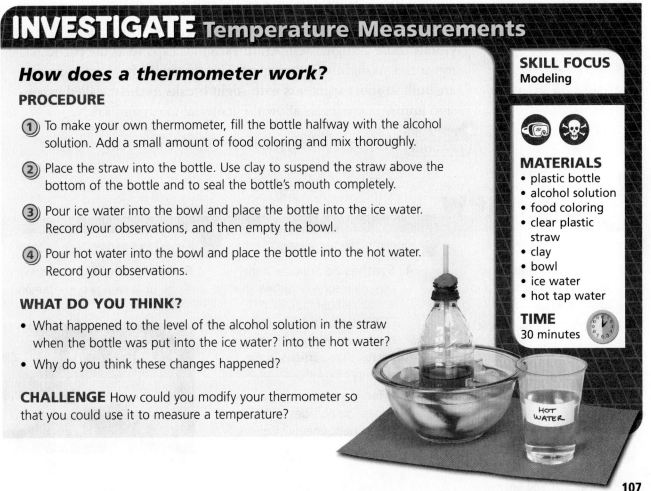

During construction of the Gateway Arch in St. Louis, engineers had to account for thermal expansion.

Thermal Expansion

The property that makes liquid-filled thermometers work is called thermal expansion. Thermal expansion affects many substances, not just alcohol and liquid mercury. All gases, many liquids, and most solids expand when their temperature increases.

Construction engineers often have to take thermal expansion into account because steel and concrete both expand with increasing temperature. An interesting example involves the construction of the Gateway Arch in St. Louis, which is built mostly of steel.

The final piece of the Arch to be put into place was the top segment joining the two legs. The Arch was scheduled to be completed in the middle of the day for its opening ceremony. However, engineers knew that the side of the Arch facing the Sun would get hot and expand due to thermal expansion.

This expansion would narrow the gap between the legs and prevent the last piece from fitting into place. In order to complete the Arch, workers sprayed water on the side facing the Sun. The water helped cool the Arch and decreased the amount of thermal expansion. Once the final segment was in place, engineers made the connection strong enough to withstand the force of the expanding material.

Thermal expansion occurs in solids because the particles of solids vibrate more at higher temperatures. Solids expand as the particles move ever so slightly farther apart. This is why bridges and highways are built in short segments with slight breaks in them, called expansion joints. These joints allow the material to expand safely.

 CHECK YOUR READING Why do objects expand when their temperatures increase?

4.1 Review

KEY CONCEPTS

1. Describe the relationship between temperature and kinetic energy.

2. Describe the way in which thermometers measure temperature.

3. How can you explain thermal expansion in terms of kinetic energy?

CRITICAL THINKING

4. **Synthesize** Suppose a mercury thermometer shows that the air temperature is 22°C (72°F). Do particles in the air have more average kinetic energy than particles in the mercury? Explain.

5. **Infer** If a puddle of water is frozen, do particles in the ice have kinetic energy? Explain.

CHALLENGE

6. **Apply** Why might a sidewalk be built with periodic breaks in it?

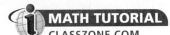

MATH TUTORIAL
CLASSZONE.COM

Click on Math Tutorial for more help with temperature conversions.

Temperatures on Earth, ranging from the extremes of frigid polar regions to the hottest deserts, can differ by more than 250°F.

How Hot Is Hot?

Temperatures on Earth can vary greatly, from extremely hot in some deserts to frigid in polar regions. The meaning of a temperature measurement depends on which temperature scale is being used. A very high temperature on the Fahrenheit scale is equal to a much lower temperature on the Celsius scale. The table shows the formulas used to convert temperatures between the two scales.

Conversion	Formula
Fahrenheit to Celsius	$°C = \frac{5}{9}(°F - 32)$
Celsius to Fahrenheit	$°F = \frac{9}{5}°C + 32$

Example

The boiling point of pure water is 212°F. Convert that temperature to a measurement on the Celsius scale.

(1) Use the correct conversion formula.

$$°C = \frac{5}{9}(°F - 32)$$

(2) Substitute the temperature given for the correct variable in the formula.

$$°C = \frac{5}{9}(212 - 32) = \frac{5}{9} \cdot 180 = 100$$

ANSWER °C = 100

Use the information in the table below to answer the questions that follow.

Highest and Lowest Temperatures Recorded on Earth			
Location	Highest Temp. (°F)	Location	Lowest Temp. (°F)
El Azizia, Libya	136	Vostok, Antarctica	−129
Death Valley, California	134	Oimekon, Russia	−90
Tirat Tsvi, Israel	129	Verkhoyansk, Russia	−90
Cloncurry, Australia	128	Northice, Greenland	−87
Seville, Spain	122	Snag, Yukon, Canada	−81

1. What is the highest temperature in °C?

2. What is the temperature difference in °C between the highest and second highest temperatures?

3. What is the difference between the highest and lowest temperatures in °F? in °C?

CHALLENGE The surface of the Sun is approximately 5500°C. What is this temperature in °F?

Energy flows from warmer to cooler objects.

 BEFORE, you learned

- All matter is made of moving particles
- Temperature is the measurement of average kinetic energy of particles in an object
- Temperature can be measured

 NOW, you will learn

- How heat is different from temperature
- How heat is measured
- Why some substances change temperature more easily than others

VOCABULARY

heat p. 110
thermal energy p. 111
calorie p. 112
joule p. 112
specific heat p. 113

THINK ABOUT

Why does water warm up so slowly?

If you have ever seen food being fried in oil or butter, you know that the metal frying pan heats up very quickly, as does the oil or butter used to coat the pan's surface.

However, if you put the same amount of water as you put oil in the same pan, the water warms up more slowly. Why does water behave so differently from the metal, oil, or butter?

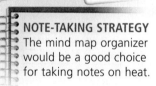
NOTE-TAKING STRATEGY
The mind map organizer would be a good choice for taking notes on heat.

Heat is different from temperature.

Heat and temperature are very closely related. As a result, people often confuse the concepts of heat and temperature. However, they are not the same. Temperature is a measurement of the average kinetic energy of particles in an object. **Heat** is a flow of energy from an object at a higher temperature to an object at a lower temperature.

If you add energy as heat to a pot of water, the water's temperature starts to increase. The added energy increases the average kinetic energy of the water molecules. Once the water starts to boil, however, adding energy no longer changes the temperature of the water. Instead, the heat goes into changing the physical state of the water from liquid to gas rather than increasing the kinetic energy of the water molecules. This fact is one demonstration that heat and temperature are not the same thing.

 What is heat?

Heat and Thermal Energy

RESOURCE CENTER
CLASSZONE.COM

Learn more about thermal energy.

Suppose you place an ice cube in a bowl on a table. At first, the bowl and the ice cube have different temperatures. However, the ice cube melts, and the water that comes from the ice will eventually have the same temperature as the bowl. This temperature will be lower than the original temperature of the bowl but higher than the original temperature of the ice cube. The water and the bowl end up at the same temperature because the particles in the ice cube and the particles in the bowl continually bump into each other and energy is transferred from the bowl to the ice.

Heat is always the transfer of energy from an object at a higher temperature to an object at a lower temperature. So energy flows from the particles in the warmer bowl to the particles in the cold ice and, later, the cooler water. If energy flowed in the opposite direction— from cooler to warmer—the ice would get colder and the bowl would get hotter, and you know that never happens.

CHECK YOUR READING   In which direction does heat always transfer energy?

When energy flows from a warmer object to a cooler object, the thermal energy of both of the objects changes. **Thermal energy** is the total random kinetic energy of particles in an object. Note that temperature and thermal energy are different from each other. Temperature is an average and thermal energy is a total. A glass of water can have the same temperature as Lake Superior, but the lake has far more thermal energy because the lake contains many more water molecules.

Energy is transferred from the warmer lemonade to the cold ice through heat until their temperatures are equal.

Another example of how energy is transferred through heat is shown on the right. Soon after you put ice cubes into a pitcher of lemonade, energy is transferred from the warmer lemonade to the colder ice. The lemonade's thermal energy decreases and the ice's thermal energy increases. Because the particles in the lemonade have transferred some of their energy to the particles in the ice, the average kinetic energy of the particles in the lemonade decreases. As a result, the temperature of the lemonade decreases.

CHECK YOUR READING   How are heat and thermal energy related to each other?

Measuring Heat

VOCABULARY
Remember to make description wheel diagrams for *calorie, joule,* and other vocabulary terms.

The most common units of heat measurement are the calorie and the joule (jool). One **calorie** is the amount of energy needed to raise the temperature of 1 gram of water by 1°C. The **joule** (J) is the standard scientific unit in which energy is measured. One calorie is equal to 4.18 joules.

You probably think of calories in terms of food. However, in nutrition, one Calorie—written with a capital C—is actually one kilocalorie, or 1000 calories. This means that one Calorie in food contains enough energy to raise the temperature of 1 kilogram of water by 1°C. So, each Calorie in food contains 1000 calories of energy.

How do we know how many Calories are in a food, such as a piece of chocolate cake? The cake is burned inside an instrument called a calorimeter. The amount of energy released from the cake through heat is the number of Calories transferred from the cake to the calorimeter. The energy transferred to the calorimeter is equal to the amount of energy originally in the cake. A thermometer inside the calorimeter measures the increase in temperature from the burning cake, which is used to calculate how much energy is released.

 CHECK YOUR READING How is heat measured?

INVESTIGATE Heat Transfer

Which substances change temperature faster?

PROCEDURE

1. Using the graduated cylinder and the balance, separately measure 20 g of room-temperature water, 20 g of pennies, and 20 g of aluminum foil. Pour the water into a beaker until it is needed.

2. Using the graduated cylinder, pour 50 mL of hot water into each of the cups. Record the water temperature in each cup.

3. Pour the room-temperature water into one cup. Place the pennies in the second cup and the foil in the third. After 5 minutes, record the temperature of the water in each of the cups.

WHAT DO YOU THINK?

- How did the temperature changes in the three cups compare?
- What might account for the differences you observed?

CHALLENGE Why might items such as pots and pans be made of materials like copper, stainless steel, or iron?

SKILL FOCUS
Measuring

MATERIALS
- graduated cylinder
- balance
- room-temperature water
- pennies
- aluminum foil
- hot tap water
- 100 mL beaker
- 3 plastic cups
- thermometer
- stopwatch

TIME
30 minutes

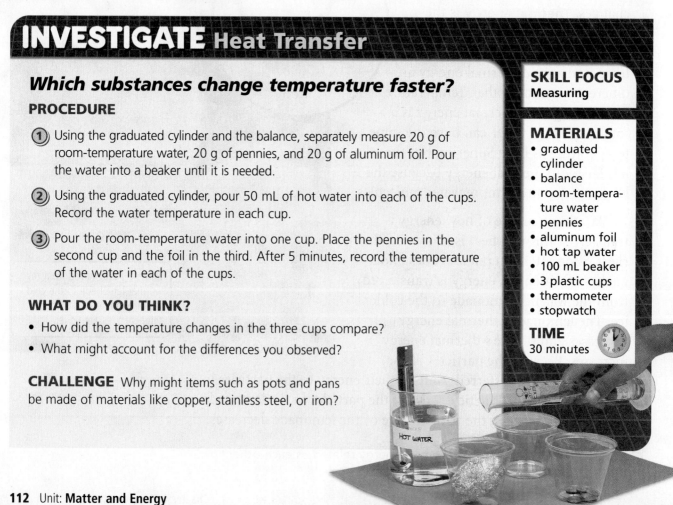

Some substances change temperature more easily than others.

Have you ever seen an apple pie taken right out of the oven? If you put a piece of pie on a plate to cool, you can touch the pie crust in a few minutes and it will feel only slightly warm. But if you try to take a bite, the hot pie filling will burn your mouth. The pie crust cools much more quickly than the filling, which is mostly water.

Specific Heat

The amount of energy required to raise the temperature of 1 gram of a substance by 1°C is the **specific heat** of that substance. Every substance has its own specific heat value. So, each substance absorbs a different amount of energy in order to show the same increase in temperature.

READING TiP

Joules per gram per °C is shown as $\frac{J}{g°C}$.

If you look back at the definition of a calorie, you will see that it is defined in terms of water—one calorie raises the temperature of 1 gram of water by 1°C. So, water has a specific heat of exactly 1.00 calorie per gram per °C. Because one calorie is equal to 4.18 J, it takes 4.18 J to raise the temperature of one gram of water by 1°C. In joules, water's specific heat is 4.18 J per gram per °C. If you look at the specific heat graph shown below, you will see that 4.18 is an unusually large value. For example, one gram of iron has to absorb only 0.45 joules for its temperature to increase by 1°C.

A substance with a high specific heat value, like water, not only has to absorb a large quantity of energy for its temperature to increase, but it also must release a large quantity of energy for its temperature to decrease. This is why the apple pie filling can still be hot while the pie crust is cool. The liquid filling takes longer to cool. The high specific heat of water is also one reason it is used as a coolant in car radiators. The water can absorb a great deal of energy and protect the engine from getting too hot.

CHECK YOUR READING How is specific heat related to a change in temperature?

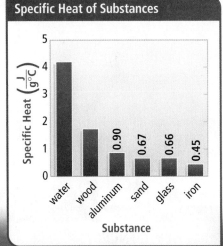

Specific Heat of Substances

Specific Heat ($\frac{J}{g°C}$) vs. Substance

- water: 4.18
- wood: (value)
- aluminum: 0.90
- sand: 0.67
- glass: 0.66
- iron: 0.45

APPLY More energy is needed to warm water than many other substances. What materials in this photograph might be warmer than the water?

Specific Heat and Mass

Recall that thermal energy is the total kinetic energy of all particles in an object. So, thermal energy depends on the object's mass. Suppose you have a cup of water at a temperature of 90°C (194°F) and a bathtub full of water at a temperature of 40°C (104°F). Which mass of water has more thermal energy? There are many more water molecules in the bathtub, so the water in the tub has more thermal energy.

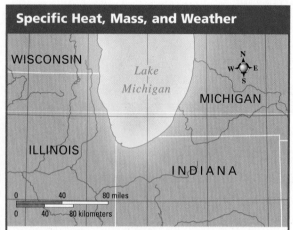

Specific Heat, Mass, and Weather

The temperature of a large body of water influences the temperature of nearby land. The green shading shows how far this effect extends.

The water in the cup has the same specific heat as the water in the tub. However, the cup of water will cool more quickly than the water in the bathtub. The tub of water has to release more thermal energy to its surroundings, through heat, to show a decrease in temperature because it has so much more mass.

This idea is particularly relevant to very large masses. For example, Lake Michigan holds 4.92 quadrillion liters (1.30 quadrillion gallons) of water. Because of the high specific heat of water and the mass of water in the lake, the temperature of Lake Michigan changes very slowly.

The temperature of the lake affects the temperatures on its shores. During spring and early summer, the lake warms slowly, which helps keep the nearby land cooler. During the winter, the lake cools slowly, which helps keep the nearby land warmer. Temperatures within about 15 miles of the lake can differ by as much as 6°C (about 10°F) from areas farther away from the lake.

As you will read in the next section, the way in which a large body of water can influence temperatures on land depends on how energy is transferred through heat.

 CHECK YOUR READING How does an object's thermal energy depend on its mass?

4.2 Review

KEY CONCEPTS

1. How is temperature related to heat?

2. How do the units that are used to measure heat differ from the units that are used to measure temperature?

3. Describe specific heat in your own words.

CRITICAL THINKING

4. **Compare and Contrast** How are a calorie and a joule similar? How are they different?

5. **Synthesize** Describe the relationships among kinetic energy, temperature, heat, and thermal energy.

◯ CHALLENGE

6. **Infer** Suppose you are spending a hot summer day by a pool. Why might the water in the pool cool the air near the pool?

Cooking with Heat

A chef makes many decisions about cooking a meal based on heat and temperature. The appropriate temperature and cooking method must be used. A chef must calculate the cooking time of each part of the meal so that everything is finished at the same time. A chef also needs to understand how heat moves through food. For example, if an oven temperature is too hot, meat can be overcooked on the outside and undercooked on the inside.

Bread vs. Meat

Chefs have to understand how energy as heat is transferred to different foods. For example, the fluffy texture of bread comes from pockets of gas that separate its fibers. The gas is a poor conductor of energy. Therefore, more energy and a longer cooking time are needed to cook bread than to cook an equal amount of meat.

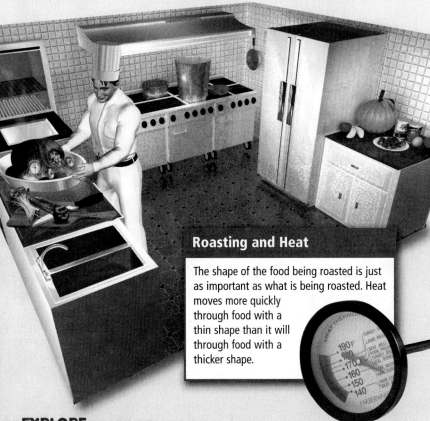

What Temperature?

Eggs cook very differently under different temperatures. For example, temperature is important when baking meringue, which is made of egg whites and sugar. A Key lime pie topped with meringue is baked at 400°F to make a meringue that is soft. However, meringue baked at 275°F makes light and crisp dessert shells.

Roasting and Heat

The shape of the food being roasted is just as important as what is being roasted. Heat moves more quickly through food with a thin shape than it will through food with a thicker shape.

EXPLORE

1. **COMPARE** Using a cookbook, find the oven temperatures for baking biscuits, potatoes, and beef. Could you successfully cook a roast and biscuits in the oven at the same time?

2. **CHALLENGE** Crack open three eggs. Lightly beat one egg in each of three separate bowls. Follow the steps below.

   1. Heat about two cups of water to 75°C in a small pan.
   2. Pour one of the eggs into the water in the pan.
   3. Observe the egg and record your observations.
   4. Repeat steps 1–3 twice, once with boiling water and then with room-temperature water.

   Describe the differences that you observed among the three eggs. What may account for these differences?

KEY CONCEPT

4.3 The transfer of energy as heat can be controlled.

◀ **BEFORE**, you learned

- Temperature is the average amount of kinetic energy of particles in an object
- Heat is the flow of energy from warmer objects to cooler objects

▶ **NOW**, you will learn

- How energy is transferred through heat
- How materials are used to control the transfer of energy through heat

VOCABULARY

conduction p. 117
conductor p. 117
insulator p. 117
convection p. 118
radiation p. 119

EXPLORE Conduction

How can you observe a flow of energy?

PROCEDURE

① Fill the large beaker halfway with hot tap water. Fill the small beaker halfway with cold water. Place a thermometer in each beaker. Record the temperature of the water in each beaker.

② Without removing the water in either beaker, place the small beaker inside the large beaker. Record the temperature in each beaker every 30 seconds for 2 minutes.

MATERIALS

- 500 mL beaker
- hot tap water
- 200 mL beaker
- cold water
- 2 thermometers
- stopwatch

WHAT DO YOU THINK?

- How did the water temperature in each beaker change?
- In which direction did energy flow? How do you know?

Energy moves as heat in three ways.

NOTE-TAKING STRATEGY
Main idea and detail notes would be a useful strategy for taking notes on how heat transfers energy.

Think about what you do to keep warm on a cold day. You may wear several layers of clothing, sit next to a heater, or avoid drafty windows. On a hot day, you may wear light clothing and sit in the shade of a tree. In all of these situations, you are trying to control the transfer of energy between yourself and your surroundings.

Recall that heat is always a transfer of energy from objects at a higher temperature to objects at a lower temperature. How does energy get transferred from a warmer object to a cooler one? There are three different ways in which this transfer of energy can occur—by conduction, convection, and radiation. So, in trying to control heat, it is necessary to control conduction, convection, and radiation.

Conduction

One way in which energy is transferred as heat is through direct contact between objects. **Conduction** is the process that moves energy from one object to another when they are touching physically. If you have ever picked up a bowl of hot soup, you have experienced conduction.

VOCABULARY
Remember to make a description wheel diagram for *conduction* and other vocabulary terms.

Conduction occurs any time that objects at different temperatures come into contact with each other. The average kinetic energy of particles in the warmer object is greater than that of the particles in the cooler object. When particles of the objects collide, some of the kinetic energy of the particles in the warmer object is transferred to the cooler object. As long as the objects are in contact, conduction continues until the temperatures of the objects are equal.

Conduction can also occur within a single object. In this case, energy is transferred from the warmer part of the object to the cooler part of the object by heat. Suppose you put a metal spoon into a cup of hot cocoa. Energy will be conducted from the warm end of the spoon to the cool end until the temperature of the entire spoon is the same.

Some materials transfer the kinetic energy of particles better than others. **Conductors** are materials that transfer energy easily. Often, conductors also have a low specific heat. For example, metals are typically good conductors. You know that when one end of a metal object gets hot, the other end quickly becomes hot as well. Consider pots or pans that have metal handles. A metal handle becomes too hot to touch soon after the pan is placed on a stove that has been turned on.

Conduction transfers energy from the cocoa to the mug to the person's hands.

Other materials, called **insulators,** are poor conductors. Insulators often have high specific heats. Some examples of insulators are wood, paper, and plastic foam. In fact, plastic foam is a good insulator because it contains many small spaces that are filled with air. A plastic foam cup will not easily transfer energy by conduction. As a result, plastic foam is often used to keep cold drinks cold or hot drinks hot. Think about the pan handle mentioned above. Often, the handle is made of a material that is an insulator, such as wood or plastic. Although a wood or plastic handle will get hot when the pan is on a stove, it takes a much longer time for wood or plastic to get hot as compared to a metal handle.

CHECK YOUR READING How are conductors and insulators different?

Convection

Energy can also be transferred through the movement of gases or liquids. **Convection** is the process that transfers energy by the movement of large numbers of particles in the same direction within a liquid or gas. In most substances, as the kinetic energy of particles increases, the particles spread out over a larger area. An increased distance between particles causes a decrease in the density of the substance. Convection occurs when a cooler, denser mass of the gas or liquid replaces a warmer, less dense mass of the gas or liquid by pushing it upward.

Convection is a cycle in nature responsible for most winds and ocean currents. When the temperature of a region of air increases, the particles in the air spread out and the air becomes less dense.

❶ Cooler, denser air flows in underneath the warmer, less dense air, and pushes the warmer air upward.

❷ When this air cools, it becomes more dense than the warmer air beneath it.

❸ The cooled air sinks and moves under the warmer air.

Convection in liquids is similar. Warm water is less dense than cold water, so the warm water is pushed upward as cooler, denser water moves underneath. When the warm water that has been pushed up cools, its density increases. The cycle continues when this more dense water sinks, pushing warmer water up again.

Recall that a large body of water, such as Lake Michigan, influences the temperature of the land nearby. This effect is due to convection. During the spring and early summer, the lake is cool and warms more slowly than the land. The air above the land gets warmer than the air over the water. The warmer air above the land is less dense than the cooler air above the water. The cooler, denser air moves onshore and pushes the warmer air up. The result is a cooling breeze from the lake.

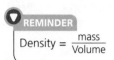
REMINDER

Density = $\dfrac{\text{mass}}{\text{Volume}}$

READING TiP

As you read about the cycle that occurs during convection, follow the steps in the illustration below.

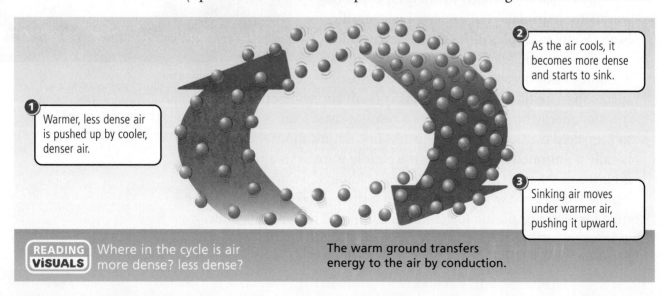

❶ Warmer, less dense air is pushed up by cooler, denser air.

❷ As the air cools, it becomes more dense and starts to sink.

❸ Sinking air moves under warmer air, pushing it upward.

READING VISUALS Where in the cycle is air more dense? less dense?

The warm ground transfers energy to the air by conduction.

Radiation

Radiation is another way in which energy can be transferred from one place to another. **Radiation** is energy that travels as electromagnetic waves, which include visible light, microwaves, and infrared (IHN-fruh-REHD) light. The Sun is the most significant source of radiation that you experience on a daily basis. However, all objects—even you—emit radiation and release energy to their surroundings.

Consider radiation from the Sun. You can feel radiation as heat when radiation from the Sun warms your skin. The radiation emitted from the Sun strikes the particles in your body and transfers energy. This transfer of energy increases the movement of particles in your skin, which you detect as an increase in temperature. Of course, you are not the only object on Earth that absorbs the Sun's radiation. Everything—from air to concrete sidewalks—absorbs radiation that increases particle motion and produces an increase in temperature.

When radiation is emitted from one object and then is absorbed by another, the result is often a transfer of energy through heat. Like both conduction and convection, radiation can transfer energy from warmer to cooler objects. However, radiation differs from conduction and convection in a very significant way. Radiation can travel through empty space, as it does when it moves from the Sun to Earth. If this were not the case, radiation from the Sun would have no effect on Earth.

When radiation from the Sun is absorbed, energy is transferred through heat.

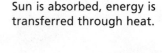

SIMULATION
CLASSZONE.COM

Identify examples of conduction, convection, or radiation.

 CHECK YOUR READING How does radiation transfer energy?

Different materials are used to control the transfer of energy.

Energy is always being transferred between objects at different temperatures. It is often important to slow this movement of energy. For example, if energy were always transferred quickly and efficiently through heat, it would not be possible to keep a building warm during a cold day or to keep cocoa hot in a thermos.

Insulation

Insulators used by people are similar to insulators in nature.
Polar bears are so well insulated that they tend to overheat.

The polar bear's hollow guard hair is an effective insulator because air inside the hair does not easily conduct energy.

hollow hair

Vacuum Flask

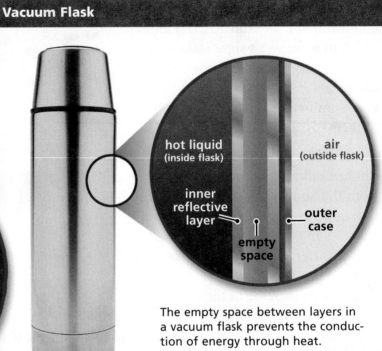

hot liquid
(inside flask)

air
(outside flask)

inner
reflective
layer

outer
case

empty
space

The empty space between layers in a vacuum flask prevents the conduction of energy through heat.

Polar bears have several layers of insulation. They have a layer of fat up to 11 cm thick, a 2.5–5.0 cm thick layer of fur, and an outer layer of hollow guard hairs.

READING VISUALS How is the polar bear's hollow hair similar to the empty space in a vacuum flask? How is it different?

Insulators are used to control and slow the transfer of energy from warmer objects to cooler objects because they are poor conductors of energy. You can think of an insulator as a material that keeps cold things cold or hot things hot.

Sometimes people say that insulation "keeps out the cold." An insulator actually works by trapping energy. During the winter, you use insulators such as wool to slow the loss of your body heat to cold air. The wool traps air against your body, and because both air and wool are poor conductors, you lose body heat at a slower rate. Fiberglass insulation in the outer walls of a building works in the same way. The fiberglass slows the movement of energy from a building to the outside during cold weather, and it slows the movement of energy into the building during hot weather.

A vacuum flask, or thermos, works in a slightly different way to keep liquids either hot or cold. Between two layers of the flask is an empty space. This space prevents conduction between the inside and outside walls of the flask. Also, the inside of the flask is covered with a shiny material that reflects much of the radiation that strikes it. This prevents radiation from either entering or leaving the flask.

Insulators that people use are often very similar to insulators in nature. Look at the photograph of the polar bear on page 120. Because of the arctic environment in which the polar bear lives, it needs several different types of insulation. The polar bear's fur helps to trap a layer of air against its body to keep warmth inside. Polar bears also have guard hairs that extend beyond the fur. These guard hairs are hollow and contain air. Because air is a poor conductor, the bear's body heat is not easily released into the air.

 How does insulation keep a building warm?

KEY CONCEPTS

1. What are three ways in which energy can be transferred through heat? Provide an example of each.

2. Explain how convection is a cycle in nature.

3. Describe how an insulator can slow a transfer of energy.

CRITICAL THINKING

4. **Compare and Contrast** Describe the similarities and differences among conduction, convection, and radiation.

5. **Synthesize** Do you think solids can undergo convection? Why or why not? Explain.

◔ CHALLENGE

6. **Infer** During the day, wind often blows from a body of water to the land. What do you think would happen at night? Explain.

CHAPTER INVESTIGATION

MATERIALS
- 2 small plastic bottles
- 2 thermometers
- modeling clay
- graduated cylinder
- tap water (hot or cold)
- foam packing peanuts
- plastic wrap
- aluminum foil
- soil
- sand
- rubber bands
- coffee can
- beaker
- stopwatch

Insulators

DESIGN
—YOUR OWN—

OVERVIEW AND PURPOSE

To keep warm in cold weather, a person needs insulation. A down-filled coat, such as the one worn by the girl in the photograph, is a very effective insulator because it contains a great deal of air. Energy is transferred rapidly through some substances and quite slowly through others. In this investigation, you will

- design and build an insulator for a bottle to maintain the temperature of the water inside
- test an unchanged bottle and your experimental bottle to see which maintains the water's temperature more effectively

▶ Problem

Write It Up

How can a bottle be insulated most effectively?

▶ Procedure

1. Create a data table similar to the one shown on the sample notebook page to record your measurements.

2. Set aside plastic bottles, thermometers, modeling clay, and a graduated cylinder. Decide whether you will test hot or cold water in your bottles.

3. From the other materials available to you, design a way to modify one of the bottles so that it will keep the temperature of the water constant for a longer period of time than the control bottle.

4. Build your modified bottle by using one or more of the insulating materials available.

5 Fill each bottle with 200 mL of hot or cold water. Make sure that the water in each bottle is the same temperature.

6 Place a thermometer into each bottle. The thermometers should touch only the water, not the bottom or sides of the bottles. Use modeling clay to hold the thermometers in place in the bottles.

7 Record the starting temperature of the water in both bottles. Continue to observe and record the temperature of the water in both bottles every 2 minutes for 30 minutes. Record these temperatures in your data table.

step 6

▶ Observe and Analyze

Write It Up

1. **COMMUNICATE** Draw the setup of your experimental bottle in your notebook. Be sure to label the materials that you used to insulate your experimental bottle.

2. **RECORD OBSERVATIONS** Make sure you record all of your measurements and observations in the data table.

3. **GRAPH** Make a double line graph of the temperature data. Graph temperature versus time. Plot the temperature on the vertical axis, or y-axis, and the time on the horizontal axis, or x-axis. Use different colors to show the data from the different bottles.

4. **IDENTIFY VARIABLES, CONTROLS, AND CONSTANTS** Which bottle was the control? What was the variable? What were the constants in both setups?

5. **ANALYZE** Obtain the experimental results from two other groups that used a different insulator. Compare your results with the results from the other groups. Which bottle changed temperature most quickly?

▶ Conclude

Write It Up

1. **EVALUATE** Explain why the materials used by different groups might have been more or less effective as insulators. How might you change your design to improve its insulating properties?

2. **IDENTIFY LIMITS** Describe possible sources of error in the procedure or any points at which errors might have occurred. Why is it important to use the same amount of water in both bottles?

3. **APPLY** Energy can be transferred as heat by radiation, conduction, and convection. Which of these processes might be slowed by the insulation around your bottle? Explain.

▶ INVESTIGATE Further

CHALLENGE We depend on our clothing to keep us from losing body heat when we go outside in cold weather. How might you determine the type of clothing that would provide the best insulation? Design an experiment that would test your hypothesis.

Insulators

Problem How can a bottle be insulated most effectively?

Observe and Analyze

Table 1. Water Temperature Measurements

Time (min)	Control Bottle Temperature (°C)	Experimental Bottle Temperature (°C)
0		
2		
4		
6		
8		
10		

Conclude

Chapter Review

the **BIG** idea

Heat is a flow of energy due to temperature differences.

CONTENT REVIEW
CLASSZONE.COM

 KEY CONCEPTS SUMMARY

4.1 Temperature depends on particle movement.
- All particles in matter have kinetic energy.
- Temperature is the measurement of the average kinetic energy of particles in an object.
- Temperature is commonly measured on the Fahrenheit or Celsius scales.

VOCABULARY
kinetic theory of matter p. 104
temperature p. 105
degree p. 106
thermometer p. 107

hot liquid

cold liquid

Particles in a warmer substance have a greater average kinetic energy than particles in a cooler substance.

4.2 Energy flows from warmer to cooler objects.
- Heat is a transfer of energy from an object at a higher temperature to an object at a lower temperature.
- Different materials require different amounts of energy to change temperature.

VOCABULARY
heat p. 110
thermal energy p. 111
calorie p. 112
joule p. 112
specific heat p. 113

Energy is transferred from the warmer lemonade to the cold ice through heat.

heat

ice

4.3 The transfer of energy as heat can be controlled.
- Energy can be transferred by conduction, convection, and radiation.
- Different materials are used to control the transfer of energy.

VOCABULARY
conduction p. 117
conductor p. 117
insulator p. 117
convection p. 118
radiation p. 119

Types of Energy Transfer		
Conduction	**Convection**	**Radiation**
• Energy transferred by direct contact • Energy flows directly from warmer object to cooler object • Can occur within one object • Continues until object temperatures are equal	• Occurs in gases and liquids • Movement of large number of particles in same direction • Occurs due to difference in density • Cycle occurs while temperature differences exist	• Energy transferred by electromagnetic waves such as light, microwaves, and infrared radiation • All objects radiate energy • Can transfer energy through empty space

Reviewing Vocabulary

Make a frame for each of the vocabulary terms listed below. Write the term in the center. Decide what information to frame it with. Use definitions, examples, descriptions, parts, or pictures.

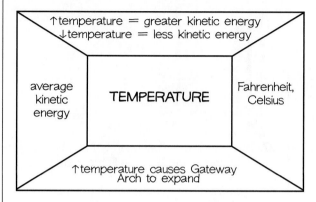

↑temperature = greater kinetic energy
↓temperature = less kinetic energy

average kinetic energy

TEMPERATURE

Fahrenheit, Celsius

↑temperature causes Gateway Arch to expand

1. kinetic theory of matter

2. heat

3. thermal energy

4. conduction

5. convection

6. radiation

In two or three sentences, describe how the terms in the following pairs are related to each other. Underline each term in your answers.

7. calorie, joule

8. conductor, insulator

Reviewing Key Concepts

Multiple Choice *Choose the letter of the best answer.*

9. What is the zero point in the Celsius scale?
   a. the freezing point of pure water
   b. the boiling point of pure water
   c. the freezing point of mercury
   d. the boiling point of alcohol

10. Energy is always transferred through heat from?
   a. an object with a lower specific heat to one with a higher specific heat
   b. a cooler object to a warmer object
   c. an object with a higher specific heat to one with a lower specific heat
   d. a warmer object to a cooler object

11. The average kinetic energy of particles in an object can be measured by its
   a. heat   **c.** calories
   b. thermal energy   **d.** temperature

12. How is energy transferred by convection?
   a. by direct contact between objects
   b. by electromagnetic waves
   c. by movement of groups of particles in gases or liquids
   d. by movement of groups of particles in solid objects

13. The total kinetic energy of particles in an object is
   a. heat   **c.** calories
   b. thermal energy   **d.** temperature

14. Water requires more energy than an equal mass of iron for its temperature to increase by a given amount because water has a greater
   a. thermal energy   **c.** temperature
   b. specific heat   **d.** kinetic energy

15. Energy from the Sun travels to Earth through which process?
   a. temperature   **c.** radiation
   b. conduction   **d.** convection

16. An insulator keeps a home warm by
   a. slowing the transfer of cold particles from outside to inside
   b. increasing the specific heat of the air inside
   c. slowing the transfer of energy from inside to outside
   d. increasing the thermal energy of the walls

17. Conduction is the transfer of energy from a warmer object to a cooler object through
   a. a vacuum   **c.** direct contact
   b. a gas   **d.** empty space

Short Answer *Write a short answer to each question.*

18. How are kinetic energy and temperature related to each other?

19. What is the difference between heat and temperature?

Thinking Critically

The illustrations below show particle movement in a substance at two different temperatures. Use the illustrations to answer the next four questions.

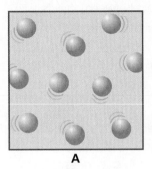 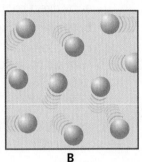

A   B

20. **OBSERVE** Which illustration represents the substance when it is at a higher temperature? Explain.

21. **PREDICT** What would happen to the particles in illustration A if the substance were chilled? What would happen if the particles in illustration B were warmed?

22. **PREDICT** If energy is transferred from one of the substances to the other through heat, in which direction would the energy flow (from A to B, or from B to A)? Why?

23. **COMMUNICATE** Suppose energy is transferred from one of the substances to the other through heat. Draw a sketch that shows what the particles of both substances would look like when the transfer of energy is complete. Explain.

24. **COMPARE AND CONTRAST** How are conduction and convection similar? How are they different?

25. **DRAW CONCLUSIONS** Suppose you are outdoors on a hot day and you move into the shade of a tree. Which form of energy transfer are you avoiding? Which type of energy transfer are you still feeling? Explain.

26. **COMMUNICATE** Draw a sketch that shows how convection occurs in a liquid. Label the sketch to indicate how the process occurs in a cycle.

Using Math Skills in Science

Use the illustrations of the two thermometers below to answer the next four questions.

A   B

27. How much of a change in temperature occurred between A and B in the Fahrenheit scale?

28. Suppose the temperatures were measured in 10 g of water. How much energy, in calories, would have been added to cause that increase in temperature? (**Hint:** 1 calorie raises the temperature of 1 g of water by 1°C.)

29. Again, suppose the temperatures shown above were measured in 10 g of water. How much energy, in joules, would have been added? (**Hint:** 1 calorie = 4.18 joules.)

30. Suppose that the temperatures were measured for 10 g of iron. How much energy, in joules, would have been added to cause the increase in temperature? (**Hint:** see graph on p. 113.)

the BIG idea

31. **ANALYZE** Look back at the photograph and the question on pages 100 and 101. How has your understanding of temperature and heat changed after reading the chapter?

32. **COMMUNICATE** Explain the kinetic theory of matter in your own words. What, if anything, about the kinetic theory of matter surprised you?

UNIT PROJECTS

Evaluate all the data, results, and information from your project folder. Prepare to present your project.

Standardized Test Practice

Interpreting Diagrams

The diagrams below illustrate the process that occurs in sea and land breezes.

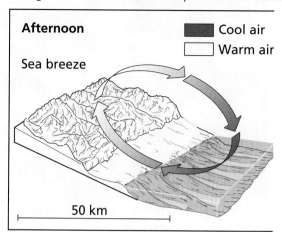

Afternoon

Sea breeze

■ Cool air
□ Warm air

50 km

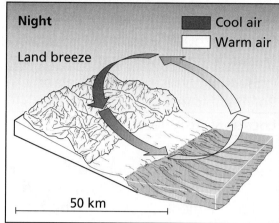

Night

Land breeze

■ Cool air
□ Warm air

50 km

Use the diagrams above to answer the next five questions.

1. What happens during the day?

  a. Cool air from the land flows out to sea.

  b. Warm air from the land flows out to sea close to sea level.

  c. Cool air from the sea flows to the land.

  d. Warm air from the sea flows to the land.

2. What characteristic of large bodies of water explains why the seawater is cooler than the land in the hot afternoon sun?

  a. Water is liquid while the land is solid.

  b. Water has a higher specific heat than land.

  c. Land is a better insulator than water.

  d. Land has a higher specific heat than water.

3. What process causes the warm air to move upward over the land during the day?

  a. convection   **c.** evaporation

  b. condensation   **d.** radiation

4. Warm air is pushed upwards by cooler air during convection because the warm air

  a. is more dense   **c.** is less dense

  b. has more mass   **d.** has less mass

5. About how far over water does this land breeze extend?

  a. 1 kilometer   **c.** 25 kilometers

  b. 10 kilometers   **d.** 50 kilometers

Extended Response

Answer the two questions below in detail. Include some of the terms from the word box on the right. Underline each term that you use in your answer.

boiling point	heat	specific heat
conduction	freezing point	zero point

6. What are the differences between the Fahrenheit and Celsius temperature scales? Which one is used in science? Why might this be the case?

7. Suppose you place three spoons—one metal, one plastic, and one wood—into a cup filled with hot water. The bowl end of the spoon is inside the cup and the handle is sticking up into the air. On each handle, you place a bead, held to the spoon by a dab of margarine. From which spoon will the bead fall first, and why?

Today's Scientist at Work

© Mark McCarty

Name:	Shirley Ann Jackson
Degree:	PhD, Physics, Massachusetts Institute of Technology
Profession:	President, Rensselaer Polytechnic Institute
Location:	Troy, New York

How can you make contributions to many areas of science all at once? One way is to promote the study of science by others. This is precisely what physicist Dr. Shirley Ann Jackson does as the president of Rensselaer Polytechnic Institute in Troy, New York.

In her early career, she was a research scientist, investigating the electrical and optical properties of matter. Her research was used by engineers and other scientists to help develop products for the telecommunications industry. She later became a professor of physics at Rutgers University in New Jersey.

In 1995, President Bill Clinton appointed Dr. Jackson to chair the U.S. Nuclear Regulatory Commission (NRC). The NRC is responsible for promoting the safe use of nuclear energy. At the NRC, Dr. Jackson used her knowledge of how the particles that make up matter interact and create energy. She also used her leadership skills. During her time at the NRC, she helped to start the International Nuclear Regulators Association. This group made it easier for officials from many nations to discuss issues of nuclear safety.

The NRC promotes the safe use of nuclear energy. Nuclear energy is produced in plants like this one. An improperly run nuclear facility can cause environmental hazards.

© AFP/Getty Images

Dr. Jackson first got interested in science by observing bees in her backyard. She is still studying the world around her, making careful observations, and taking actions based on what she learns. These steps for learning were the foundation for all her later contributions to science. As a student, Dr. Jackson learned the same things about matter and energy that you are learning.

Student Resource Handbooks

Making Observations

An **observation** is an act of noting and recording an event, characteristic, behavior, or anything else detected with an instrument or with the senses.

Observations allow you to make informed hypotheses and to gather data for experiments. Careful observations often lead to ideas for new experiments. There are two categories of observations:

- **Quantitative observations** can be expressed in numbers and include records of time, temperature, mass, distance, and volume.

- **Qualitative observations** include descriptions of sights, sounds, smells, and textures.

EXAMPLE

A student dissolved 30 grams of Epsom salts in water, poured the solution into a dish, and let the dish sit out uncovered overnight. The next day, she made the following observations of the Epsom salt crystals that grew in the dish.

> To determine the mass, the student found the mass of the dish before and after growing the crystals and then used subtraction to find the difference.

> The student measured several crystals and calculated the mean length. (To learn how to calculate the mean of a data set, see page R36.)

Table 1. Observations of Epsom Salt Crystals

Quantitative Observations	Qualitative Observations
• mass = 30 g	• Crystals are clear.
• mean crystal length = 0.5 cm	• Crystals are long, thin, and rectangular.
• longest crystal length = 2 cm	• White crust has formed around edge of dish.

> Photographs or sketches are useful for recording qualitative observations.

 Epsom salt crystals

MORE ABOUT OBSERVING

- Make quantitative observations whenever possible. That way, others will know exactly what you observed and be able to compare their results with yours.

- It is always a good idea to make qualitative observations too. You never know when you might observe something unexpected.

Predicting and Hypothesizing

A **prediction** is an expectation of what will be observed or what will happen. A **hypothesis** is a tentative explanation for an observation or scientific problem that can be tested by further investigation.

EXAMPLE

Suppose you have made two paper airplanes and you wonder why one of them tends to glide farther than the other one.

1. Start by asking a question.

2. Make an educated guess. After examination, you notice that the wings of the airplane that flies farther are slightly larger than the wings of the other airplane.

3. Write a prediction based upon your educated guess, in the form of an "If . . . , then . . ." statement. Write the independent variable after the word *if*, and the dependent variable after the word *then*.

4. To make a hypothesis, explain why you think what you predicted will occur. Write the explanation after the word *because*.

1. Why does one of the paper airplanes glide farther than the other?

2. The size of an airplane's wings may affect how far the airplane will glide.

3. Prediction: If I make a paper airplane with larger wings, then the airplane will glide farther.

> To read about independent and dependent variables, see page R30.

4. Hypothesis: If I make a paper airplane with larger wings, then the airplane will glide farther, because the additional surface area of the wing will produce more lift.

> Notice that the part of the hypothesis after *because* adds an explanation of why the airplane will glide farther.

MORE ABOUT HYPOTHESES

• The results of an experiment cannot prove that a hypothesis is correct. Rather, the results either support or do not support the hypothesis.

• Valuable information is gained even when your hypothesis is not supported by your results. For example, it would be an important discovery to find that wing size is not related to how far an airplane glides.

• In science, a hypothesis is supported only after many scientists have conducted many experiments and produced consistent results.

Inferring

An **inference** is a logical conclusion drawn from the available evidence and prior knowledge. Inferences are often made from observations.

EXAMPLE

A student observing a set of acorns noticed something unexpected about one of them. He noticed a white, soft-bodied insect eating its way out of the acorn.

The student recorded these observations.

Observations

- There is a hole in the acorn, about 0.5 cm in diameter, where the insect crawled out.
- There is a second hole, which is about the size of a pinhole, on the other side of the acorn.
- The inside of the acorn is hollow.

Here are some inferences that can be made on the basis of the observations.

Inferences

- The insect formed from the material inside the acorn, grew to its present size, and ate its way out of the acorn.
- The insect crawled through the smaller hole, ate the inside of the acorn, grew to its present size, and ate its way out of the acorn.
- An egg was laid in the acorn through the smaller hole. The egg hatched into a larva that ate the inside of the acorn, grew to its present size, and ate its way out of the acorn.

When you make inferences, be sure to look at all of the evidence available and combine it with what you already know.

MORE ABOUT INFERENCES

Inferences depend both on observations and on the knowledge of the people making the inferences. Ancient people who did not know that organisms are produced only by similar organisms might have made an inference like the first one. A student today might look at the same observations and make the second inference. A third student might have knowledge about this particular insect and know that it is never small enough to fit through the smaller hole, leading her to the third inference.

Identifying Cause and Effect

In a **cause-and-effect relationship,** one event or characteristic is the result of another. Usually an effect follows its cause in time.

There are many examples of cause-and-effect relationships in everyday life.

Cause	Effect
Turn off a light.	Room gets dark.
Drop a glass.	Glass breaks.
Blow a whistle.	Sound is heard.

Scientists must be careful not to infer a cause-and-effect relationship just because one event happens after another event. When one event occurs after another, you cannot infer a cause-and-effect relationship on the basis of that information alone. You also cannot conclude that one event caused another if there are alternative ways to explain the second event. A scientist must demonstrate through experimentation or continued observation that an event was truly caused by another event.

EXAMPLE

Make an Observation

Suppose you have a few plants growing outside. When the weather starts getting colder, you bring one of the plants indoors. You notice that the plant you brought indoors is growing faster than the others are growing. You cannot conclude from your observation that the change in temperature was the cause of the increased plant growth, because there are alternative explanations for the observation. Some possible explanations are given below.

- The humidity indoors caused the plant to grow faster.

- The level of sunlight indoors caused the plant to grow faster.

- The indoor plant's being noticed more often and watered more often than the outdoor plants caused it to grow faster.

- The plant that was brought indoors was healthier than the other plants to begin with.

To determine which of these factors, if any, caused the indoor plant to grow faster than the outdoor plants, you would need to design and conduct an experiment.

See pages R28–R35 for information about designing experiments.

Recognizing Bias

Television, newspapers, and the Internet are full of experts claiming to have scientific evidence to back up their claims. How do you know whether the claims are really backed up by good science?

Bias is a slanted point of view, or personal prejudice. The goal of scientists is to be as objective as possible and to base their findings on facts instead of opinions. However, bias often affects the conclusions of researchers, and it is important to learn to recognize bias.

When scientific results are reported, you should consider the source of the information as well as the information itself. It is important to critically analyze the information that you see and read.

SOURCES OF BIAS

There are several ways in which a report of scientific information may be biased. Here are some questions that you can ask yourself:

1. **Who is sponsoring the research?**

   Sometimes, the results of an investigation are biased because an organization paying for the research is looking for a specific answer. This type of bias can affect how data are gathered and interpreted.

2. **Is the research sample large enough?**

   Sometimes research does not include enough data. The larger the sample size, the more likely that the results are accurate, assuming a truly random sample.

3. **In a survey, who is answering the questions?**

   The results of a survey or poll can be biased. The people taking part in the survey may have been specifically chosen because of how they would answer. They may have the same ideas or lifestyles. A survey or poll should make use of a random sample of people.

4. **Are the people who take part in a survey biased?**

   People who take part in surveys sometimes try to answer the questions the way they think the researcher wants them to answer. Also, in surveys or polls that ask for personal information, people may be unwilling to answer questions truthfully.

SCIENTIFIC BIAS

It is also important to realize that scientists have their own biases because of the types of research they do and because of their scientific viewpoints. Two scientists may look at the same set of data and come to completely different conclusions because of these biases. However, such disagreements are not necessarily bad. In fact, a critical analysis of disagreements is often responsible for moving science forward.

Identifying Faulty Reasoning

Faulty reasoning is wrong or incorrect thinking. It leads to mistakes and to wrong conclusions. Scientists are careful not to draw unreasonable conclusions from experimental data. Without such caution, the results of scientific investigations may be misleading.

EXAMPLE

Scientists try to make generalizations based on their data to explain as much about nature as possible. If only a small sample of data is looked at, however, a conclusion may be faulty. Suppose a scientist has studied the effects of the El Niño and La Niña weather patterns on flood damage in California from 1989 to 1995. The scientist organized the data in the bar graph below.

The scientist drew the following conclusions:

1. The La Niña weather pattern has no effect on flooding in California.

2. When neither weather pattern occurs, there is almost no flood damage.

3. A weak or moderate El Niño produces a small or moderate amount of flooding.

4. A strong El Niño produces a lot of flooding.

Flood and Storm Damage in California

y-axis: Estimated damage (millions of dollars) — 0, 500, 1000, 1500, 2000

x-axis: Starting year of season (July 1–June 30) — 1989, 1992, 1995

Legend: Weak–moderate El Niño; Strong El Niño

SOURCE: *Governor's Office of Emergency Services, California*

For the six-year period of the scientist's investigation, these conclusions may seem to be reasonable. However, a six-year study of weather patterns may be too small of a sample for the conclusions to be supported. Consider the following graph, which shows information that was gathered from 1949 to 1997.

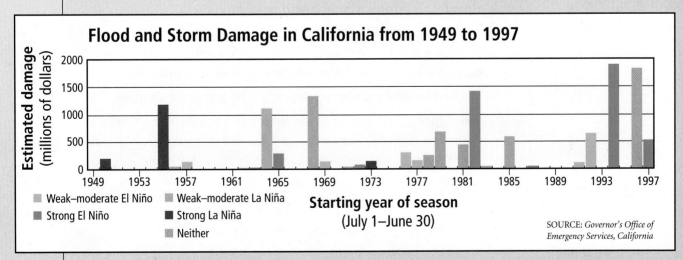

Flood and Storm Damage in California from 1949 to 1997

y-axis: Estimated damage (millions of dollars) — 0, 500, 1000, 1500, 2000

x-axis: Starting year of season (July 1–June 30) — 1949, 1953, 1957, 1961, 1965, 1969, 1973, 1977, 1981, 1985, 1989, 1993, 1997

Legend: Weak–moderate El Niño; Strong El Niño; Weak–moderate La Niña; Strong La Niña; Neither

SOURCE: *Governor's Office of Emergency Services, California*

The only one of the conclusions that all of this information supports is number 3: a weak or moderate El Niño produces a small or moderate amount of flooding. By collecting more data, scientists can be more certain of their conclusions and can avoid faulty reasoning.

Analyzing Statements

To **analyze** a statement is to examine its parts carefully. Scientific findings are often reported through media such as television or the Internet. A report that is made public often focuses on only a small part of research. As a result, it is important to question the sources of information.

Evaluate Media Claims

To **evaluate** a statement is to judge it on the basis of criteria you've established. Sometimes evaluating means deciding whether a statement is true.

Reports of scientific research and findings in the media may be misleading or incomplete. When you are exposed to this information, you should ask yourself some questions so that you can make informed judgments about the information.

1. **Does the information come from a credible source?**

   Suppose you learn about a new product and it is stated that scientific evidence proves that the product works. A report from a respected news source may be more believable than an advertisement paid for by the product's manufacturer.

2. **How much evidence supports the claim?**

   Often, it may seem that there is new evidence every day of something in the world that either causes or cures an illness. However, information that is the result of several years of work by several different scientists is more credible than an advertisement that does not even cite the subjects of the experiment.

3. **How much information is being presented?**

   Science cannot solve all questions, and scientific experiments often have flaws. A report that discusses problems in a scientific study may be more believable than a report that addresses only positive experimental findings.

4. **Is scientific evidence being presented by a specific source?**

   Sometimes scientific findings are reported by people who are called experts or leaders in a scientific field. But if their names are not given or their scientific credentials are not reported, their statements may be less credible than those of recognized experts.

Differentiate Between Fact and Opinion

Sometimes information is presented as a fact when it may be an opinion. When scientific conclusions are reported, it is important to recognize whether they are based on solid evidence. Again, you may find it helpful to ask yourself some questions.

1. What is the difference between a fact and an opinion?

A **fact** is a piece of information that can be strictly defined and proved true. An **opinion** is a statement that expresses a belief, value, or feeling. An opinion cannot be proved true or false. For example, a person's age is a fact, but if someone is asked how old they feel, it is impossible to prove the person's answer to be true or false.

2. Can opinions be measured?

Yes, opinions can be measured. In fact, surveys often ask for people's opinions on a topic. But there is no way to know whether or not an opinion is the truth.

HOW TO DIFFERENTIATE FACT FROM OPINION

Human Activities and the Environment

Opinions

Notice words or phrases that express beliefs or feelings. The words *unfortunately* and *careless* show that opinions are being expressed.

Unfortunately, human use of fossil fuels is one of the most significant developments of the past few centuries. Humans rely on fossil fuels, a non-renewable energy resource, for more than 90 percent of their energy needs.

Facts

Statements that contain statistics tend to be facts. Writers often use facts to support their opinions.

This careless misuse of our planet's resources has resulted in pollution, global warming, and the destruction of fragile ecosystems. For example, oil pipelines carry more than one million barrels of oil each day across tundra regions. Transporting oil across such areas can only result in oil spills that poison the land for decades.

Opinion

Look for statements that speculate about events. These statements are opinions, because they cannot be proved.

Lab Handbook

Safety Rules

Before you work in the laboratory, read these safety rules twice. Ask your teacher to explain any rules that you do not completely understand. Refer to these rules later on if you have questions about safety in the science classroom.

Directions

- Read all directions and make sure that you understand them before starting an investigation or lab activity. If you do not understand how to do a procedure or how to use a piece of equipment, ask your teacher.
- Do not begin any investigation or touch any equipment until your teacher has told you to start.
- Never experiment on your own. If you want to try a procedure that the directions do not call for, ask your teacher for permission first.
- If you are hurt or injured in any way, tell your teacher immediately.

Dress Code

goggles

apron

gloves

- Wear goggles when
  — using glassware, sharp objects, or chemicals
  — heating an object
  — working with anything that can easily fly up into the air and hurt someone's eye
- Tie back long hair or hair that hangs in front of your eyes.
- Remove any article of clothing—such as a loose sweater or a scarf—that hangs down and may touch a flame, chemical, or piece of equipment.
- Observe all safety icons calling for the wearing of eye protection, gloves, and aprons.

Heating and Fire Safety

fire safety

heating safety

- Keep your work area neat, clean, and free of extra materials.
- Never reach over a flame or heat source.
- Point objects being heated away from you and others.
- Never heat a substance or an object in a closed container.
- Never touch an object that has been heated. If you are unsure whether something is hot, treat it as though it is. Use oven mitts, clamps, tongs, or a test-tube holder.
- Know where the fire extinguisher and fire blanket are kept in your classroom.
- Do not throw hot substances into the trash. Wait for them to cool or use the container your teacher puts out for disposal.

Electrical Safety

electrical safety

- Never use lamps or other electrical equipment with frayed cords.
- Make sure no cord is lying on the floor where someone can trip over it.
- Do not let a cord hang over the side of a counter or table so that the equipment can easily be pulled or knocked to the floor.
- Never let cords hang into sinks or other places where water can be found.
- Never try to fix electrical problems. Inform your teacher of any problems immediately.
- Unplug an electrical cord by pulling on the plug, not the cord.

Chemical Safety

chemical safety

poison

fumes

- If you spill a chemical or get one on your skin or in your eyes, tell your teacher right away.
- Never touch, taste, or sniff any chemicals in the lab. If you need to determine odor, waft. Wafting consists of holding the chemical in its container 15 centimeters (6 in.) away from your nose, and using your fingers to bring fumes from the container to your nose.
- Keep lids on all chemicals you are not using.
- Never put unused chemicals back into the original containers. Throw away extra chemicals where your teacher tells you to.
- Pour chemicals over a sink or your work area, not over the floor.
- If you get a chemical in your eye, use the eyewash right away.
- Always wash your hands after handling chemicals, plants, or soil.

Wafting

Glassware and Sharp-Object Safety

sharp objects

- If you break glassware, tell your teacher right away.
- Do not use broken or chipped glassware. Give these to your teacher.
- Use knives and other cutting instruments carefully. Always wear eye protection and cut away from you.

Animal Safety

- Never hurt an animal.
- Touch animals only when necessary. Follow your teacher's instructions for handling animals.
- Always wash your hands after working with animals.

Cleanup

disposal

- Follow your teacher's instructions for throwing away or putting away supplies.
- Clean your work area and pick up anything that has dropped to the floor.
- Wash your hands.

Using Lab Equipment

Different experiments require different types of equipment. But even though experiments differ, the ways in which the equipment is used are the same.

Beakers

- Use beakers for holding and pouring liquids.
- Do not use a beaker to measure the volume of a liquid. Use a graduated cylinder instead. (See page R16.)
- Use a beaker that holds about twice as much liquid as you need. For example, if you need 100 milliliters of water, you should use a 200- or 250-milliliter beaker.

Test Tubes

- Use test tubes to hold small amounts of substances.
- Do not use a test tube to measure the volume of a liquid.
- Use a test tube when heating a substance over a flame. Aim the mouth of the tube away from yourself and other people.
- Liquids easily spill or splash from test tubes, so it is important to use only small amounts of liquids.

Test-Tube Holder

- Use a test-tube holder when heating a substance in a test tube.
- Use a test-tube holder if the substance in a test tube is dangerous to touch.
- Make sure the test-tube holder tightly grips the test tube so that the test tube will not slide out of the holder.
- Make sure that the test-tube holder is above the surface of the substance in the test tube so that you can observe the substance.

Test-Tube Rack

- Use a test-tube rack to organize test tubes before, during, and after an experiment.

- Use a test-tube rack to keep test tubes upright so that they do not fall over and spill their contents.

- Use a test-tube rack that is the correct size for the test tubes that you are using. If the rack is too small, a test tube may become stuck. If the rack is too large, a test tube may lean over, and some of its contents may spill or splash.

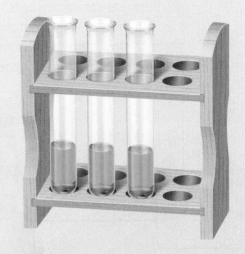

Forceps

- Use forceps when you need to pick up or hold a very small object that should not be touched with your hands.

- Do not use forceps to hold anything over a flame, because forceps are not long enough to keep your hand safely away from the flame. Plastic forceps will melt, and metal forceps will conduct heat and burn your hand.

Hot Plate

- Use a hot plate when a substance needs to be kept warmer than room temperature for a long period of time.

- Use a hot plate instead of a Bunsen burner or a candle when you need to carefully control temperature.

- Do not use a hot plate when a substance needs to be burned in an experiment.

- Always use "hot hands" safety mitts or oven mitts when handling anything that has been heated on a hot plate.

Microscope

Scientists use microscopes to see very small objects that cannot easily be seen with the eye alone. A microscope magnifies the image of an object so that small details may be observed. A microscope that you may use can magnify an object 400 times—the object will appear 400 times larger than its actual size.

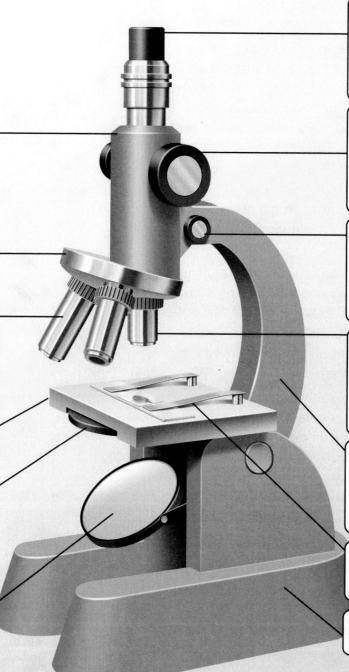

Body The body separates the lens in the eyepiece from the objective lenses below.

Nosepiece The nosepiece holds the objective lenses above the stage and rotates so that all lenses may be used.

High-Power Objective Lens This is the largest lens on the nosepiece. It magnifies an image approximately 40 times.

Stage The stage supports the object being viewed.

Diaphragm The diaphragm is used to adjust the amount of light passing through the slide and into an objective lens.

Mirror or Light Source Some microscopes use light that is reflected through the stage by a mirror. Other microscopes have their own light sources.

Eyepiece Objects are viewed through the eyepiece. The eyepiece contains a lens that commonly magnifies an image 10 times.

Coarse Adjustment This knob is used to focus the image of an object when it is viewed through the low-power lens.

Fine Adjustment This knob is used to focus the image of an object when it is viewed through the high-power lens.

Low-Power Objective Lens This is the smallest lens on the nosepiece. It magnifies an image approximately 10 times.

Arm The arm supports the body above the stage. Always carry a microscope by the arm and base.

Stage Clip The stage clip holds a slide in place on the stage.

Base The base supports the microscope.

VIEWING AN OBJECT

1. Use the coarse adjustment knob to raise the body tube.

2. Adjust the diaphragm so that you can see a bright circle of light through the eyepiece.

3. Place the object or slide on the stage. Be sure that it is centered over the hole in the stage.

4. Turn the nosepiece to click the low-power lens into place.

5. Using the coarse adjustment knob, slowly lower the lens and focus on the specimen being viewed. Be sure not to touch the slide or object with the lens.

6. When switching from the low-power lens to the high-power lens, first raise the body tube with the coarse adjustment knob so that the high-power lens will not hit the slide.

7. Turn the nosepiece to click the high-power lens into place.

8. Use the fine adjustment knob to focus on the specimen being viewed. Again, be sure not to touch the slide or object with the lens.

MAKING A SLIDE, OR WET MOUNT

1 Place the specimen in the center of a clean slide.

2 Place a drop of water on the specimen.

3 Place a cover slip on the slide. Put one edge of the cover slip into the drop of water and slowly lower it over the specimen.

4 Remove any air bubbles from under the cover slip by gently tapping the cover slip.

5 Dry any excess water before placing the slide on the microscope stage for viewing.

Spring Scale (Force Meter)

- Use a spring scale to measure a force pulling on the scale.

- Use a spring scale to measure the force of gravity exerted on an object by Earth.

- To measure a force accurately, a spring scale must be zeroed before it is used. The scale is zeroed when no weight is attached and the indicator is positioned at zero.

- Do not attach a weight that is either too heavy or too light to a spring scale. A weight that is too heavy could break the scale or exert too great a force for the scale to measure. A weight that is too light may not exert enough force to be measured accurately.

Graduated Cylinder

- Use a graduated cylinder to measure the volume of a liquid.

- Be sure that the graduated cylinder is on a flat surface so that your measurement will be accurate.

- When reading the scale on a graduated cylinder, be sure to have your eyes at the level of the surface of the liquid.

- The surface of the liquid will be curved in the graduated cylinder. Read the volume of the liquid at the bottom of the curve, or meniscus (muh-NIHS-kuhs).

- You can use a graduated cylinder to find the volume of a solid object by measuring the increase in a liquid's level after you add the object to the cylinder.

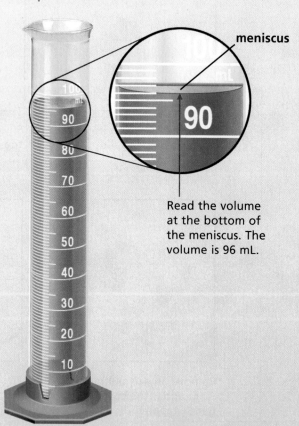

meniscus

Read the volume at the bottom of the meniscus. The volume is 96 mL.

LAB HANDBOOK

Metric Rulers

- Use metric rulers or meter sticks to measure objects' lengths.

- Do not measure an object from the end of a metric ruler or meter stick, because the end is often imperfect. Instead, measure from the 1-centimeter mark, but remember to subtract a centimeter from the apparent measurement.

- Estimate any lengths that extend between marked units. For example, if a meter stick shows centimeters but not millimeters, you can estimate the length that an object extends between centimeter marks to measure it to the nearest millimeter.

- **Controlling Variables** If you are taking repeated measurements, always measure from the same point each time. For example, if you're measuring how high two different balls bounce when dropped from the same height, measure both bounces at the same point on the balls—either the top or the bottom. Do not measure at the top of one ball and the bottom of the other.

EXAMPLE

How to Measure a Leaf

1. Lay a ruler flat on top of the leaf so that the 1-centimeter mark lines up with one end. Make sure the ruler and the leaf do not move between the time you line them up and the time you take the measurement.

2. Look straight down on the ruler so that you can see exactly how the marks line up with the other end of the leaf.

3. Estimate the length by which the leaf extends beyond a marking. For example, the leaf below extends about halfway between the 4.2-centimeter and 4.3-centimeter marks, so the apparent measurement is about 4.25 centimeters.

4. Remember to subtract 1 centimeter from your apparent measurement, since you started at the 1-centimeter mark on the ruler and not at the end. The leaf is about 3.25 centimeters long (4.25 cm – 1 cm = 3.25 cm).

Triple-Beam Balance

This balance has a pan and three beams with sliding masses, called riders. At one end of the beams is a pointer that indicates whether the mass on the pan is equal to the masses shown on the beams.

1. Make sure the balance is zeroed before measuring the mass of an object. The balance is zeroed if the pointer is at zero when nothing is on the pan and the riders are at their zero points. Use the adjustment knob at the base of the balance to zero it.

2. Place the object to be measured on the pan.

3. Move the riders one notch at a time away from the pan. Begin with the largest rider. If moving the largest rider one notch brings the pointer below zero, begin measuring the mass of the object with the next smaller rider.

4. Change the positions of the riders until they balance the mass on the pan and the pointer is at zero. Then add the readings from the three beams to determine the mass of the object.

300 g	position of largest rider
90 g	position of middle rider
+ 3 g	position of smallest rider
393 g	mass of beaker

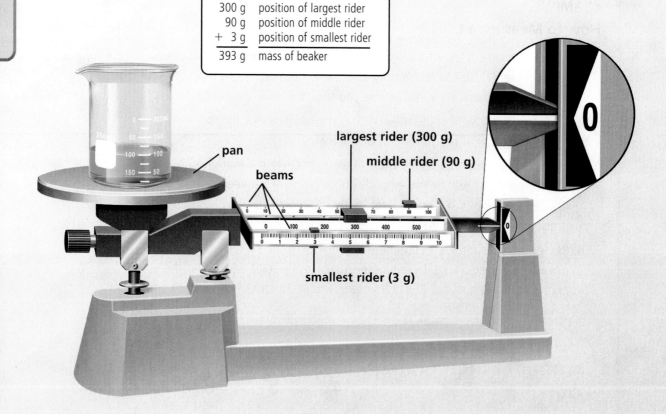

pan

beams

largest rider (300 g)

middle rider (90 g)

smallest rider (3 g)

LAB HANDBOOK

Double-Pan Balance

This type of balance has two pans. Between the pans is a pointer that indicates whether the masses on the pans are equal.

1. Make sure the balance is zeroed before measuring the mass of an object. The balance is zeroed if the pointer is at zero when there is nothing on either of the pans. Many double-pan balances have sliding knobs that can be used to zero them.

2. Place the object to be measured on one of the pans.

3. Begin adding standard masses to the other pan. Begin with the largest standard mass. If this adds too much mass to the balance, begin measuring the mass of the object with the next smaller standard mass.

4. Add standard masses until the masses on both pans are balanced and the pointer is at zero. Then add the standard masses together to determine the mass of the object being measured.

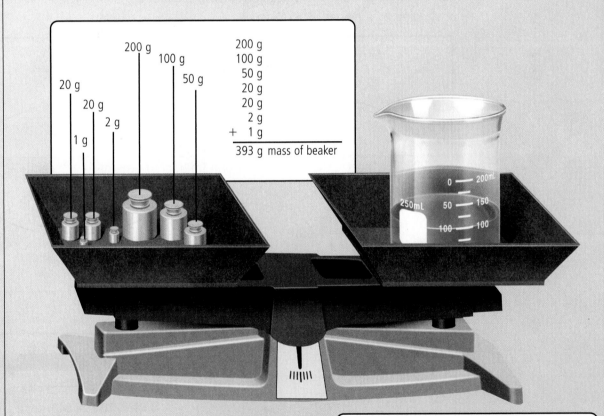

```
         200 g        200 g
            100 g     100 g
                       50 g
               50 g    20 g
  20 g                 20 g
       20 g             2 g
          2 g    +      1 g
                      ─────────
   1 g                393 g  mass of beaker
```

Never place chemicals or liquids directly on a pan. Instead, use the following procedure:

1 Determine the mass of an empty container, such as a beaker.

2 Pour the substance into the container, and measure the total mass of the substance and the container.

3 Subtract the mass of the empty container from the total mass to find the mass of the substance.

The Metric System and SI Units

Scientists use International System (SI) units for measurements of distance, volume, mass, and temperature. The International System is based on multiples of ten and the metric system of measurement.

Basic SI Units		
Property	Name	Symbol
length	meter	m
volume	liter	L
mass	kilogram	kg
temperature	kelvin	K

SI Prefixes		
Prefix	Symbol	Multiple of 10
kilo-	k	1000
hecto-	h	100
deca-	da	10
deci-	d	$0.1 \left(\frac{1}{10}\right)$
centi-	c	$0.01 \left(\frac{1}{100}\right)$
milli-	m	$0.001 \left(\frac{1}{1000}\right)$

Changing Metric Units

You can change from one unit to another in the metric system by multiplying or dividing by a power of 10.

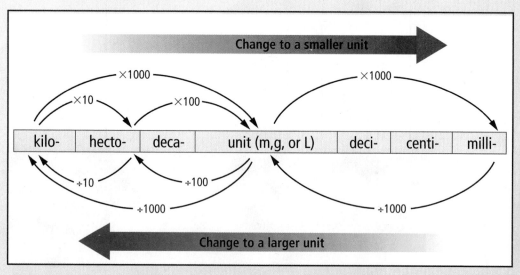

Example

Change 0.64 liters to milliliters.

(1) Decide whether to multiply or divide.

(2) Select the power of 10.

ANSWER 0.64 L = 640 mL

Change to a smaller unit by multiplying.

mL ◄—— × 1000 —— L

0.64 × 1000 = **640.**

Example

Change 23.6 grams to kilograms.

(1) Decide whether to multiply or divide.

(2) Select the power of 10.

ANSWER 23.6 g = 0.0236 kg

Change to a larger unit by dividing.

g —— ÷ 1000 —► kg

23.6 ÷ 1000 = **0.0236**

Temperature Conversions

Even though the kelvin is the SI base unit of temperature, the degree Celsius will be the unit you use most often in your science studies. The formulas below show the relationships between temperatures in degrees Fahrenheit (°F), degrees Celsius (°C), and kelvins (K).

$$°C = \frac{5}{9}(°F - 32)$$

$$°F = \frac{9}{5}°C + 32$$

$$K = °C + 273$$

See page R42 for help with using formulas.

Examples of Temperature Conversions

Condition	Degrees Celsius	Degrees Fahrenheit
Freezing point of water	0	32
Cool day	10	50
Mild day	20	68
Warm day	30	86
Normal body temperature	37	98.6
Very hot day	40	104
Boiling point of water	100	212

Converting Between SI and U.S. Customary Units

Use the chart below when you need to convert between SI units and U.S. customary units.

SI Unit	From SI to U.S. Customary			From U.S. Customary to SI		
Length	**When you know**	**multiply by**	**to find**	**When you know**	**multiply by**	**to find**
kilometer (km) = 1000 m	kilometers	0.62	miles	miles	1.61	kilometers
meter (m) = 100 cm	meters	3.28	feet	feet	0.3048	meters
centimeter (cm) = 10 mm	centimeters	0.39	inches	inches	2.54	centimeters
millimeter (mm) = 0.1 cm	millimeters	0.04	inches	inches	25.4	millimeters
Area	**When you know**	**multiply by**	**to find**	**When you know**	**multiply by**	**to find**
square kilometer (km²)	square kilometers	0.39	square miles	square miles	2.59	square kilometers
square meter (m²)	square meters	1.2	square yards	square yards	0.84	square meters
square centimeter (cm²)	square centimeters	0.155	square inches	square inches	6.45	square centimeters
Volume	**When you know**	**multiply by**	**to find**	**When you know**	**multiply by**	**to find**
liter (L) = 1000 mL	liters	1.06	quarts	quarts	0.95	liters
	liters	0.26	gallons	gallons	3.79	liters
	liters	4.23	cups	cups	0.24	liters
	liters	2.12	pints	pints	0.47	liters
milliliter (mL) = 0.001 L	milliliters	0.20	teaspoons	teaspoons	4.93	milliliters
	milliliters	0.07	tablespoons	tablespoons	14.79	milliliters
	milliliters	0.03	fluid ounces	fluid ounces	29.57	milliliters
Mass	**When you know**	**multiply by**	**to find**	**When you know**	**multiply by**	**to find**
kilogram (kg) = 1000 g	kilograms	2.2	pounds	pounds	0.45	kilograms
gram (g) = 1000 mg	grams	0.035	ounces	ounces	28.35	grams

Precision and Accuracy

When you do an experiment, it is important that your methods, observations, and data be both precise and accurate.

low precision

precision,
but not accuracy

precision and
accuracy

LAB HANDBOOK

Precision

In science, **precision** is the exactness and consistency of measurements. For example, measurements made with a ruler that has both centimeter and millimeter markings would be more precise than measurements made with a ruler that has only centimeter markings. Another indicator of precision is the care taken to make sure that methods and observations are as exact and consistent as possible. Every time a particular experiment is done, the same procedure should be used. Precision is necessary because experiments are repeated several times and if the procedure changes, the results will change.

EXAMPLE

Suppose you are measuring temperatures over a two-week period. Your precision will be greater if you measure each temperature at the same place, at the same time of day, and with the same thermometer than if you change any of these factors from one day to the next.

Accuracy

In science, it is possible to be precise but not accurate. **Accuracy** depends on the difference between a measurement and an actual value. The smaller the difference, the more accurate the measurement.

EXAMPLE

Suppose you look at a stream and estimate that it is about 1 meter wide at a particular place. You decide to check your estimate by measuring the stream with a meter stick, and you determine that the stream is 1.32 meters wide. However, because it is hard to measure the width of a stream with a meter stick, it turns out that you didn't do a very good job. The stream is actually 1.14 meters wide. Therefore, even though your estimate was less precise than your measurement, your estimate was actually more accurate.

Making Data Tables and Graphs

Data tables and graphs are useful tools for both recording and communicating scientific data.

Making Data Tables

You can use a **data table** to organize and record the measurements that you make. Some examples of information that might be recorded in data tables are frequencies, times, and amounts.

EXAMPLE

Suppose you are investigating photosynthesis in two elodea plants. One sits in direct sunlight, and the other sits in a dimly lit room. You measure the rate of photosynthesis by counting the number of bubbles in the jar every ten minutes.

1. Title and number your data table.
2. Decide how you will organize the table into columns and rows.
3. Any units, such as seconds or degrees, should be included in column headings, not in the individual cells.

Table 1. Number of Bubbles from Elodea

Always number and title data tables.

Time (min)	Sunlight	Dim Light
0	0	0
10	15	5
20	25	8
30	32	7
40	41	10
50	47	9
60	42	9

The data in the table above could also be organized in a different way.

Table 1. Number of Bubbles from Elodea

Put units in column heading.

Light Condition	Time (min)						
	0	10	20	30	40	50	60
Sunlight	0	15	25	32	41	47	42
Dim light	0	5	8	7	10	9	9

Making Line Graphs

You can use a **line graph** to show a relationship between variables. Line graphs are particularly useful for showing changes in variables over time.

EXAMPLE

Suppose you are interested in graphing temperature data that you collected over the course of a day.

Table 1. Outside Temperature During the Day on March 7

	Time of Day						
	7:00 A.M.	9:00 A.M.	11:00 A.M.	1:00 P.M.	3:00 P.M.	5:00 P.M.	7:00 P.M.
Temp (°C)	8	9	11	14	12	10	6

1. Use the vertical axis of your line graph for the variable that you are measuring—temperature.

2. Choose scales for both the horizontal axis and the vertical axis of the graph. You should have two points more than you need on the vertical axis, and the horizontal axis should be long enough for all of the data points to fit.

3. Draw and label each axis.

4. Graph each value. First find the appropriate point on the scale of the horizontal axis. Imagine a line that rises vertically from that place on the scale. Then find the corresponding value on the vertical axis, and imagine a line that moves horizontally from that value. The point where these two imaginary lines intersect is where the value should be plotted.

5. Connect the points with straight lines.

Be sure to add a number and a title to your graph.

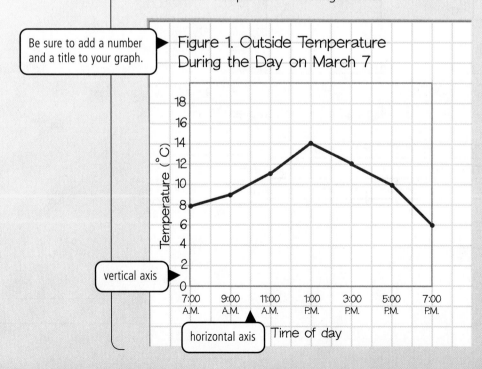

Figure 1. Outside Temperature During the Day on March 7

vertical axis

horizontal axis

Making Circle Graphs

You can use a **circle graph,** sometimes called a pie chart, to represent data as parts of a circle. Circle graphs are used only when the data can be expressed as percentages of a whole. The entire circle shown in a circle graph is equal to 100 percent of the data.

EXAMPLE

Suppose you identified the species of each mature tree growing in a small wooded area. You organized your data in a table, but you also want to show the data in a circle graph.

1. To begin, find the total number of mature trees.

    $56 + 34 + 22 + 10 + 28 = 150$

2. To find the degree measure for each sector of the circle, write a fraction comparing the number of each tree species with the total number of trees. Then multiply the fraction by 360°.

    Oak: $\frac{56}{150} \times 360° = 134.4°$

3. Draw a circle. Use a protractor to draw the angle for each sector of the graph.

4. Color and label each sector of the graph.

5. Give the graph a number and title.

Table 1. Tree Species in Wooded Area

Species	Number of Specimens
Oak	56
Maple	34
Birch	22
Willow	10
Pine	28

Figure 1. Tree Species in Wooded Area

Willow 10
Birch 22
Pine 28
Oak 56
Maple 34

Instead of labeling each sector, you could make a color key.

- Oak 56
- Maple 34
- Pine 28
- Birch 22
- Willow 10

Bar Graph

A **bar graph** is a type of graph in which the lengths of the bars are used to represent and compare data. A numerical scale is used to determine the lengths of the bars.

EXAMPLE

To determine the effect of water on seed sprouting, three cups were filled with sand, and ten seeds were planted in each. Different amounts of water were added to each cup over a three-day period.

Table 1. Effect of Water on Seed Sprouting

Daily Amount of Water (mL)	Number of Seeds That Sprouted After 3 Days in Sand
0	1
10	4
20	8

1. Choose a numerical scale. The greatest value is 8, so the end of the scale should have a value greater than 8, such as 10. Use equal increments along the scale, such as increments of 2.

2. Draw and label the axes. Mark intervals on the vertical axis according to the scale you chose.

3. Draw a bar for each data value. Use the scale to decide how long to make each bar.

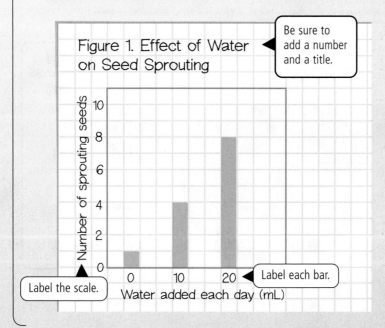

Figure 1. Effect of Water on Seed Sprouting

Be sure to add a number and a title.

Label the scale.

Label each bar.

Double Bar Graph

A **double bar graph** is a bar graph that shows two sets of data. The two bars for each measurement are drawn next to each other.

EXAMPLE

The seed-sprouting experiment was done using both sand and potting soil. The data for sand and potting soil can be plotted on one graph.

1. Draw one set of bars, using the data for sand, as shown below.
2. Draw bars for the potting-soil data next to the bars for the sand data. Shade them a different color. Add a key.

Table 2. Effect of Water and Soil on Seed Sprouting

Daily Amount of Water (mL)	Number of Seeds That Sprouted After 3 Days in Sand	Number of Seeds That Sprouted After 3 Days in Potting Soil
0	1	2
10	4	5
20	8	9

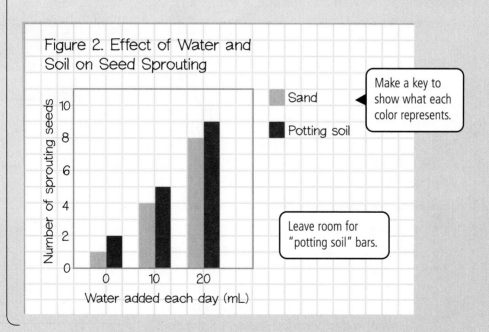

Figure 2. Effect of Water and Soil on Seed Sprouting

Make a key to show what each color represents.

Leave room for "potting soil" bars.

Designing an Experiment

Use this section when designing or conducting an experiment.

Determining a Purpose

You can find a purpose for an experiment by doing research, by examining the results of a previous experiment, or by observing the world around you. An **experiment** is an organized procedure to study something under controlled conditions.

Don't forget to learn as much as possible about your topic before you begin.

1. Write the purpose of your experiment as a question or problem that you want to investigate.

2. Write down research questions and begin searching for information that will help you design an experiment. Consult the library, the Internet, and other people as you conduct your research.

EXAMPLE

Middle school students observed an odor near the lake by their school. They also noticed that the water on the side of the lake near the school was greener than the water on the other side of the lake. The students did some research to learn more about their observations. They discovered that the odor and green color in the lake

came from algae. They also discovered that a new fertilizer was being used on a field nearby. The students inferred that the use of the fertilizer might be related to the presence of the algae and designed a controlled experiment to find out whether they were right.

> **Problem**
>
> How does fertilizer affect the presence of algae in a lake?
>
> **Research Questions**
>
> - Have other experiments been done on this problem? If so, what did those experiments show?
> - What kind of fertilizer is used on the field? How much?
> - How do algae grow?
> - How do people measure algae?
> - Can fertilizer and algae be used safely in a lab? How?

Research
As you research, you may find a topic that is more interesting to you than your original topic, or learn that a procedure you wanted to use is not practical or safe. It is OK to change your purpose as you research.

LAB HANDBOOK

Writing a Hypothesis

A **hypothesis** is a tentative explanation for an observation or scientific problem that can be tested by further investigation. You can write your hypothesis in the form of an "If . . . , then . . . , because . . ." statement.

Hypothesis

If the amount of fertilizer in lake water is increased, then the amount of algae will also increase, because fertilizers provide nutrients that algae need to grow.

> **Hypotheses**
> For help with hypotheses, refer to page R3.

Determining Materials

Make a list of all the materials you will need to do your experiment. Be specific, especially if someone else is helping you obtain the materials. Try to think of everything you will need.

Materials

- 1 large jar or container
- 4 identical smaller containers
- rubber gloves that also cover the arms
- sample of fertilizer-and-water solution
- eyedropper
- clear plastic wrap
- scissors
- masking tape
- marker
- ruler

Determining Variables and Constants

EXPERIMENTAL GROUP AND CONTROL GROUP

An experiment to determine how two factors are related always has two groups—a control group and an experimental group.

1. Design an experimental group. Include as many trials as possible in the experimental group in order to obtain reliable results.

2. Design a control group that is the same as the experimental group in every way possible, except for the factor you wish to test.

Experimental Group: two containers of lake water with one drop of fertilizer solution added to each

Control Group: two containers of lake water with no fertilizer solution added

Go back to your materials list and make sure you have enough items listed to cover both your experimental group and your control group.

VARIABLES AND CONSTANTS

Identify the variables and constants in your experiment. In a controlled experiment, a **variable** is any factor that can change. **Constants** are all of the factors that are the same in both the experimental group and the control group.

1. Read your hypothesis. The **independent variable** is the factor that you wish to test and that is manipulated or changed so that it can be tested. The independent variable is expressed in your hypothesis after the word *if*. Identify the independent variable in your laboratory report.

2. The **dependent variable** is the factor that you measure to gather results. It is expressed in your hypothesis after the word *then*. Identify the dependent variable in your laboratory report.

Hypothesis
If the amount of fertilizer in lake water is increased, then the amount of algae will also increase, because fertilizers provide nutrients that algae need to grow.

Table 1. Variables and Constants in Algae Experiment

Independent Variable	Dependent Variable	Constants
Amount of fertilizer in lake water	Amount of algae that grow	• Where the lake water is obtained • Type of container used • Light and temperature conditions where water will be stored

Set up your experiment so that you will test only one variable.

MEASURING THE DEPENDENT VARIABLE

Before starting your experiment, you need to define how you will measure the dependent variable. An **operational definition** is a description of the one particular way in which you will measure the dependent variable.

Your operational definition is important for several reasons. First, in any experiment there are several ways in which a dependent variable can be measured. Second, the procedure of the experiment depends on how you decide to measure the dependent variable. Third, your operational definition makes it possible for other people to evaluate and build on your experiment.

EXAMPLE 1

An operational definition of a dependent variable can be qualitative. That is, your measurement of the dependent variable can simply be an observation of whether a change occurs as a result of a change in the independent variable. This type of operational definition can be thought of as a "yes or no" measurement.

Table 2. Qualitative Operational Definition of Algae Growth

Independent Variable	Dependent Variable	Operational Definition
Amount of fertilizer in lake water	Amount of algae that grow	Algae grow in lake water

A qualitative measurement of a dependent variable is often easy to make and record. However, this type of information does not provide a great deal of detail in your experimental results.

EXAMPLE 2

An operational definition of a dependent variable can be quantitative. That is, your measurement of the dependent variable can be a number that shows how much change occurs as a result of a change in the independent variable.

Table 3. Quantitative Operational Definition of Algae Growth

Independent Variable	Dependent Variable	Operational Definition
Amount of fertilizer in lake water	Amount of algae that grow	Diameter of largest algal growth (in mm)

A quantitative measurement of a dependent variable can be more difficult to make and analyze than a qualitative measurement. However, this type of data provides much more information about your experiment and is often more useful.

Writing a Procedure

Write each step of your procedure. Start each step with a verb, or action word, and keep the steps short. Your procedure should be clear enough for someone else to use as instructions for repeating your experiment.

If necessary, go back to your materials list and add any materials that you left out.

Procedure

1. Put on your gloves. Use the large container to obtain a sample of lake water.

2. Divide the sample of lake water equally among the four smaller containers.

Controlling Variables
The same amount of fertilizer solution must be added to two of the four containers. ▶

3. Use the eyedropper to add one drop of fertilizer solution to two of the containers.

4. Use the masking tape and the marker to label the containers with your initials, the date, and the identifiers "Jar 1 with Fertilizer," "Jar 2 with Fertilizer," "Jar 1 without Fertilizer," and "Jar 2 without Fertilizer."

5. Cover the containers with clear plastic wrap. Use the scissors to punch ten holes in each of the covers.

Controlling Variables
All four containers must receive the same amount of light. ▶

6. Place all four containers on a window ledge. Make sure that they all receive the same amount of light.

7. Observe the containers every day for one week.

8. Use the ruler to measure the diameter of the largest clump of algae in each container, and record your measurements daily.

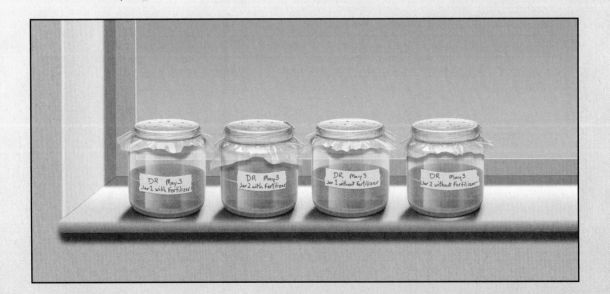

Recording Observations

Once you have obtained all of your materials and your procedure has been approved, you can begin making experimental observations. Gather both quantitative and qualitative data. If something goes wrong during your procedure, make sure you record that too.

Observations
For help with making qualitative and quantitative observations, refer to page R2.

For more examples of data tables, see page R23.

Table 4. Fertilizer and Algae Growth

Date and Time	Experimental Group		Control Group		Observations
	Jar 1 with Fertilizer (diameter of algae in mm)	Jar 2 with Fertilizer (diameter of algae in mm)	Jar 1 without Fertilizer (diameter of algae in mm)	Jar 2 without Fertilizer (diameter of algae in mm)	
5/3 4:00 P.M.	0	0	0	0	condensation in all containers
5/4 4:00 P.M.	0	3	0	0	tiny green blobs in jar 2 with fertilizer
5/5 4:15 P.M.	4	5	0	3	green blobs in jars 1 and 2 with fertilizer and jar 2 without fertilizer
5/6 4:00 P.M.	5	6	0	4	water light green in jar 2 with fertilizer
5/7 4:00 P.M.	8	10	0	6	water light green in jars 1 and 2 with fertilizer and in jar 2 without fertilizer
5/8 3:30 P.M.	10	18	0	6	cover off jar 2 with fertilizer
5/9 3:30 P.M.	14	23	0	8	drew sketches of each container

Notice that on the sixth day, the observer found that the cover was off one of the containers. It is important to record observations of unintended factors because they might affect the results of the experiment.

Use technology, such as a microscope, to help you make observations when possible.

Drawings of Samples Viewed Under Microscope on 5/9 at 100×

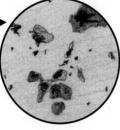
Jar 1 with Fertilizer

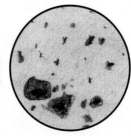
Jar 2 with Fertilizer

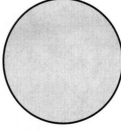
Jar 1 without Fertilizer

Jar 2 without Fertilizer

LAB HANDBOOK

Summarizing Results

To summarize your data, look at all of your observations together. Look for meaningful ways to present your observations. For example, you might average your data or make a graph to look for patterns. When possible, use spreadsheet software to help you analyze and present your data. The two graphs below show the same data.

EXAMPLE 1

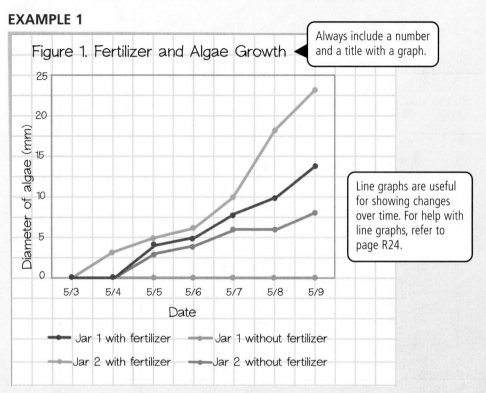

Figure 1. Fertilizer and Algae Growth

Always include a number and a title with a graph.

Line graphs are useful for showing changes over time. For help with line graphs, refer to page R24.

EXAMPLE 2

Bar graphs are useful for comparing different data sets. This bar graph has four bars for each day. Another way to present the data would be to calculate averages for the tests and the controls, and to show one test bar and one control bar for each day.

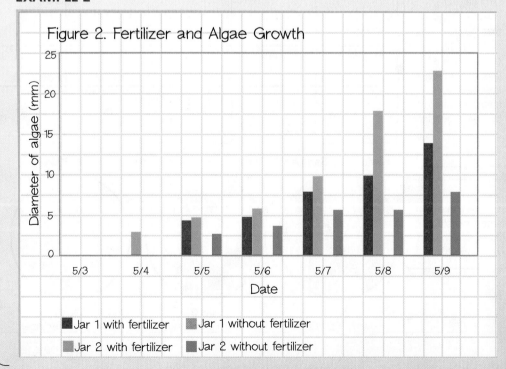

Figure 2. Fertilizer and Algae Growth

Drawing Conclusions

RESULTS AND INFERENCES

To draw conclusions from your experiment, first write your results. Then compare your results with your hypothesis. Do your results support your hypothesis? Be careful not to make inferences about factors that you did not test.

> For help with making inferences, see page R4.

Results and Inferences

The results of my experiment show that more algae grew in lake water to which fertilizer had been added than in lake water to which no fertilizer had been added. My hypothesis was supported. I infer that it is possible that the growth of algae in the lake was caused by the fertilizer used on the field.

> Notice that you cannot conclude from this experiment that the presence of algae in the lake was due only to the fertilizer.

QUESTIONS FOR FURTHER RESEARCH

Write a list of questions for further research and investigation. Your ideas may lead you to new experiments and discoveries.

Questions for Further Research

• What is the connection between the amount of fertilizer and algae growth?
• How do different brands of fertilizer affect algae growth?
• How would algae growth in the lake be affected if no fertilizer were used on the field?
• How do algae affect the lake and the other life in and around it?
• How does fertilizer affect the lake and the life in and around it?
• If fertilizer is getting into the lake, how is it getting there?

Math Handbook

Describing a Set of Data

Means, medians, modes, and ranges are important math tools for describing data sets such as the following widths of fossilized clamshells.

13 mm   25 mm   14 mm   21 mm   16 mm   23 mm   14 mm

Mean

The **mean** of a data set is the sum of the values divided by the number of values.

Example

To find the mean of the clamshell data, add the values and then divide the sum by the number of values.

$$\frac{13 \text{ mm} + 25 \text{ mm} + 14 \text{ mm} + 21 \text{ mm} + 16 \text{ mm} + 23 \text{ mm} + 14 \text{ mm}}{7} = \frac{126 \text{ mm}}{7} = 18 \text{ mm}$$

ANSWER The mean is 18 mm.

Median

The **median** of a data set is the middle value when the values are written in numerical order. If a data set has an even number of values, the median is the mean of the two middle values.

Example

To find the median of the clamshell data, arrange the values in order from least to greatest. The median is the middle value.

13 mm   14 mm   14 mm   16 mm   21 mm   23 mm   25 mm

ANSWER The median is 16 mm.

MATH HANDBOOK

Mode

The **mode** of a data set is the value that occurs most often.

Example

To find the mode of the clamshell data, arrange the values in order from least to greatest and determine the value that occurs most often.

13 mm   14 mm   14 mm   16 mm   21 mm   23 mm   25 mm

ANSWER The mode is 14 mm.

A data set can have more than one mode or no mode. For example, the following data set has modes of 2 mm and 4 mm:

2 mm   2 mm   3 mm   4 mm   4 mm

The data set below has no mode, because no value occurs more often than any other.

2 mm   3 mm   4 mm   5 mm

Range

The **range** of a data set is the difference between the greatest value and the least value.

Example

To find the range of the clamshell data, arrange the values in order from least to greatest.

13 mm   14 mm   14 mm   16 mm   21 mm   23 mm   25 mm

Subtract the least value from the greatest value.

13 mm is the least value.
25 mm is the greatest value.

25 mm − 13 mm = 12 mm

ANSWER The range is 12 mm.

Using Ratios, Rates, and Proportions

You can use ratios and rates to compare values in data sets. You can use proportions to find unknown values.

Ratios

A **ratio** uses division to compare two values. The ratio of a value a to a nonzero value b can be written as $\frac{a}{b}$.

Example

The height of one plant is 8 centimeters. The height of another plant is 6 centimeters. To find the ratio of the height of the first plant to the height of the second plant, write a fraction and simplify it.

$$\frac{8 \text{ cm}}{6 \text{ cm}} = \frac{4 \times \overset{1}{\cancel{2}}}{3 \times \underset{1}{\cancel{2}}} = \frac{4}{3}$$

ANSWER The ratio of the plant heights is $\frac{4}{3}$.

You can also write the ratio $\frac{a}{b}$ as "a to b" or as $a:b$. For example, you can write the ratio of the plant heights as "4 to 3" or as $4:3$.

Rates

A **rate** is a ratio of two values expressed in different units. A unit rate is a rate with a denominator of 1 unit.

Example

A plant grew 6 centimeters in 2 days. The plant's rate of growth was $\frac{6 \text{ cm}}{2 \text{ days}}$. To describe the plant's growth in centimeters per day, write a unit rate.

$$\textit{Divide numerator and} \atop \textit{denominator by 2:} \quad \frac{6 \text{ cm}}{2 \text{ days}} = \frac{6 \text{ cm} \div 2}{2 \text{ days} \div 2}$$

You divide 2 days by 2 to get 1 day, so divide 6 cm by 2 also.

$$\textit{Simplify:} \qquad = \frac{3 \text{ cm}}{1 \text{ day}}$$

ANSWER The plant's rate of growth is 3 centimeters per day.

Proportions

A **proportion** is an equation stating that two ratios are equivalent. To solve for an unknown value in a proportion, you can use cross products.

Example

If a plant grew 6 centimeters in 2 days, how many centimeters would it grow in 3 days (if its rate of growth is constant)?

$$\textit{Write a proportion:} \quad \frac{6 \text{ cm}}{2 \text{ days}} = \frac{x}{3 \text{ days}}$$

$$\textit{Set cross products:} \quad 6 \text{ cm} \cdot 3 = 2x$$

$$\textit{Multiply 6 and 3:} \quad 18 \text{ cm} = 2x$$

$$\textit{Divide each side by 2:} \quad \frac{18 \text{ cm}}{2} = \frac{2x}{2}$$

$$\textit{Simplify:} \quad 9 \text{ cm} = x$$

ANSWER The plant would grow 9 centimeters in 3 days.

Using Decimals, Fractions, and Percents

Decimals, fractions, and percentages are all ways of recording and representing data.

Decimals

A **decimal** is a number that is written in the base-ten place value system, in which a decimal point separates the ones and tenths digits. The values of each place is ten times that of the place to its right.

Example

A caterpillar traveled from point A to point C along the path shown.

A — 36.9 cm — B — 52.4 cm — C

ADDING DECIMALS To find the total distance traveled by the caterpillar, add the distance from A to B and the distance from B to C. Begin by lining up the decimal points. Then add the figures as you would whole numbers and bring down the decimal point.

```
  36.9 cm
+ 52.4 cm
  89.3 cm
```

ANSWER The caterpillar traveled a total distance of 89.3 centimeters.

Example *continued*

SUBTRACTING DECIMALS To find how much farther the caterpillar traveled on the second leg of the journey, subtract the distance from *A* to *B* from the distance from *B* to *C*.

$$
\begin{array}{r}
52.4 \text{ cm} \\
- \ 36.9 \text{ cm} \\
\hline
15.5 \text{ cm}
\end{array}
$$

ANSWER The caterpillar traveled 15.5 centimeters farther on the second leg of the journey.

Example

A caterpillar is traveling from point *D* to point *F* along the path shown. The caterpillar travels at a speed of 9.6 centimeters per minute.

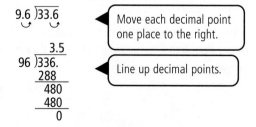

D   E   **33.6 cm**   F

MULTIPLYING DECIMALS You can multiply decimals as you would whole numbers. The number of decimal places in the product is equal to the sum of the number of decimal places in the factors.

For instance, suppose it takes the caterpillar 1.5 minutes to go from *D* to *E*. To find the distance from *D* to *E*, multiply the caterpillar's speed by the time it took.

Align as shown. ▶

$$
\begin{array}{r}
9.6 \qquad\quad 1 \quad \text{decimal place} \\
\times \ 1.5 \qquad + \ 1 \quad \text{decimal place} \\
\hline
480 \qquad\qquad\qquad\qquad\quad \\
96 \qquad\qquad\qquad\qquad\quad \\
\hline
14.40 \qquad\quad 2 \quad \text{decimal places}
\end{array}
$$

ANSWER The distance from *D* to *E* is 14.4 centimeters.

DIVIDING DECIMALS When you divide by a decimal, move the decimal points the same number of places in the divisor and the dividend to make the divisor a whole number.

For instance, to find the time it will take the caterpillar to travel from *E* to *F*, divide the distance from *E* to *F* by the caterpillar's speed.

$$9.6\,\overline{)33.6}$$

Move each decimal point one place to the right.

$$
\begin{array}{r}
3.5 \\
96\,\overline{)336.} \\
\underline{288} \\
480 \\
\underline{480} \\
0
\end{array}
$$

Line up decimal points.

ANSWER The caterpillar will travel from *E* to *F* in 3.5 minutes.

Fractions

A **fraction** is a number in the form $\frac{a}{b}$, where b is not equal to 0. A fraction is in **simplest form** if its numerator and denominator have a greatest common factor (GCF) of 1. To simplify a fraction, divide its numerator and denominator by their GCF.

Example

A caterpillar is 40 millimeters long. The head of the caterpillar is 6 millimeters long. To compare the length of the caterpillar's head with the caterpillar's total length, you can write and simplify a fraction that expresses the ratio of the two lengths.

Write the ratio of the two lengths:
$$\frac{\text{Length of head}}{\text{Total length}} = \frac{6 \text{ mm}}{40 \text{ mm}}$$

Write numerator and denominator as products of numbers and the GCF:
$$= \frac{3 \times 2}{20 \times 2}$$

Divide numerator and denominator by the GCF:
$$= \frac{3 \times \overset{1}{2}}{20 \times \underset{1}{2}}$$

Simplify:
$$= \frac{3}{20}$$

ANSWER In simplest form, the ratio of the lengths is $\frac{3}{20}$.

Percents

A **percent** is a ratio that compares a number to 100. The word *percent* means "per hundred" or "out of 100." The symbol for *percent* is %.

For instance, suppose 43 out of 100 caterpillars are female. You can represent this ratio as a percent, a decimal, or a fraction.

Percent	Decimal	Fraction
43%	0.43	$\frac{43}{100}$

Example

In the preceding example, the ratio of the length of the caterpillar's head to the caterpillar's total length is $\frac{3}{20}$. To write this ratio as a percent, write an equivalent fraction that has a denominator of 100.

Multiply numerator and denominator by 5:
$$\frac{3}{20} = \frac{3 \times 5}{20 \times 5}$$
$$= \frac{15}{100}$$

Write as a percent:
$$= 15\%$$

ANSWER The caterpillar's head represents 15 percent of its total length.

Using Formulas

A **formula** is an equation that shows the general relationship between two or more quantities.

In science, a formula often has a word form and a symbolic form. The formula below expresses Ohm's law.

Word Form

$$\text{Current} = \frac{\text{voltage}}{\text{resistance}}$$

Symbolic Form

$$I = \frac{V}{R}$$

The term *variable* is also used in science to refer to a factor that can change during an experiment.

In this formula, I, V, and R are variables. A mathematical **variable** is a symbol or letter that is used to represent one or more numbers.

Example

Suppose that you measure a voltage of 1.5 volts and a resistance of 15 ohms. You can use the formula for Ohm's law to find the current in amperes.

Write the formula for Ohm's law: $I = \dfrac{V}{R}$

Substitute 1.5 volts for V and 15 ohms for R: $I = \dfrac{1.5 \text{ volts}}{15 \text{ ohms}}$

Simplify: $I = 0.1 \text{ amp}$

ANSWER The current is 0.1 ampere.

If you know the values of all variables but one in a formula, you can solve for the value of the unknown variable. For instance, Ohm's law can be used to find a voltage if you know the current and the resistance.

Example

Suppose that you know that a current is 0.2 amperes and the resistance is 18 ohms. Use the formula for Ohm's law to find the voltage in volts.

Write the formula for Ohm's law: $I = \dfrac{V}{R}$

Substitute 0.2 amp for I and 18 ohms for R: $0.2 \text{ amp} = \dfrac{V}{18 \text{ ohms}}$

Multiply both sides by 18 ohms: $0.2 \text{ amp} \cdot 18 \text{ ohms} = V$

Simplify: $3.6 \text{ volts} = V$

ANSWER The voltage is 3.6 volts.

Finding Areas

The area of a figure is the amount of surface the figure covers.

Area is measured in square units, such as square meters (m^2) or square centimeters (cm^2). Formulas for the areas of three common geometric figures are shown below.

Area = (side length)^2
$A = s^2$

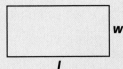

Area = length × width
$A = lw$

Area = $\frac{1}{2}$ × base × height
$A = \frac{1}{2} bh$

Example

Each face of a halite crystal is a square like the one shown. You can find the area of the square by using the steps below.

3 mm

3 mm

Write the formula for the area of a square: $A = s^2$

Substitute 3 mm for s: $= (3 \text{ mm})^2$

Simplify: $= 9 \text{ mm}^2$

ANSWER The area of the square is 9 square millimeters.

Finding Volumes

The volume of a solid is the amount of space contained by the solid.

Volume is measured in cubic units, such as cubic meters (m^3) or cubic centimeters (cm^3). The volume of a rectangular prism is given by the formula shown below.

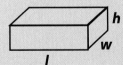

Volume = length × width × height
$V = lwh$

Example

A topaz crystal is a rectangular prism like the one shown. You can find the volume of the prism by using the steps below.

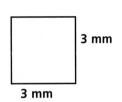

10 mm

12 mm

20 mm

Write the formula for the volume of a rectangular prism: $V = lwh$

Substitute dimensions: $= 20 \text{ mm} \times 12 \text{ mm} \times 10 \text{ mm}$

Simplify: $= 2400 \text{ mm}^3$

ANSWER The volume of the rectangular prism is 2400 cubic millimeters.

Using Significant Figures

The **significant figures** in a decimal are the digits that are warranted by the accuracy of a measuring device.

When you perform a calculation with measurements, the number of significant figures to include in the result depends in part on the number of significant figures in the measurements. When you multiply or divide measurements, your answer should have only as many significant figures as the measurement with the fewest significant figures.

Example

Using a balance and a graduated cylinder filled with water, you determined that a marble has a mass of 8.0 grams and a volume of 3.5 cubic centimeters. To calculate the density of the marble, divide the mass by the volume.

Write the formula for density: $\text{Density} = \dfrac{\text{mass}}{\text{Volume}}$

Substitute measurements: $= \dfrac{8.0 \text{ g}}{3.5 \text{ cm}^3}$

Use a calculator to divide: $\approx 2.285714286 \text{ g/cm}^3$

ANSWER Because the mass and the volume have two significant figures each, give the density to two significant figures. The marble has a density of 2.3 grams per cubic centimeter.

Using Scientific Notation

Scientific notation is a shorthand way to write very large or very small numbers. For example, 73,500,000,000,000,000,000,000 kg is the mass of the Moon. In scientific notation, it is 7.35×10^{22} kg.

Example

You can convert from standard form to scientific notation.

Standard Form	Scientific Notation
720,000	7.2×10^5
5 decimal places left	Exponent is 5.
0.000291	2.91×10^{-4}
4 decimal places right	Exponent is −4.

You can convert from scientific notation to standard form.

Scientific Notation	Standard Form
4.63×10^7	46,300,000
Exponent is 7.	7 decimal places right
1.08×10^{-6}	0.00000108
Exponent is −6.	6 decimal places left

Note-Taking Handbook

Note-Taking Strategies

Taking notes as you read helps you understand the information. The notes you take can also be used as a study guide for later review. This handbook presents several ways to organize your notes.

Content Frame

1. Make a chart in which each column represents a category.
2. Give each column a heading.
3. Write details under the headings.

NAME	GROUP	CHARACTERISTICS	DRAWING
snail	mollusks	mantle, shell	
ant	arthropods	six legs, exoskeleton	
earthworm	segmented worms	segmented body, circulatory and digestive systems	
heartworm	roundworms	digestive system	
sea star	echinoderms	spiny skin, tube feet	
jellyfish	cnidarians	stinging cells	

categories

details

Combination Notes

1. For each new idea or concept, write an informal outline of the information.
2. Make a sketch to illustrate the concept, and label it.

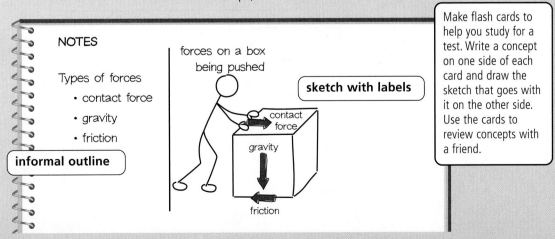

NOTES

Types of forces
- contact force
- gravity
- friction

informal outline

forces on a box being pushed

sketch with labels

contact force

gravity

friction

Make flash cards to help you study for a test. Write a concept on one side of each card and draw the sketch that goes with it on the other side. Use the cards to review concepts with a friend.

Main Idea and Detail Notes

1. In the left-hand column of a two-column chart, list main ideas. The blue headings express main ideas throughout this textbook.

2. In the right-hand column, write details that expand on each main idea.

You can shorten the headings in your chart. Be sure to use the most important words.

When studying for tests, cover up the detail notes column with a sheet of paper. Then use each main idea to form a question—such as "How does latitude affect climate?" Answer the question, and then uncover the detail notes column to check your answer.

MAIN IDEAS	DETAIL NOTES
1. Latitude affects climate. **main idea 1**	1. Places close to the equator are usually warmer than places close to the poles. 1. Latitude has the same effect in both hemispheres. **details about main idea 1**
2. Altitude affects climate. **main idea 2**	2. Temperature decreases with altitude. 2. Altitude can overcome the effect of latitude on temperature. **details about main idea 2**

Main Idea Web

1. Write a main idea in a box.

2. Add boxes around it with related vocabulary terms and important details.

You can find definitions near highlighted terms.

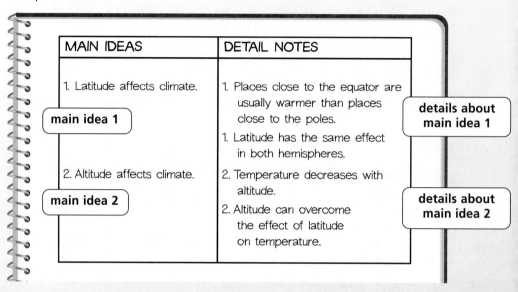

definition of *work*
Work is the use of force to move an object.

formula
Work = force · distance

main idea
Force is necessary to do work.

The joule is the unit used to measure work.
definition of *joule*

Work depends on the size of a force.
important detail

Mind Map

1. Write a main idea in the center.

2. Add details that relate to one another and to the main idea.

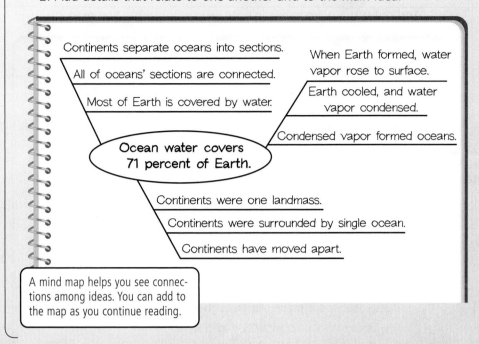

Continents separate oceans into sections.

All of oceans' sections are connected.

Most of Earth is covered by water.

When Earth formed, water vapor rose to surface.

Earth cooled, and water vapor condensed.

Condensed vapor formed oceans.

Ocean water covers 71 percent of Earth.

Continents were one landmass.

Continents were surrounded by single ocean.

Continents have moved apart.

A mind map helps you see connections among ideas. You can add to the map as you continue reading.

Supporting Main Ideas

1. Write a main idea in a box.

2. Add boxes underneath with information—such as reasons, explanations, and examples—that supports the main idea.

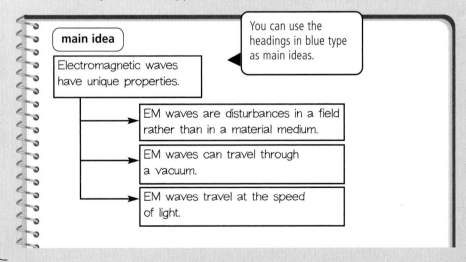

main idea

Electromagnetic waves have unique properties.

You can use the headings in blue type as main ideas.

EM waves are disturbances in a field rather than in a material medium.

EM waves can travel through a vacuum.

EM waves travel at the speed of light.

Outline

1. Copy the chapter title and headings from the book in the form of an outline.
2. Add notes that summarize in your own words what you read.

Cell Processes

I. Cells capture and release energy. — 1st key idea
   A. All cells need energy. — 1st subpoint of I
   B. Some cells capture light energy. — 2nd subpoint of I
      1. Process of photosynthesis — 1st detail about B
      2. Chloroplasts (site of photosynthesis) — 2nd detail about B
      3. Carbon dioxide and water as raw materials
      4. Glucose and oxygen as products
   C. All cells release energy.
      1. Process of cellular respiration
      2. Fermentation of sugar to carbon dioxide
      3. Bacteria that carry out fermentation
II. Cells transport materials through membranes.
   A. Some materials move by diffusion.
      1. Particle movement from higher to lower concentrations
      2. Movement of water through membrane (osmosis)
   B. Some transport requires energy.
      1. Active transport
      2. Examples of active transport

Correct Outline Form
Include a title.

Arrange key ideas, subpoints, and details as shown.

Indent the divisions of the outline as shown.

Use the same grammatical form for items of the same rank. For example, if A is a sentence, B must also be a sentence.

You must have at least two main ideas or subpoints. That is, every A must be followed by a B, and every 1 must be followed by a 2.

NOTE-TAKING HANDBOOK

Concept Map

1. Write an important concept in a large oval.
2. Add details related to the concept in smaller ovals.
3. Write linking words on arrows that connect the ovals.

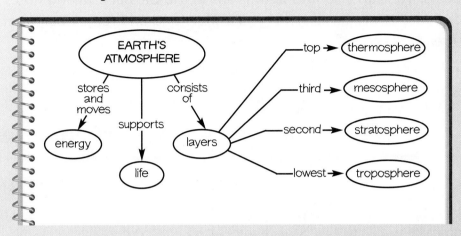

The main ideas or concepts can often be found in the blue headings. An example is "The atmosphere stores and moves energy." Use nouns from these concepts in the ovals, and use the verb or verbs on the lines.

Venn Diagram

1. Draw two overlapping circles, one for each item that you are comparing.
2. In the overlapping section, list the characteristics that are shared by both items.
3. In the outer sections, list the characteristics that are peculiar to each item.
4. Write a summary that describes the information in the Venn diagram.

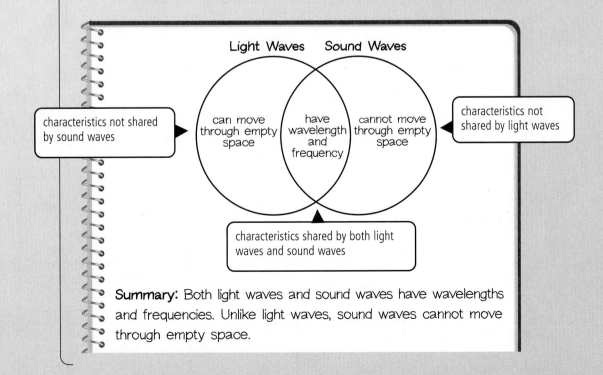

Summary: Both light waves and sound waves have wavelengths and frequencies. Unlike light waves, sound waves cannot move through empty space.

Vocabulary Strategies

Important terms are highlighted in this book. A definition of each term can be found in the sentence or paragraph where the term appears. You can also find definitions in the Glossary. Taking notes about vocabulary terms helps you understand and remember what you read.

Description Wheel

1. Write a term inside a circle.
2. Write words that describe the term on "spokes" attached to the circle.

When studying for a test with a friend, read the phrases on the spokes one at a time until your friend identifies the correct term.

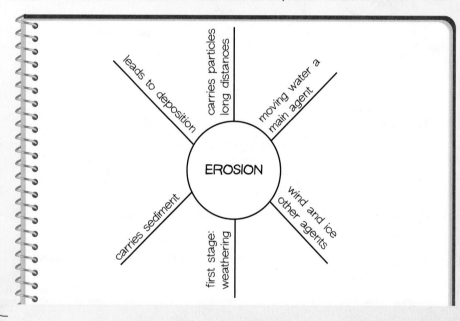

carries particles long distances

leads to deposition

moving water a main agent

EROSION

carries sediment

wind and ice other agents

first stage: weathering

Four Square

1. Write a term in the center.
2. Write details in the four areas around the term.

Definition	Characteristics
any living thing	needs food, water, air; needs energy; grows, develops, reproduces

ORGANISM

Examples	Nonexamples
dogs, cats, birds, insects, flowers, trees	rocks, water, dirt

Include a definition, some characteristics, and examples. You may want to add a formula, a sketch, or examples of things that the term does *not* name.

NOTE-TAKING HANDBOOK

Frame Game

1. Write a term in the center.
2. Frame the term with details.

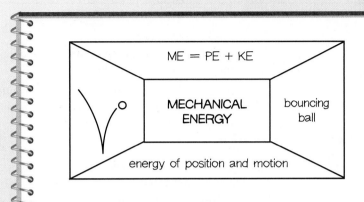

Include examples, descriptions, sketches, or sentences that use the term in context. Change the frame to fit each new term.

Magnet Word

1. Write a term on the magnet.
2. On the lines, add details related to the term.

You can also use phrases or sentences on the lines.

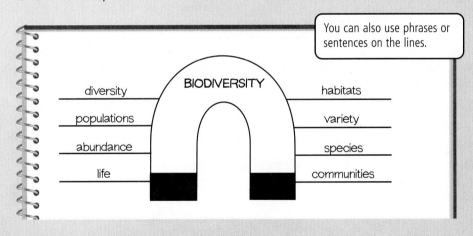

Word Triangle

1. Write a term and its definition in the bottom section.
2. In the middle section, write a sentence in which the term is used correctly.
3. In the top section, draw a small picture to illustrate the term.

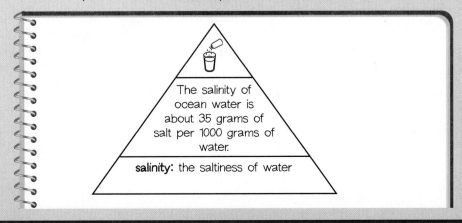

NOTE-TAKING HANDBOOK

Glossary

GLOSSARY

A

atom
The smallest particle of an element that has the chemical properties of that element. (p. 16)

átomo La partícula más pequeña de un elemento que tiene las propiedades químicas de ese elemento.

B

boiling
A process by which a substance changes from its liquid state to its gas state. The liquid is heated to a specific temperature at which bubbles of vapor form within the liquid. (p. 54)

ebullición Un proceso mediante el cual una sustancia cambia de su estado líquido a su estado gaseoso se calienta el líquido a una determinada temperatura a la cual se forman burbujas de vapor dentro del líquido.

boiling point
The temperature at which a substance changes from its liquid state to its gas state through boiling. (p. 54)

punto de ebullición La temperatura a la cual una sustancia cambia de su estado líquido a su estado gaseoso mediante ebullición.

C

calorie
The amount of energy needed to increase the temperature of one gram of water by one degree Celsius. (p. 112)

caloría La cantidad de energía que se necesita para aumentar la temperatura de un gramo de agua un grado centígrado.

chemical change
A change of one substance into another substance. (p. 46)

cambio químico La transformación de una sustancia a otra sustancia.

chemical property
A characteristic of a substance that describes how it can form a new substance. (p. 46)

propiedad química Una característica de una sustancia que describe como puede formar una nueva sustancia.

compound
A substance made up of two or more different types of atoms bonded together. (p. 23)

compuesto Una sustancia formada por dos o más diferentes tipos de átomos enlazados.

condensation
The process by which a gas becomes a liquid. (p. 55)

condensación El proceso mediante el cual un gas se convierte en un líquido.

conduction
The process by which energy is transferred from a warmer object to a cooler object by means of physical contact. (p. 117)

conducción El proceso mediante el cual se transfiere energía de un objeto más caliente a un objeto más frío por medio de contacto físico.

conductor
1. A material that transfers energy easily. (p. 117)
2. A material that transfers electric charge easily.

conductor 1. Un material que transfiere energía fácilmente. 2. Un material que transfiere cargas eléctricas fácilmente.

convection
A process by which energy is transferred in gases and liquids, occurring when a warmer, less dense area of gas or liquid is pushed up by a cooler, more dense area of the gas or liquid. (p. 118)

convección Un proceso mediante el cual se transfiere energía en los gases y los líquidos; ocurre cuando un área más fría y más densa del gas o del líquido empuja hacia arriba un área más caliente y menos densa de gas o de líquido.

cycle

n. A series of events or actions that repeat themselves regularly; a physical and/or chemical process in which one material continually changes locations and/or forms. Examples include the water cycle, the carbon cycle, and the rock cycle.

v. To move through a repeating series of events or actions.

ciclo *s.* Una serie de eventos o acciones que se repiten regularmente; un proceso físico y/o químico en el cual un material cambia continuamente de lugar y/o forma. Ejemplos: el ciclo del agua, el ciclo del carbono y el ciclo de las rocas.

D

data

Information gathered by observation or experimentation that can be used in calculating or reasoning. *Data* is a plural word; the singular is datum.

datos Información reunida mediante observación o experimentación y que se puede usar para calcular o para razonar.

degree

Evenly divided units of a temperature scale. (p. 106)

grado Unidades de una escala de temperatura distribuidas uniformemente.

density

A property of matter representing the mass per unit volume. (p. 43)

densidad Una propiedad de la materia que representa la masa por unidad de volumen.

E

element

A substance that cannot be broken down into a simpler substance by ordinary chemical changes. An element consists of atoms of only one type. (p. 22)

elemento Una sustancia que no puede descomponerse en otra sustancia más simple por medio de cambios químicos normales. Un elemento consta de átomos de un solo tipo.

energy

The ability to do work or to cause a change. For example, the energy of a moving bowling ball knocks over pins; energy from food allows animals to move and to grow; and energy from the Sun heats Earth's surface and atmosphere, which causes air to move. (p. 72)

energía La capacidad para trabajar o causar un cambio. Por ejemplo, la energía de una bola de boliche en movimiento tumba los pinos; la energía proveniente de su alimento permite a los animales moverse y crecer; la energía del Sol calienta la superficie y la atmósfera de la Tierra, lo que ocasiona que el aire se mueva.

energy efficiency

A measurement of usable energy after an energy conversion; the ratio of usable energy to the total energy after an energy conversion. (p. A83)

eficiencia energética Una medida de la energía utilizable después de una conversión energética; la razón entre la energía utilizable y el total de energía después de una conversión energética.

evaporation

A process by which a substance changes from its liquid state to its gas state by random particle movement. Evaporation usually occurs at the surface of a liquid over a wide range of temperatures. (p. 53)

evaporación Un proceso mediante el cual una sustancia cambia de su estado líquido a su estado gaseoso por medio del movimiento aleatorio de las partículas. La evaporación normalmente ocurre en la superficie de un líquido en una amplia gama de temperaturas.

experiment

An organized procedure to study something under controlled conditions. (p. xxiv)

experimento Un procedimiento organizado para estudiar algo bajo condiciones controladas.

F

force

A push or a pull; something that changes the motion of an object. (p. xxi)

fuerza Un empuje o un jalón; algo que cambia el movimiento de un objeto.

freezing

The process by which a substance changes from its liquid state into its solid state. (p. 52)

congelación El proceso mediante el cual una sustancia cambia de su estado líquido a su estado sólido.

freezing point

The temperature at which a substance changes from its liquid state to its solid state through freezing. (p. 52)

punto de congelación La temperatura a la cual una sustancia cambia de su estado líquido a su estado sólido mediante congelación.

friction

A force that resists the motion between two surfaces in contact. (p. xxi)

fricción Una fuerza que resiste el movimiento entre dos superficies en contacto.

G

gas

Matter with no definite volume and no definite shape. The molecules in a gas are very far apart, and the amount of space between them can change easily. (p. 28)

gas Materia sin volumen definido ni forma definida. Las moléculas en un gas están muy separadas unas de otras, y la cantidad de espacio entre ellas puede cambiar fácilmente.

gravity

The force that objects exert on each other because of their mass. (p. xxi)

gravedad La fuerza que los objetos ejercen entre sí debido a su masa.

H

heat

1. The flow of energy from an object at a higher temperature to an object at a lower temperature. (p. 110)
2. Energy that is transferred from a warmer object to a cooler object.

calor 1. El flujo de energía de un objeto a mayor temperatura a un objeto a menor temperatura. 2. Energía que se transfiere de un objeto más caliente a un objeto más frío.

hypothesis

A tentative explanation for an observation or phenomenon. A hypothesis is used to make testable predictions. (p. xxiv)

hipótesis Una explicación provisional de una observación o de un fenómeno. Una hipótesis se usa para hacer predicciones que se pueden probar.

I

insulator

1. A material that does not transfer energy easily. (p. 117)
2. A material that does not transfer electric charge easily.

aislante 1. Un material que no transfiere energía fácilmente. 2. Un material que no transfiere cargas eléctricas fácilmente.

J

joule (jool) J

A unit used to measure energy and work. One calorie is equal to 4.18 joules of energy; one joule of work is done when a force of one newton moves an object one meter. (p. 112)

julio Una unidad que se usa para medir la energía y el trabajo. Una caloría es igual a 4.18 julios de energía; se hace un joule de trabajo cuando una fuerza de un newton mueve un objeto un metro.

K

kinetic energy

The energy of motion. A moving object has the most kinetic energy at the point where it moves the fastest. (p. 74)

energía cinética La energía del movimiento. Un objeto que se mueve tiene su mayor energía cinética en el punto en el cual se mueve con mayor rapidez.

kinetic theory of matter

A theory stating that all matter is made of particles in motion. (p. 104)

teoría cinética de la materia Una teoría que establece que toda materia está compuesta de partículas en movimiento.

L

law
In science, a rule or principle describing a physical relationship that always works in the same way under the same conditions. The law of conservation of energy is an example.

ley En las ciencias, una regla o un principio que describe una relación física que siempre funciona de la misma manera bajo las mismas condiciones. La ley de la conservación de la energía es un ejemplo.

law of conservation of energy
A law stating that no matter how energy is transferred or transformed, it continues to exist in one form or another. (p. 82)

ley de la conservación de la energía Una ley que establece que no importa cómo se transfiere o trans-forma la energía, toda la energía sigue presente en alguna forma u otra.

liquid
Matter that has a definite volume but does not have a definite shape. The molecules in a liquid are close together but not bound to one another. (p. 28)

líquido Materia que tiene un volumen definido pero no tiene una forma definida. Las moléculas en un líquido están cerca unas de otras pero no están ligadas.

M, N, O

mass
A measure of how much matter an object is made of. (p. 10)

masa Una medida de la cantidad de materia de la que está compuesto un objeto.

matter
Anything that has mass and volume. Matter exists ordinarily as a solid, a liquid, or a gas. (p. 9)

materia Todo lo que tiene masa y volumen. Generalmente la materia existe como sólido, líquido o gas.

melting
The process by which a substance changes from its solid state to its liquid state. (p. 51)

fusión El proceso mediante el cual una sustancia cambia de su estado sólido a su estado líquido.

melting point
The temperature at which a substance changes from its solid state to its liquid state through melting. (p. 51)

punto de fusión La temperatura a la cual una sustancia cambia de su estado sólido a su estado líquido mediante fusión.

mixture
A combination of two or more substances that do not combine chemically but remain the same individual substances. Mixtures can be separated by physical means. (p. 23)

mezcla Una combinación de dos o más sustancias que no se combinan químicamente sino que permanecen como sustancias individuales. Las mezclas se pueden separar por medios físicos.

molecule
A group of atoms that are held together by covalent bonds so that they move as a single unit. (p. 18)

molécula Un grupo de átomos que están unidos mediante enlaces covalentes de tal manera que se mueven como una sola unidad.

P, Q

particle
A very small piece of matter, such as an atom, molecule, or ion.

partícula Una cantidad muy pequeña de materia, como un átomo, una molécula o un ión.

physical change
A change in a substance that does not change the sub-stance into a different one. (p. 44)

cambio físico Un cambio en una sustancia que no transforma la sustancia a otra sustancia.

physical property
A characteristic of a substance that can be observed with-out changing the identity of the substance. (p. 41)

propiedad física Una característica de una sustancia que se puede observar sin cambiar la identidad de la sustancia.

potential energy
Stored energy; the energy an object has due to its position, molecular arrangement, or chemical composition. (p. 75)

energía potencial Energía almacenada; o la energía que tiene un objeto debido a su posición, arreglo molecular o composición química.

R

radiation
Energy that travels across distances in the form of electromagnetic waves. (p. 119)

radiación Energía que viaja a través de la distancia en forma de ondas electromagnéticas.

S

solar cell
A type of technology in which light-sensitive materials convert sunlight into electrical energy. (p. 88)

celda solar Un tipo de tecnología en el cual materiales sensibles a la luz convierten luz solar a energía eléctrica.

solid
Matter that has a definite shape and a definite volume. The molecules in a solid are in fixed positions and are close together. (p. 28)

sólido La materia que tiene una forma definida y un volumen definido. Las moléculas en un sólido están en posiciones fijas y cercanas unas a otras.

specific heat
The amount of energy required to raise the temperature of one gram of a substance by one degree Celsius. (p. 113)

calor específico La cantidad de energía que se necesita para aumentar la temperatura de un gramo de una sustancia un grado centígrado.

states of matter
The different forms in which matter can exist. Three familiar states are solid, liquid, and gas. (p. 27)

estados de la materia Las diferentes formas en las cuales puede existir la materia. Los tres estados conocidos son sólido, líquido y gas.

sublimation
The process by which a substance changes directly from its solid state to its gas state without becoming a liquid first. (p. 53)

sublimación El proceso mediante el cual una sustancia cambia directamente de su estado sólido a su estado gaseoso sin convertirse primero en líquido.

substance
Matter of a particular type. Elements, compounds, and mixtures are all substances.

sustancia La materia de cierto tipo. Los elementos, los compuestos y las mezclas son sustancias.

system
A group of objects or phenomena that interact. A system can be as simple as a rope, a pulley, and a mass. It also can be as complex as the interaction of energy and matter in the four spheres of the Earth system.

sistema Un grupo de objetos o fenómenos que interactúan. Un sistema puede ser algo tan sencillo como una cuerda, una polea y una masa. También puede ser algo tan complejo como la interacción de la energía y la materia en las cuatro esferas del sistema de la Tierra.

T, U

technology
The use of scientific knowledge to solve problems or engineer new products, tools, or processes.

tecnología El uso de conocimientos científicos para resolver problemas o para diseñar nuevos productos, herramientas o procesos.

temperature
A measure of the average amount of kinetic energy of the particles in an object. (p. 105)

temperatura Una medida de la cantidad promedio de energía cinética de las partículas en un objeto.

theory
In science, a set of widely accepted explanations of observations and phenomena. A theory is a well-tested explanation that is consistent with all available evidence.

teoría En las ciencias, un conjunto de explicaciones de observaciones y fenómenos que es ampliamente aceptado. Una teoría es una explicación bien probada que es consecuente con la evidencia disponible.

thermal energy
The energy an object has due to the motion of its particles; the total amount of kinetic energy of particles in an object. (p. 111)

energía térmica La energía que tiene un objeto debido al movimiento de sus partículas; la cantidad total de energía cinética de las partículas en un objeto.

thermometer
A device for measuring temperature. (p. 107)

termómetro Un aparato para medir la temperatura.

V

variable
Any factor that can change in a controlled experiment, observation, or model. (p. R30)

    variable Cualquier factor que puede cambiar en un experimento controlado, en una observación o en un modelo.

volume
An amount of three-dimensional space, often used to describe the space that an object takes up. (p. 11)

    volumen Una cantidad de espacio tridimensional; a menudo se usa este término para describir el espacio que ocupa un objeto.

W, X, Y, Z

weight
The force of gravity on an object. (p. 11)

    peso La fuerza de la gravedad sobre un objeto.

Index

Page numbers for definitions are printed in **boldface** type.
Page numbers for illustrations, maps, and charts are printed in *italics*.

INDEX

Acknowledgments

Photography

Cover © Scott T. Smith/Corbis; **i** © Scott T. Smith/Corbis; **iii** *left (top to bottom)* Photograph of James Trefil by Evan Cantwell; Photograph of Rita Ann Calvo by Joseph Calvo; Photograph of Linda Carnine by Amilcar Cifuentes; Photograph of Sam Miller by Samuel Miller; *right (top to bottom)* Photograph of Kenneth Cutler by Kenneth A. Cutler; Photograph of Donald Steely by Marni Stamm; Photograph of Vicky Vachon by Redfern Photographics; **vi** © David Leahy/Getty Images; **vii** AP/Wide World Photos; **ix** Photographs by Sharon Hoogstraten; **xiv–xv** © Larry Hamill/age fotostock america, inc.; **xvi–xvii** © Fritz Poelking/age fotostock america, inc.; **xviii–xix** © Galen Rowell/Corbis; **xx–xxi** © Jack Affleck/SuperStock; **xxii** AP/Wide World Photos; **xxiii** © David Parker/IMI/University of Birmingham High, TC Consortium/Photo Researchers; **xxiv** *left* AP/Wide World Photos; *right* *Washington University Record*; **xxv** *top* © Kim Steele/Getty Images; *bottom* Reprinted with permission from S. Zhou et al., *SCIENCE* 291:1944–47. © 2001 AAAS; **xxvi–xxvii** © Mike Fiala/Getty Images; **xxvii** *left* © Derek Trask/Corbis; *right* AP/Wide World Photos; **xxxii** © The Chedd-Angier Production Company; **2–3, 3** Courtesy of NASA/JPL/Caltech; **4** *top* © Babakin Space Center, The Planetary Society; *bottom* © The Chedd-Angier Production Company; **6–7** © Steve Allen/Brand X Pictures; **7, 9** Photographs by Sharon Hoogstraten; **10** *left* © Antonio Mo/Getty Images; *right* © ImageState/Alamy; **11** © Tom Stewart/Corbis; **12, 13** Photographs by Sharon Hoogstraten; **14** *top* © Stewart Cohen/Getty Images; *bottom* Photograph by Sharon Hoogstraten; **14–15, 15** Photographs by Sharon Hoogstraten; **16** © Royalty-Free/Corbis; **17** Photograph by Sharon Hoogstraten; **18** © NatPhotos/Tony Sweet/Digital Vision; **19** © Jake Rajs/Getty Images; **20** Courtesy IBM Archives; **21** Photograph by Sharon Hoogstraten; **22** *left* © James L. Amos/Corbis; *right* © Omni Photo Communications, Inc./Index Stock; **23** © Richard Laird/Getty Images; **24** Photograph by Sharon Hoogstraten; **25** © Royalty-Free/Corbis; **26** © Nik Wheeler/Corbis; **27** Photograph by Sharon Hoogstraten; **30** © Robert F. Sisson/Getty Images; **31** Photograph by Sharon Hoogstraten; **34** *top* Photograph by Sharon Hoogstraten; *bottom left* © James L. Amos/Corbis; *bottom right* © Royalty-Free/Corbis; **36** Photographs by Sharon Hoogstraten; **38–39** © David Leahy/Getty Images; **39, 41** Photographs by Sharon Hoogstraten; **42** *left* Photograph by Sharon Hoogstraten; *right* © Dan Lim/Masterfile; **45** *top left* © Maryellen McGrath/Bruce Coleman Inc.; *top center* © Jean-Bernard Vernier/Corbis Sygma; *top right* © Angelo Cavalli/Getty Images; *bottom* © Garry Black/Masterfile; *inset* Photograph by Sharon Hoogstraten; **46** © Mark C. Burnett/Stock, Boston Inc./PictureQuest; **47** Photograph by Sharon Hoogstraten; **48** © J. Westrich/Masterfile; **49** *left* © Owen Franken/Corbis; *right* © Erich Lessing/Art Resource, New York; **50** © ImageState/Alamy; **51** *left* © Brand X Pictures; *right* © Peter Bowater/Alamy; **52** © Royalty-Free/Corbis; **53** © Winifred Wisniewski/Frank Lane Picture Agency/Corbis; **54** © A. Pasieka/Photo Researchers; **55** © Sean Ellis/Getty Images; **56** *top* © Royalty-Free/Corbis; *bottom* Photograph by Sharon Hoogstraten; **57, 58** Photographs by Sharon Hoogstraten; **59** © Lawrence Livermore National Laboratory/Photo Researchers; **60** *top left* © SPL/Photo Researchers; *top right* © Felix St. Clair Renard/Getty Images; *bottom* © David Young-Wolff/PhotoEdit; **61** Photograph by Sharon Hoogstraten; **62** © Alan Towse/Ecoscene/Corbis; **63** © Robert Essel NYC/Corbis; *inset* © The Cover Story/Corbis; **64** *top left* © Dan Lim/Masterfile; *top right* © Mark C. Burnett/Stock, Boston Inc./PictureQuest; *bottom* © David Young-Wolff/PhotoEdit; **66** © Winifred Wisniewski/Frank Lane Picture Agency/Corbis; **68–69** AP/Wide World Photos; **69, 71** Photographs by Sharon Hoogstraten; **72** © Alan Schein Photography/Corbis; **73** *top* © Patrick Ward/Corbis; *bottom* © NASA/Photo Researchers; **74** AP/Wide World Photos; **75** *top* © George H. H. Huey/Corbis; *bottom* Photograph by Sharon Hoogstraten; **76** *top* © Vladimir Pcholkin/Getty Images; *bottom* © Thomas Beach; **77** © Adam Gault/Digital Vision; **78** © Bill Aron/PhotoEdit; **79** © TempSport/Corbis; **80** © Robert Cameron/Getty Images; **81** *left* © Gunter Marx Photography/Corbis; *right* © Lester Lefkowitz/Corbis; **82** © Left Lane Productions/Corbis; **83** © Dorling Kindersley; **84** *top* © Grant Klotz/Alaska Stock Images/PictureQuest; *bottom* Photograph by Sharon Hoogstraten; **85, 86** Photographs by Sharon Hoogstraten; **87** *top left* © Royalty-Free/Corbis; *top right* Thinkstock, LLC; *bottom* AP/Wide World Photos; **88** © AFP/Corbis; *inset* © John Farmar; Cordaiy Photo Library Ltd./Corbis; **89** *top* © Sally A. Morgan; Ecoscene/Corbis; *bottom* Photograph by Sharon Hoogstraten; **90** © Joe Sohm/Visions of America, LLC/PictureQuest; **91** © Michael S. Lewis/Corbis; **92** *top* © Vladimir Pcholkin/Getty Images; *bottom* © AFP/Corbis; **96** © Don Farrall/Getty Images; **97** *top left* © Sheila Terry/Photo Researchers; *top center, top right* © Dorling Kindersley; *bottom* © SEF/Art Resource, New York; **98** *top left* Mary Evans Picture Library; *top right, bottom* © Dorling Kindersley; **99** *top right* © 1913 Debris Yearbook, Purdue University; *left* © Mark Wiens/Masterfile; **100–101** © Steve Bloom/stevebloom.com; **101, 103** Photographs by Sharon Hoogstraten; **104** © Tracy Frankel/Getty Images; **105** Photographs by Sharon Hoogstraten; **106** © Daryl Benson/Masterfile; *inset* © Spencer Grant/PhotoEdit; **107** Photograph by Sharon Hoogstraten; **108** *top* © Steve Vidler/SuperStock; *bottom* © Chase Jarvis/Getty Images; **109** © FogStock/Alamy; *inset* © Gordon Wiltsie/Getty Images; **110** © David Bishop/Getty Images; **111** Thinkstock, LLC; **112** Photograph by Sharon Hoogstraten; **113** © Richard Bickel/Corbis; **115** *top left* © Jeremy Samuelson/FoodPix; *bottom left* © William Reavell-StockFood Munich/StockFood; *right* © Martin Jacobs/FoodPix; **116** Photograph by Sharon Hoogstraten; **117** © Brand X Pictures/Alamy; **119** © ImageState Royalty Free/Alamy; **120** *top left* E.C. Humphrey; *top right* Creatas®; *bottom* © Uwe Walz Gdt/age fotostock america, inc.; **122** *top* © Nancy Ney/Corbis; *bottom* Photograph by Sharon Hoogstraten; **123** Photograph by Sharon Hoogstraten; **124** *top* Photographs by Sharon Hoogstraten; *bottom* Thinkstock, LLC; **R28** © Photodisc/Getty Images.

Illustrations and Maps

Accurate Art, Inc. **127**; Ampersand Design Group **29, 115**; Stephen Durke **10, 11, 18, 20, 22, 30, 32, 33, 34, 81**; MapQuest.com, Inc. **114**; Dan Stuckenschneider **R11–R19, R22, R32**